COUNSELING STRATEGIES
AND INTERVENTIONS

SIXTH EDITION

COUNSELING STRATEGIES AND INTERVENTIONS

SHERRY CORMIER

West Virginia University

HAROLD HACKNEY

Syracuse University

PEARSON

Boston ▪ New York ▪ San Francisco
Mexico City ▪ Montreal ▪ Toronto ▪ London ▪ Madrid ▪ Munich ▪ Paris
Hong Kong ▪ Singapore ▪ Tokyo ▪ Cape Town ▪ Sydney

Executive Editor: *Virginia Lanigan*
Editorial Assistant: *Scott Blaszak*
Marketing Manager: *Tara Whorf*
Production Editor: *Michelle Limoges*
Editorial Production Service: *Lynda Griffiths*
Compositor: *Omegatype Typography, Inc.*
Composition and Prepress Buyer: *Linda Cox*
Manufacturing Buyer: *Andrew Turso*
Cover Designer: *Kristina Mose-Libon*

For related titles and support materials, visit our online catalog at www.ablongman.com.

Between the time Website information is gathered and then published, it is not unusual for some sites to have closed. Also, the transcription of URLs can result in typographical errors. The publisher would appreciate notification where these errors occur so that they may be corrected in subsequent editions.

Library of Congress Cataloging-in-Publication Data

Cormier, L. Sherilyn (Louise Sherilyn).
    Counseling strategies and interventions / Sherry Cormier, Harold Hackney.—6th ed.
      p. cm.
    Includes bibliographical references and index.
    ISBN 0-205-37052-7
    1. Counseling.   I. Hackney, Harold.

   BF637.C6H25 2004
   158'.3—dc22   2003068700

Printed in the United States of America

10 9 8 7 6 5 4 3 2 1   08 07 06 05 04

*This book is lovingly dedicated
to our children:*

*Christiane and Lisanne
Kristen, Jason, and Curtis*

CONTENTS

CHAPTER SIX
Responding to Cognitive Content   80

CHAPTER SEVEN
Responding to Affective Content   95

CHAPTER EIGHT

Conceptualizing Issues and Setting Goals 116

CHAPTER NINE

**Using Integrative Counseling Strategies
and Interventions** 132

APPLICATION EXERCISES

■ ■ ■ ■ ■

PREFACE

Since the fifth edition of *Counseling Strategies and Interventions*, the helping professions have continued to expand and evolve. An increasing number of training programs have been recognized by various accrediting bodies. For example, professional counseling programs are now accredited by the Council for Accreditation of Counseling and Related Educational Programs (CACREP); counseling and clinical psychology programs are accredited by the American Psychological Association (APA); marriage and family counseling programs are accredited by the American Association of Marriage and Family Therapists (AAMFT); social work programs are accredited by the Council on Social Work Education (CSWE); and rehabilitation counseling programs are accredited by the Council on Rehabilitation Education (CORE). All of these organizations monitor the type, duration, and quality of training that helpers receive throughout their training and educational processes.

In writing this sixth edition, we have kept several well-grounded features from the previous editions. First, we have tried to be comprehensive yet concise. Second, the book has been written with upper-class undergraduates or beginning-level graduate students in mind. Also, we have included a variety of learning exercises to help students apply and review what they have learned. We have also added more examples.

At the same time, we have made some changes, including deletions and additions. We have eliminated out-of-date material and added content that reflects new sources and new thinking about the field. Many recently published sources are included.

A perusal of *new* content includes the following topics:

Professional identity and organizations and credentialing

Cultural competence, social justice, power, and privilege

Cultural empathy

Cultural narratives

Culture and language

Gender-sensitive communication

Positive feedback statements

Ethics of self-disclosure and privacy

Structuring the counseling sessions

Boundary issues in terminating interviews

Challenges and ethical issues in termination

Affective competence and affect regulation

Stages of change model

Cultural and ecological intervention strategies such as cultural genograms, ecomaps, and indigenous practices

Additionally, we have included a new chapter, Chapter 10, Common Challenges for Beginning Counselors. This chapter, coauthored by T. Anne Hawkins, Sherry Cormier, and Janine Bernard, features common concerns of beginning counselors, and preparing for ethical challenges and supervision challenges. Also new to this edition is an on-line Instructor's Manual, authored by Beth Robinson, which contains test questions, chapter summaries, recommended readings, and additional classroom and homework activities. This supplement may be accessed for printing or download. Contact your sales representative for more details. We also recommend that instructors consult the Allyn and Bacon supersite for helpful PowerPoint slides for this and other course areas, helpful counseling websites, and convenient links to listings of other counseling texts: www.ablongman.com/helpingprofessions.

Chapter 1 identifies the context of the helping profession—who the helping professional is, what kinds of activities he or she enters, qualities and skills of helpers such as cultural competence, and professional identity, training, and credentialing. This context includes a wide variety of roles and functions. It might even seem to the untrained eye that the differences among helpers are greater than the similarities. We attempt to dispel that impression in Chapter 2, where we discuss the helping relationship. It is this helping relationship that proves to be the unifying force for disparate roles and functions.

Although the helping relationship connotes a sense of shared purpose, there is an added expectation for the counselor—the expectation that he or she be both responsible and responsive in exploring the client's needs and concerns. In Chapters 3 through 9, we identify the skills and interventions expected of a beginning professional counselor. Some of these skills are rudimentary; others are more advanced and require coaching and practice. Chapters 3 and 4 define the counselor's responsibility to be aware of and attentive to the client's communication patterns, especially silence. This responsibility is examined in Chapter 5, which deals with session management.

Chapters 6 and 7 delineate the basic counseling strategies designed to elicit, support, or direct client change. Whether the focus be the client's thoughts or feelings, or more likely a combination of both, the counselor has certain tools or skills that facilitate the client's growth. Often, these skills enable the counselor to understand the client's concerns or the client's world.

Chapter 8 is a pivotal point in the book. It builds on the fundamentals of the early chapters and is the foundation for the remaining chapters of the book. Although the counselor is instrumental in conceptualizing issues (usually with the assistance of a particular theoretical orientation), the goal-setting process is inherently dependent on *mutual* discussion and agreement between counselor and client. Drawing upon mutually accepted counseling goals, the counselor begins the most crucial portion of the relationship: the focus on overt change. This calls for more than relationship skills and more than active listening. There are many counseling interventions—derived both from theory and practice and supported by research—that are synonymous with effective counseling. In Chapters 8 and 9, we explain and suggest classroom activities that will help the counselor understand and begin practicing these interventions.

Finally, Chapter 10, a new chapter, focuses on several areas pertinent to beginning helpers. We explore common concerns of beginning helpers, such as managing anxiety and personal issues, bridging the gulf between theory and practice, and managing all flavors and combinations of anxiety. This chapter also discusses preparing for ethical challenges, such as confidentiality, informed consent, privacy, and dual relationships. Finally, the chapter focuses on the process of clinical supervision and how beginning counselors may use it to enhance their personal and professional development.

As you begin the process of understanding the role of helper and as you acquire the necessary skills required for effective helping, you will come to realize that the ultimate goal is to develop your abilities to the point that they are a natural extension of your existing interpersonal skills. But this will not be the case in the beginning. The interventions and even the conceptualizations may seem unnatural, inconsistent with your existing behaviors, or inappropriate. As you become more accomplished in the craft of counseling, these counseling skills will begin to feel more comfortable, appropriate, and effective. Ultimately, they will become a natural part of your professional practice.

Acknowledgments

We extend our thanks and appreciation to several people who have helped make this sixth edition possible. We thank our editor, Virginia Lanigan, who is an accomplished and experienced editor as well as a wonderful human being. Thanks also to our editorial assistant, Robert Champagne, whose timely and expert help made our jobs so much easier. We also gratefully acknowledge Janine Bernard and T. Anne Hawkins for their valued contributions to Chapter 10, and Beth Robinson for her wonderful work on the new Instructor's Manual. In addition, we are grateful to the following reviewers for their comments: Patricia Bethea-Whitfield, North Carolina A & T State University; Laura Foster, Southwest Texas State University; Stella Beatriz Kerl, Southwest Texas State University; and Glenda P. Reynolds, Auburn University Montgomery.

S. C.
H. H.

CHAPTER ONE

THE HELPING PROFESSION

The helping profession includes a broadly knit collection of professionals, each fitting a particular need or segment of society. Some are directly identified as helping professionals, such as psychiatrists, psychologists, professional counselors, marriage and family therapists, and social workers. Others are professionals from other disciplines who enter the helping network for temporary periods of time. Most notable among these are ministers, physicians, nurses, and teachers.

Professional helpers can be distinguished from nonprofessional helpers by their identification with a professional organization, their use of an ethical code and standards of practice, and an accrediting body that governs training, credentialing, and licensing of their practice (Gale & Austin, 2003, p. 3). This constitutes a major way in which a professional helper develops a sense of professional identity. *Professional identity* is defined as the identity assumed by a particular discipline that is reflected in the title, role, and intention of the profession and results from a cohesive decision of the members of the profession (Sweeney, 1995; Myers, Sweeney, & White, 2002, p. 396). One of the ways that helping professionals achieve a sense of professional identity is with membership in a professional organization. As Vacc and Loesch (2000) pointed out, there are a number of relevant professional organizations for helping professionals, such as the American Counseling Association (ACA) for counselors, the American Psychological Association (APA) for psychologists, and the National Association of Social Workers (NASW) for social workers. (See Appendix A for a list of websites for these and other organizations.)

Most counseling textbooks devote at least a portion of one chapter to the subject of helping. You might think that a process so inherent to human nature as this act of extending oneself to another person should be self-evident. And yet, people continue to belabor the subject in ways not unlike the poet who talks about love. In a psychotherapeutic context, the process has carried many labels, among which are *treatment, analysis, facilitation,* and *modification*. In the company of such terms, the label *helping* seems innocently harmless, if not simplistic. In fact, the act of helping proves not to be so simple or clear to the participant or observer. In this chapter, we examine the many facets of the helping profession.

WHAT IS HELPING?

The process of helping has several dimensions, each of which contributes to the definition of *helping*. One dimension specifies the conditions under which helping occurs. Another dimension specifies the preconditions that lead one person to seek help and another to provide help. A third dimension relates to the results of the interaction between these two persons.

Helping Conditions

The conditions under which helping occurs are quite complex, but in their simplest terms may be described as involving "(a) someone seeking help, (b) someone willing to give help who is (c) capable of, or trained to help (d) in a setting that permits help to be given and received" (Hackney & Cormier, 1996, p. 2).

The first of these conditions is obvious; one cannot help without the presence of someone seeking help. If I do not want to be helped, nothing you can do will be helpful. If I am not sure I want to be helped, then perhaps you will be helpful, provided you can enjoin me to make a commitment to accept help.

The second condition requires the willingness or intention to be helpful. Here, it would be good to differentiate between the *intention* to be helpful and the *need* to be helpful. Many would-be helpers are driven by the need to be helpful and use the helping relationship for their own needs. This is rarely a conscious act. Neediness has a way of camouflaging itself in more respectable attire. But when the relationship is dictated by the helper's needs, the possibilities for helping are minimal.

It is important to recognize and accept your needs. All people have needs for such things as intimacy, power, esteem, admiration, and so on. It is also important to be certain that you are not dependent on your interactions with clients for fulfilling these needs in a primary way. One of the best ways to ensure that you do not depend on clients inappropriately to meet your needs is to take care of yourself and to live a balanced life in which your needs are met through relationships with a partner, family, friends, or even a support group of other helpers. If you are living your own life in a healthy and balanced way, then your clients will not have to provide you with intimacy, approval, and admiration and will be free to receive from you the kinds of things that *they* need.

The third condition reflects the helper's skills, either learned or natural. It is not enough to be well intentioned if your awareness and behaviors drive people away. Indeed, the primary purpose of pursuing training in the field of helping is to develop, expand, and refine your therapeutic skills.

The fourth condition, a setting in which help may occur, refers to the physical surroundings in which the helper and client meet. Privacy, comfort, aesthetic character of the room, and timing of the encounter all contribute to the setting in which helping transpires.

All four of these conditions occur within a cultural and environmental context in which individual clients may present with a variety of concerns and individual differences, along such dimensions as race, ethnicity, socioeconomic level, gender, religious and spiritual affiliation, sexual orientation, age, developmental stage of life, and so on. Naturally, such differences affect the help-giving and help-receiving process in a variety of ways. For example, some clients' cultural affiliations have a great impact on even the decision to seek or not seek help from a helping professional. Instead, they may turn to family or tribal elders, religious and spiritual elders, or close family confidants for guidance. Cultural variables also affect the setting in which help giving occurs. For some clients, the idea of going to see a helper in a professional office is too foreign to consider it as a viable option. These clients may prefer a setting that is more informal and less structured. Also, even your best intentions to be helpful are influenced by your own cultural affiliations and may affect the degree to which some clients perceive you as able and qualified to help. If you do not understand your clients' expressions or subtle nuances of their communication patterns, or their cultural values, or their culturally related views of their problems, your best intentions may not be enough.

SETTINGS IN WHICH COUNSELORS WORK

As we mentioned at the beginning of this chapter, there are a variety of trained persons and specializations in the helping professions. According to Gale and Austin (2003), counselors are entering "new employment arenas" and are providing services to diverse kinds of clients (p. 7). The following discussion of representative settings and the services they perform will provide some sense of the helping spectrum.

School Settings

School counselors are found in elementary, middle or junior high, as well as high schools. Elementary school counselors do provide some individual counseling with children, but they are more likely to work with the total school environment. Much of the elementary school counselor's focus is on preventive and developmental guidance programs and activities such as classroom guidance units, small group counseling, and parent-teacher conferences (Baker, 1999).

Middle school and junior high school counselors share this total school perspective but tend to spend more time with students, individually and in groups, and somewhat less time with teachers and parents. This slight shift in focus reflects the developmental changes that occur with preteens, who find themselves involved in self-exploration and identity crises. Two common programs in middle schools include peer facilitation and teacher-as-advisor programs (Vacc & Loesch, 2000).

Counseling in the high school reflects a noticeable shift to the students as individuals. Career and college planning, interpersonal concerns, family matters, substance use, and personal identity issues tend to dominate the students' awareness, and the counseling process attempts to provide an environment in which these issues may be addressed. The counselor's day is therefore much more task oriented. Some students are referred by teachers, but many are self-referrals. The high school counselor often works with student groups on career and college issues, although counseling focuses on all types of secondary students, not just those who are college bound. Secondary school counselors also engage in much consultation with teachers and administrators (Vacc & Loesch, 2000).

In general, the current force of school counseling is in comprehensive programs that focus on primary prevention and healthy development for all students (Paisley & Borders, 1995). There is also an increasing emphasis on providing multiculturally effective school guidance programs that are inclusive of and relevant to a diverse group of students. An unfortunate newer focus in school counseling involves recognition of and responses to school violence.

College Settings

Although much college counseling occurs in counseling centers or psychological services centers, some counselors in higher education settings also work in offices related to student affairs, such as residence halls, career services, academic advising, and so on. A wide variety of problems are addressed, including career counseling, personal adjustment counseling, crisis counseling, and substance abuse counseling. College counselors also see students with mild to severe pathological problems, such as anxiety, depression, suicide gestures, eating disorders, and trauma. In addition to individual counseling, much reliance is placed on group counseling and on the needs of special student populations and student retention. For example, most college counseling centers have a special focus and staff person to engage in counseling-related services for students with disabilities.

Historically, college counseling has emphasized a developmental framework resulting in "creative outreach and support work on campuses" (Dean & Meadows, 1995, p. 139). Increasingly, however, college counselors are faced with a rising tide of greater psychopathology among college students, a greater diversity among college students, and an increased need for services stemming from societal issues, such as AIDS, sexual abuse and violence, and dysfunctional family experiences (Dean & Meadows, 1995, p. 141). At the same time that the needs for counseling services are at an all-time high, college counseling faces budget cuts and external pressures for accountability. Increasingly, as a result of the shift in health care to "managed care" or health maintenance organizations (HMOs), some colleges are replacing college counselors with off-campus mental health professionals. Currently, many college counselors are faced with survival!

Community Settings

Counselors working in community settings usually are master's degree–level social workers (M.S.W.) or mental health counselors (M.A.). Their places of employment are the most diverse of all counseling settings. Family service agencies, youth service bureaus, satellite mental health centers, YWCA counseling services, homeless shelters, and substance abuse centers are examples of community settings. Much of what is done is psychotherapy, whether with individuals, families, or groups. In addition, the community counselor may become involved in community advocacy efforts and direct community intervention. The types of problems seen by community counselors encompass the spectrum of mental health issues. Clients include children, adolescents, adults, couples, families, and the elderly. In other words, community counselors see an enormous variety of clients and problems in a typical month. The work demands are often heavy, with caseloads ranging from 20 to 40 clients per week.

Currently, mental health counselors are concerned with the delivery and implementation of services that are both therapeutic and cost effective and are based on developmental notions as much as remediation (Smith & Robinson, 1995). Couples and family counselors as well as addiction specialists also offer services through a variety of community agencies.

Religious Settings

Vacc and Loesch (2000) noted that "an interesting mixture of professions is evident in the growing number of clerics (e.g., rabbis, priests, ministers, sisters) who have completed counselor-in-preparation programs" (p. 344). Counseling in religious settings is in many ways similar and in some ways different from that in other counseling settings. The similarities include the range of individual and family problems seen, the types and quality of therapy provided, and the counselors' professional qualifications. The differences reflect the reasons why some religious groups establish their own counseling services. There is at least some acknowledgment of the role of religion or spirituality in the individual's life problems. Many religious counselors believe that human problems must be examined and changes introduced within a context of spiritual and religious beliefs and values. The religious counseling center is undeniably attractive for many clients who, because of their backgrounds, place greater trust in the counselor who works within a religious affiliation. According to Vacc and Loesch (2000), the three major activities engaged in by clerics include bereavement counseling, marriage and family counseling, and referrals to other professionals.

Counselors in religious settings often are ordained ministers who have obtained postgraduate training in counseling. However, increasing numbers of the laity are also entering religious counseling settings. Their training may be similar to that of the community mental health counselor or the couples and family therapist. Indeed, at the Invitational Summit Meeting on Spirituality in Counseling (American Counseling Association, 1995b), a set of spiritual competencies were proposed for all counselors, including the ability to use spiritual, religious, and transpersonal beliefs in the practice of counseling. Also included was the need for counselors to understand other spiritual and religious orientations in addition to their own. Wehrly (1995) noted that "belief systems related to religion and spirituality play vital roles in the lives of many people of color. Western-trained therapists may downplay or ignore the importance of these belief systems because minimal attention is given to the importance of religion or spirituality in most U.S. counselor training programs" (p. 11). All of the world's major religions—Buddhism, Christianity, Confucianism, Hinduism, Islam, Judaism, Shintoism, and Taoism—as well as various tribal beliefs have their own core belief systems and life philosophy (see also Axelson, 1999).

Industrial and Employment Settings

Many professionals consider the private sector to be the new frontier for counseling services. Counseling services occur primarily in the form of employee assistance programs (EAPs) that are administered either within the setting or through a private contract with a counseling agency. These programs are occurring with increasing frequency in business, industries, governmental units, hospitals, and schools. Many EAPs focus on the treatment of substance abuse issues, whereas others have expanded services to include individual, couple, and family concerns. To make the workplace a psychologically healthy environment, EAPs also deal with counterproductive workplace behaviors and stress management issues. Some research has found a connection between work stress and infectious disease (Hewlett, 2001).

In addition to employee assistance programs, another type of counseling service has appeared in industry settings: the outplacement counseling service. *Outplacement* refers to the process of facilitating the transition from employment to unemployment or from employment in one corporation to employment in another. The need for outplacement counseling has increased as corporations downsize their operations to cut costs or to address new goals and objectives. The client may be a top executive, middle manager, line supervisor, or laborer. Counseling takes the form of career counseling and includes the administration of career and personality inventories. The objectives for management clients are (1) to provide data and counseling that will help executives assess their career options and develop plans for obtaining new positions and (2) to support clients through that transition period. The objectives for employees who may be affected by plant closings are (1) to identify career alternatives for the employees and (2) to assist the company in designing retraining programs that will help the unemployed workers obtain new jobs. The outplacement counselor is often a person who has worked in an industry setting and understands the characteristics of this clientele from firsthand experience. Counselors in employment settings also often focus on career issues and the interaction between the individuals and their work roles (Power & Rothausen, 2003).

Health Care and Rehabilitation Settings

An increasing number of counselors are finding employment in health care settings such as hospitals, hospices, vocational rehabilitation centers, departments of behavioral medicine, rehabilitation clinics, and so on. Responsibilities of helpers in these settings include such diverse things as providing counseling to patients and/or patients' families, crisis management, grief work with the terminally ill, and the implementation of psychological and educational interventions for patients with chronic illnesses, people with physical challenges, and so on. An increasing number of addictions specialists are working in health care settings as well. "Wellness" programs are also increasing in numbers in these settings. It is believed that the number of counselors in health care and rehabilitation settings will continue to rise as human service needs and advances in medicine increase. For example, the need for rehabilitation counselors now exceeds the supply by over 25 percent across the United States.

■ ■ ■ ■ ■

APPLICATION EXERCISE 1.1
WORK SETTINGS AND JOB FUNCTIONS

Determine a setting in which counselors work that interests you. Interview a particular person employed as a counselor in this setting. Explore the job responsibilities, types of clients served, unique aspects of the setting, and joys and frustrations of the counselor. Your instructor may have you either present to your class an oral summary on your visit or write a summary of your interview. In constructing this summary, note whether your findings about this setting are consistent with your expectations. If so, how? If not, why?

COUNSELOR QUALITIES AND SKILLS

We have described six settings in which helping and counseling occur. There are many others, of course, including couples and family therapy, correctional institution counseling, geriatric counseling, and the emerging area of sports counseling (Miller & Wooten, 1995). In all of these settings, and with the variety of presenting issues that are seen, there is a common core of counselor characteristics, skills, and abilities. These common ingredients may be categorized as the counselor's personal qualities, and his or her interpersonal skills, conceptual skills, intervention skills, and cultural competence skills.

Personal Qualities

What are the raw materials, the predisposing conditions that contribute to the development of a highly skilled counselor? Do all counselor trainees possess these raw materials? Hackney and Cormier (2001) identified five personal qualities that are found in effective counselors:

Self-awareness and understanding
Good psychological health
Sensitivity to and understanding of racial, ethnic, and cultural factors in self and others
Open-mindedness
Objectivity (p. 13)

In addition to these qualities, one other is very important, and that is the counselor's ability to promote the welfare of the client. We discuss the role of ethics throughout the book and specifically in Chapter 10. Counselors are also guided by professional *standards of practice*, which describe minimally required behaviors for professional counselors (Corey, Corey, & Callanan, 2003). Most of the ethical codes of the major professional organizations also contain these standards of practice (see Appendix A). For counselors, the standards of practice "reflect a strong identification with prevention, human development over the life span, and interventions not only to remediate" but also to enhance the well-being of "all persons living in a diverse society and world" (West, Osborn, & Bubenzer, 2003, p. 34).

As we discussed earlier in this chapter, part of being an effective counselor involves the awareness of your own needs and the ability to put the well-being of your clients first. Helpers in all fields are guided by various codes of ethical behavior (*Code of Ethics*, American Counseling Association, 1995a; *Ethical Principles of Psychologists*, American Psychological Association, 2003; *Code of Ethics*, National Association of Social Workers, 1996; *Code of Ethical Principles for Marriage and Family Therapists*, American Association for Marriage and Family Therapy, 1998; *Ethical Standards for School Counselors*, American School Counselor Association, 1998; and "Professional Standards for the Training of Group Workers," Association for Specialists in Group Work, 2000). A major guiding principle of all of these ethical codes and standards is the recognition of the importance of being committed to the client's well-being.

Interpersonal Skills

Although personal qualities are basic ingredients for good counseling, possession of these qualities alone does not ensure success as a counselor. There is a second level of characteristics that determine how a counselor is able to relate to others. Egan (2002) described some of these qualities as empathy, respect, genuineness, and the promotion of client empowerment and self-responsibility. Other interpersonal skills include the ability to listen and to communicate accurately what one has heard without becoming dominant in the interaction and the ability to communicate competence and trustworthiness. This array of characteristics must contribute to a general ability to put clients at ease, to elicit client trust, and to work through difficult moments, tasks, and problems. These qualities enable the helper to form a collaborative and respectful relationship with clients. This kind of relationship has received some empirical support in recent years (Norcross, 2002).

Conceptualization Skills

As the counseling relationship evolves, the counselor becomes increasingly involved in the client's personal world. From the client's perspective, the counselor *becomes* part of his or her world. This involvement challenges the counselor to be in the relationship and yet to remain objective. Such a challenge is very difficult because it requires the counselor to exhibit congruence, honesty, and professional responsibility, all at the same time.

The counselor must be able to listen, to comprehend, to relate, to think through, to recognize connections and contradictions, to conceptualize what these might mean within some theoretical framework, to react, to instigate, to support, to challenge, and to empathize—all within the span of a counseling session. Conceptualization skills involve the ability of the helper to be reflective about his or her work and about clients and their issues, as well as to have a spirit of inquiry.

Intervention Skills

Counselors must also be able to implement their conceptualization of what would facilitate a client's growth and success with presenting problems. We believe that "all counselors, regardless of theoretical orientation, have a therapeutic plan that they follow, a plan that is related to the assessment of the presenting problem, to their view of human nature and change processes, and to the resulting goals that have been agreed upon" (Hackney & Cormier, 2001, p. 31). These interventions may address the client's feelings and attitudes, the client's thought processes and assessments of life situations, the client's behaviors or efforts to change, or the client's interpersonal relationships and the effect those relationships have.

Some intervention skills are nothing more than common sense and are as common among friends as they are in counseling. Other interventions are unique to the therapeutic relationship and are formed out of the theoretical conceptualizations of human relationships. Intervention skills are like therapeutic "tools" and are necessary to develop a repertoire of skills for varying needs of diverse clients and to provide flexibility in service delivery approaches.

Cultural Competence Skills

Counselors are seeing an increasingly diverse group of clients. It is certainly realistic that such diversity will continue to grow in this century. As the dimensions of client diversity expand, the competence of counselors to deal with complex cultural issues must also grow.

As Robinson (1997) noted, diversity and multiculturalism are not synonymous. *Diversity* describes the experiences of clients who are different across dimensions such as age, gender, race, religion, ethnicity, sexual orientation, health status, social class, and so on. *Multiculturalism* involves an awareness and understanding of the principles of *power and privilege*. Power and privilege can be defined in many ways, but we especially like the definitions that Lott (2002, p. 101) has offered: Power is "access to resources" and privilege is "unearned advantage" and thereby "dominance." As you can see from these definitions, power and privilege are linked together in important ways. Those who have unearned privilege often use or abuse their power to dominate and subordinate (or oppress) those who do not have privilege and power. Multiculturalism is "willingly sharing power with those who have less power" and using "unearned privilege to empower others" (Robinson, 1997, p. 6).

Lott (2002, p. 101) stated that "categorization of groups of people into upper and lower strata, into superior and inferior, is done by those who require such categorization to maintain their power, prevent others from sharing and obtaining an equal share of resources, and sustain the myth of superiority." There are several unfortunate results from this. First is the result of "isms"—racism, sexism, ageism, and so on. That is, people who hold unearned privilege and power often seek to maintain their power by labeling, judging, and discriminating against those who do not. This discrimination usually occurs on the basis of various dimensions of diversity, such as race, social class, religion, age, gender, sexual orientation, health status, and so on. Those who are discriminated against on the basis of these dimensions not only feel excluded and disempowered but they also have, in reality, fewer resources. For example, poor people have less access to employment, decent housing, health care, benefits, and even such resources as technology.

Another unfortunate result of power and privilege is the possibility that someone could have a professional commitment to diversity without a corresponding commitment to multiculturalism. When this occurs, differences usually pull people apart rather than bring them together, and often the excluded person feels scapegoated and alienation results. As an example, consider the client who comes to see you after a particularly volatile staff meeting at her worksite. Her colleagues are primarily white men with the exception of one African American woman. Your client reports that during the meeting, one of the men (not the boss) publicly shamed her female colleague in front of the group for a particular way that this woman had handled a situation. Your client has also been publicly criticized by this same man. The same man who has done this also professes publicly to a strong commitment to diversity, yet his continuing behavior suggests he has no commitment to multiculturalism. Moreover, he has engaged in "pulling rank" on the basis of his unearned privilege (race and gender) to maintain his power and privilege as well as to disempower the female worker, and, as a result, he has engaged in both racism and sexism. Your client feels so intimidated and abused by this male colleague that she said nothing in the meeting after the public attack (nor did any of the other men, including the male boss). She is in a quandary about what she should now do—should she attempt to talk to her boss, speak with her female colleague, or file some sort of complaint? In spite of her intimidation, your client feels strongly that she must do something, not just on behalf of herself, but also on behalf of her female colleague and in protest of the values reflected in this organizational behavior that have been permitted to continue over time.

This scenario reflects an emerging trend in the development of cultural competence that is referred to as *social justice*—or "how advantages and disadvantages are distributed to individuals in a society" (Miller, 1999, p. 11). Vera and Speight (2003, p. 254) have suggested that "social justice is at the heart of multiculturalism" because the existence of institutionalized discrimination, such as racism, sexism, religious persecution, homophobia, and so on, is what accounts for the unfair experiences for diverse groups of persons. They asserted that "any multicultural movement that underemphasizes social justice is likely to do little to eradicate oppression and will maintain the status quo to the detriment of historically marginalized people" (p. 255). We return to this concept throughout the book and particularly in Chapter 9.

In 1992, D. W. Sue, Arredondo, and McDavis developed a set of multicultural competencies that focused on attitudes, knowledge, and skill areas for the development of culturally sensitive counselors. These competencies were updated in a 2002 guidebook (Roysircar et al., 2002). There are many other ideas of what it means to be a culturally competent counselor. Montalvo (as cited in Daw, 1997) stated that cultural competence "is the business of spotting obstacles and facilitators to treatments" within a client's culture (p. 9). He illustrated this definition with the following story of a client who was a Vietnam veteran suffering from posttraumatic stress disorder (PTSD):

> The man was shunned by his family because they saw the spirits of the people he had killed in Vietnam. His therapist did some checking around in the man's ethnic group and discovered that the Navajos had a ritual dance for warriors dealing with the spirits of those they had harmed. Rather than EMDR [eye movement desensitization and reprocessing] or another treatment that had probably already been tried, the therapist connected the veteran to a medicine man. When the man opened up to his culture it was helpful to him and also to his family. The family opened their doors to him again. (p. 9)

D. W. Sue (2001) has suggested that cultural competence is multidimensional. It includes not just the three general competency areas of attitudes, knowledge, and skills, but also specific race and culture attributes of various minority groups. It also includes a focus on different levels or targets of change—thus, cultural competence does not apply just to an individual client but also to systems as well.

How do counselors develop cultural competence? The answers to this question are not always simple ones. D. W. Sue (2001) noted that "cultural competence for one group is not necessarily the same for another group" (p. 816). However, we can make the following recommendations, as summarized by Daw (1997):

1. Become aware of your own cultural heritage and affiliations and of the impact your own culture has on the counseling relationship. Remember that culture affects you and your clients. Pipher (as cited by Farberman, 1997) observed that it is no longer therapeutically useful to focus just on an individual client or on the client's family of origin without consideration of the client's culture.

2. Become immersed in the cultures of people who differ from yourself. Seek opportunities to interact with people who represent different cultural dimensions and be open to what they have to say.

3. Be realistic and honest about your own range of experiences as well as issues of power, privilege, and poverty. Become aware of the great impact that poverty has on ethnicity. Think about the positions you have or hold that contribute to oppression, power, and privilege. Hardy (as cited in Daw, 1997) observed, "It's easier to talk about one's culture than one's power, one's ethnicity than one's privilege" (p. 9).

4. Remember, as a counselor, it is incumbent on *you*, not your clients, to educate yourself about various dimensions of culture. For example, if you are uninformed about a sexual orientation different from your own and you ask your client to inform you, this essentially constitutes a role reversal and the client is likely to feel frustrated. One thing related to cultural competence that emerges consistently from much literature is how important it is for counselors to *demonstrate an interest in a client's culture.*

In recent years, all major professional organizations for helping professionals have offered descriptions of various multicultural competencies required for helpers. (These are usually available from the organizations' websites, many of which are listed in Appendix A.) We strongly encourage you to familiarize yourself with these competencies and to work on areas in which you need to develop more awareness and greater proficiency and sensitivity.

APPLICATION EXERCISE 1.2
SKILLS OF COUNSELORS

Observe the day-to-day work of several counselors and/or helping professionals or the counselor you observed for Exercise 1.1. What do you conclude about their skills? Were you aware of particular personal qualities that stood out for you? What did you notice about the way they interacted with other people in their work setting? Did anything about the interventions they used seem especially useful? From your observations, could you draw any conclusions about their cultural competence and commitment to social justice? What kinds of diverse clients do they serve?

TRAINING AND CREDENTIALING
OF PROFESSIONAL COUNSELORS

Professional counseling has been defined as "the application of mental health, psychological, and human development principles through cognitive, affective, behavioral, and systemic intervention strategies, that address wellness, personal growth, and career development, as well as pathology" (American Counseling Association, 1997). Credentialing of professionals usually involves three activities:

1. Graduation from an accredited program;
2. Certification; and
3. Licensure (Vacc & Loesch, 2000, p. 304)

Gale and Austin (2003) have argued that despite the diversity of settings in which counselors practice, their training should be based on a "foundation of basic skills" (p. 6).

Professional counselors are trained in graduate programs, usually affiliated with higher education institutions, that lead to a master's degree. Traditionally, these programs require 48 to 60 semester credits and usually are designed to meet professional criteria established by the Council for Accreditation of Counseling and Related Educational Programs (CACREP). *Accreditation* refers to the process in which a private association grants public recognition to a program that meets established guidelines, based on evaluative data (Sweeney, 1995).

Most training programs begin with a series of courses that introduce the helping professions, settings, client populations, and professional ethics. Early in most programs, a counseling techniques laboratory or prepracticum introduces students to communication skills and entry-level counseling interventions, and provides opportunities to try out these skills in an observable setting (either through a two-way mirror or a closed-circuit video). Such a course includes content that is presented in this text. Typically, this course is followed by a counseling practicum in which students work with real clients under the supervision of a skilled counselor or therapist. That supervision may include live observation, videotaped review, or audiotaped review. Whatever the medium, sessions are reviewed by the supervisor, and feedback is provided to the trainee to permit assessment and professional growth.

Concurrent with these courses, most students take courses in group counseling (sometimes including a group practicum), educational and psychological testing, career counseling and development research, human development, multicultural counseling, and substance abuse. Toward the end of the program, most trainees are required to complete a one-year internship in a counseling setting related to their program. This may be in school counseling, agency counseling, college counseling, or another related setting. Programs in rehabilitation counseling, social work, and marriage and family therapy differ in some of the didactic content, but the experiential portions are similar. These programs are also accredited by their respective accrediting organization.

In addition to receiving a degree in counseling or a related field, most counselors and other help-giving professionals also seek a means by which they can become a credentialed counselor following their training and degree. Credentialing has become an important issue in recent years because of health care reforms (i.e., managed care) in which the credentials of the counselor are important for obtaining third-party reimbursement. Sweeney (1995) defined *credentialing* as "a method of identifying individuals by occupational group" (p. 120). It involves either certification and/or licensing. Although certification and licensing are similar processes, they differ in several important ways. *Certification*, unlike licensure, is established through independent, nonlegislative organizations that help to regulate the use of a particular *title*. Vacc and Loesch (2000) noted that "application of this title is more than self-anointment by those who refer to themselves as counselors" (p. 228). Counselors can be certified through the National Board of Certified Counselors (NBCC), rehabilitation counselors are certified through the Commission for Rehabilitation Counselor Certification (CRCC), and social workers are certified through the National Association of Social Workers (NASW). School counselors are also credentialed by the state in which they work (Myers, Sweeney, & White, 2002).

Licensure is a legislatively established basis of credentialing that is considered even more desirable than certification because it regulates not only the *title* but also the *practice* of the profession. Almost all states have passed legislation to license professional counselors. Social workers also can obtain social work licenses through state legislation, and some states have passed legislation to license marriage and family therapists. It is important to note that licensing laws, in particular, vary among different states and "only by examining a specific law and the rules by which it is administered can one determine the full implications of the law in a given state" (Sweeney, 1995, p. 121).

Myers, Sweeney, and White (2002) summarized a number of advantages to the credentialing process. First, it invokes a sense of pride that is important both for advocacy and job satisfaction. Second, credentialing increases a feeling of competence. Such competence not only helps professionals but it also should be reassuring to the public or clients who see credentialed practitioners. Finally, credentialing promotes accountability within a profession and its members.

■ ■ ■ ■ ■ ▬▬▬▬▬▬▬▬▬▬▬▬▬▬▬▬▬▬▬▬▬▬▬▬▬▬▬▬▬▬▬▬▬▬▬

APPLICATION EXERCISE 1.3
CREDENTIALING AND PROFESSIONAL IDENTITY

Continue with the counseling interview you began in the first exercise of this chapter (1.1). Ask the counselor you interviewed about his or her sense of professional identity. How was this person trained? What certification and/or license does this person have? What professional standards of practice and codes of ethics does this person use? With what professional organizations does this person affiliate? Present an oral summary of your findings to your class or write your finding in a written report.

SUMMARY

This chapter has examined the meaning of helping in the context of human concerns and who the helpers are. Professional helpers are found in many settings and encounter a wide variety of human issues. Professional helpers can be distinguished from non-professional helpers by their identification with a professional organization, their use of an ethical code and standards of practice, and an accrediting body that regulates their training, certification, and licensing of their practice. The effective helper brings to the setting certain personal qualities, without which the client would not likely enter into the alliance in which help occurs. But more than personal qualities are necessary to become a professional helper. A person must possess certain interpersonal skills, conceptual skills, intervention skills, and cultural competence skills to be an effective counselor. The effective counselor is committed to the sharing of resources, power, and privilege, across diverse clients. While the exact parameters of these skills may be defined by the counselor's theoretical orientation, there is no denying that the effective counselor has them and the ineffective counselor does not. Increasingly, counselors are entering new employment settings and encountering diverse groups of clients.

In the chapters that follow, we shall examine these skills and provide you with exercises and discussion questions to help in your integration of the material. Chapter 2 will look at the helping relationship and conditions that enable it to develop in positive directions to facilitate the client's progress. Chapters 3, 4, and 5 address the interpersonal skills of the counselor in regard to attending to clients, recognizing communication patterns, and managing the counseling session. Chapters 6 and 7 focus on the cognitive and affective messages of clients and ways in which counselors can differentiate between and respond to these two types of messages. Chapters 8 and 9 address the counselor's skills in conceptualizing issues and selecting and implementing strategies and interventions. Finally, Chapter 10 looks at common challenges for counselors. It is important to note that all of the skills and processes we describe in the following chapters are affected by both the social milieu and the multicultural context of the counselor and client.

REFLECTIVE QUESTIONS

1. In a small group of three to five class members, each of you should identify a preferred setting in which you would choose to be a professional counselor. Discuss among yourselves why you chose the particular setting. Does it have to do with your personal qualities? Your perception of the demands of the setting? Your perception of the rewards of working in that setting?

2. Now choose a second-most-preferred setting (other than your first choice). Continue the discussion as directed in Question 1. How did you find your reactions to be different in this second discussion? What might you learn from these differences? Did you perceive the other group members as having similar or different reactions to the second choice? What did you learn about them as a result? Share your reactions candidly.

3. Identify a person you have known who was, in your opinion, an exceptional helper. What qualities did this person possess that contributed to his or her helping nature? How do you think these qualities were acquired? Do you have any of these qualities?

4. In your opinion, what does it mean to help? To give help? To receive help? How are these processes related?

5. What has had an impact on your decision to become a helper? Consider the following sources of influence: your family of origin (the one in which you grew up), life experiences, role models, personal qualities, needs, motivations, and pragmatic concerns.

6. What do you have to offer to people struggling both with life issues and with societal issues? How do your gender, race, and cultural affiliation(s) affect this?

RECOMMENDED READINGS

Anderson, J., & Carter, R. (2003). *Diversity perspectives for social work practice*. Boston: Allyn and Bacon.

Brammer, R. (2004). *Diversity in counseling*. Pacific Grove, CA: Brooks/Cole.

Capuzzi, D., & Gross, P. (2001). *Introduction to the counseling profession* (3rd ed.). Boston: Allyn and Bacon.

Gale, A. U., & Austin, B. D. (2003). Professionalism's challenges to professional counselors' collective identity. *Journal of Counseling and Development, 81*, 3–10.

Hepworth, D., Rooney, R., & Larsen, J. (2002). *Direct social work practice* (6th ed.). Pacific Grove, CA: Brooks/Cole.

Myers, J. E., Sweeney, T. J., & White, V. E. (2002). Advocacy for counseling and counselors: A professional imperative. *Journal of Counseling and Development, 80*, 394–402.

Roysircar, G., Sandhu, D. S., & Bibbins, V. (2003). *Multicultural competencies: A guidebook of practices*. Washington DC: American Counseling Association.

Sue, D. W. (2001). Multidimensional facets of cultural competence. *The Counseling Psychologist, 29*, 790–821.

Vacc, N. A., & Loesch, L. C. (2000). *Professional orientation to counseling* (3rd ed.). Philadelphia: Brunner-Routledge.

Vera, E. M., & Speight, S. L. (2003). Multicultural competence, social justice, and counseling psychology: Expanding our roles. *The Counseling Psychologist, 31*, 253–272.

West, J. D., Osborn, C. J., & Bubenzer, D. L. (2003). *Leaders and legacies: Contributions to the profession of counseling*. New York: Brunner-Routledge.

CHAPTER TWO

THE HELPING RELATIONSHIP

Much of what is accomplished in counseling is dependent on the quality of the relationship between the counselor and the client. In all the writing on this subject, none offers more than an approach to helping known as the *person-centered approach*. This approach has been described by Corey (2001):

> The person-centered approach focuses on the client's responsibility and capacity to discover ways to more fully encounter reality. Clients, who know themselves best, are the ones to discover more appropriate behavior for themselves based on a growing self-awareness. The approach emphasizes the phenomenal world of the client. With an attempt to apprehend the client's internal frame of reference, therapists concern themselves mainly with the client's perception of self and of the world. (p. 173)

The person-centered approach derives principally from the work of one individual: Carl Rogers. Rogers emerged on the counseling scene at a time when two psychological approaches, psychoanalysis and behaviorism, were dominant. Through his influence, the profession began to focus on the relationship between therapist and client, as opposed to the existing emphasis on the client's intrapsychic experience or patterns of behavior. In one of his early writings, Rogers (1957) defined what he believed to be the "necessary and sufficient conditions" for positive personality change to occur. These conditions referred to characteristics inherent in a constructive interpersonal relationship, including accurate empathy, unconditional positive regard, and congruence. These concepts have evolved over the years, and today they are generally acknowledged by most theoretical approaches as core conditions in the therapeutic process (Glauser & Bozarth, 2001). Recent exploration of a task force on empirically supported relationship variables has reemphasized the contributions of these core conditions and the helping relationship to effective therapy processes and outcomes (Norcross, 2001). Norcross (2002) has observed that all communication skills as well as therapeutic strategies and interventions (such as the ones we describe in later chapters) are "relational acts" (p. 98).

In working with victims of the September 11, 2001, World Trade Center tragedy, Gladding (2002) observed "how crucial the *personhood* of the counselor" became (p. 10). This sense of personhood requires that, as helpers, we learn how to use ourselves in relationships in order to give a healing and growth-oriented experience in the counseling process (Moursund & Erskine, 2004). This involves being aware of our own feelings as helpers and also attuned to the feelings and experiences of our clients through the core or facilitative conditions previously mentioned. In the following sections of this chapter, we describe these core conditions in depth.

ACCURATE EMPATHY

There are numerous definitions of *empathy* in the counseling literature. In fact, an entire volume has been written just on the concept of empathy (Bohart & Greenberg, 1997a). The definition that we like is the following: the ability to (1) understand the client's experience and (2) feel with or emotionally resonate to the client's experience as if it were your own but without losing the "as if" quality (Rogers, 1957; Bozarth, 1997). Watson (2002) noted that empathy is a complex process and is often used in different ways and for different purposes in the helping relationship. When used effectively, empathy increases clients' sense of safety, their feelings of being understood, and their satisfaction with the helping process. Effective use of this core condition also decreases premature termination and promotes client exploration (Bohart, Elliott, Greenberg, & Watson, 2002).

Empathic understanding involves two primary steps:

1. "Empathic rapport"—that is, accurately sensing the client's world and being able to see things the way he or she does (Bohart & Greenberg, 1997a, p. 13)
2. "Communicative attunement"—that is, verbally sharing your understanding with the client (Bohart & Greenberg, 1997a, p. 14)

How do you know when the client feels you have understood? Client responses such as "Yes, that's it" or "That's exactly right" indicate some sort of recognition by the client of the level of your understanding. When your clients say something like that after one of your responses, you are assured that they feel you are following and understanding what is occurring.

Learning to understand is not an easy process. It involves the capacity to switch from your own set of experiences to those of your clients, as seen through their eyes, not yours. It involves sensing the feelings they have, not the feelings you have or might have had in the same or similar circumstances. It involves skillful listening, so that you can hear not only the obvious but also the subtle shadings of which the client is perhaps not yet aware.

Empathy also involves having good internal boundaries for yourself. An internal boundary helps to separate personal thoughts, feelings, and behavior from the thoughts, feelings, and behaviors of others (Mellody, 1989, p. 11). Rogers (1957) asserted that empathy is being sensitive to a client's experiencing a feeling. This is sometimes called *resonant empathy* (Buie, 1981). You can feel with the client yet you do not take on the client's feelings and actually feel them yourself. This is an area that occasionally poses problems, especially for beginning counselors. In your eagerness to be helpful, you may find yourself becoming so involved with the client that you get disconnected from yourself and what you are feeling. Instead, you take on the client's feelings and perhaps even find yourself obsessing about the client long after the session is over. Such *immersion* is not helpful because you lose your capacity to be objective in a subjective way about the client's experience. As a result, you may avoid seeing, hearing, or saying important things in the session. If you feel this is happening to you, you can talk it over with a supervisor. You also can get reconnected to yourself during a session by taking a minute to focus internally and privately on what you are feeling and by taking some deep breaths.

Understanding clients' perspectives alone is not sufficient. You also must express verbally to clients your sense of understanding about them. This kind of communication is, in effect, a kind of mirror—feeding back clients' feelings to them, without agreeing or disagreeing, reassuring or denying. Accurate empathy involves not only mirroring your clients' feelings but also some parts of the immediate process. For example, if clients continually ask many questions, rather than discuss the issues that brought them to counseling, it would be appropriate to reflect on the obvious with statements such as:

> "You have a lot of questions to ask right now."
>
> "You seem to be wanting a lot of information about this."
>
> "You are asking a lot of questions. I wonder if you are uncertain about what to expect."

Learning to develop accurate empathy with your client and with other people takes time and practice. You must experience the client's feeling first, understand it as best you can, then react to it using your own words. Effectively used, empathy helps clients to "symbolize, organize, and make sense" of their experiences (Bohart & Greenberg, 1997a, p. 15).

Several caveats about the effective use of empathy are worth noting. First, the effects of empathy are most useful when the other two core conditions of positive regard and congruence are also present. Second, empathy is not the same as sympathy. *Empathy* is about communicating your understanding of the client and her or his experience. *Sympathy* is about feeling sorry for or sad about the client. Finally, not all clients will perceive empathic understanding as useful—some may experience empathy as intrusive, directive, or foreign to them (Bohart et al., 2002, p. 102). We elaborate on this in the following section.

Cultural and Relational Empathy

In addition to understanding the client's verbal message, it is also important to consider the impact of gender and cultural backgrounds. There is increasing evidence that men and women talk in different ways (Tannen, 1990) and that cultural/historical backgrounds affect the meaning the client conveys as well as the meaning the therapist interprets. O'Hara (1997) observed that "there is good evidence that people are not all in the world in the same way and that the way people experience themselves and their phenomenal world has differed historically across time and still differs from context to context" (p. 301). Chung and Bemak (2002) noted that in North America, the concept of empathy is derived largely from Western Eurocentric values. They believe there is a need for culturally sensitive empathy. "Cultural empathy is, therefore, a way of relating interpersonally as well as understanding and communicating across cultures" and extends "the boundaries of traditional empathy" (pp. 156, 157).

Cultural empathy includes consideration of context and society in which both the counselor and the client live. When context is ignored and attempts to understand are made solely from an individualistic frame of reference, "blaming the victim" can result (O'Hara, 1997, p. 311). As an example of this, consider the way in which the understanding of unwed teenage pregnancy is often confined to the individual teenage girl who presents with the pregnancy. Absent from this empathic quotient is the understanding of larger system issues about why the girl became pregnant in the first place (O'Hara, 1997). Ignoring social context overlooks the relational world in which clients live—the dyads, families, racial/ethnic/religious groups, social class, occupational groups, and genders to which clients belong. As O'Hara noted, effective counseling is more than just a venture of two people—it is a "multilevel, relational situation" (p. 311). Theorists have coined the term *relational empathy* to describe this process (Jordan, 1997). Relational empathy involves empathy for oneself, other people, and the counseling relationship. In empathic interactions with the therapist, the client develops self-empathy as well as an increase in empathic attunement to others. This leads to "enhanced relational capacity and to an increase in self-esteem" (Jordan, 1997, p. 345). For therapists to work effectively with clients from cultures different from their own, they must be able to step back from the usual ways of knowing and be open to different ways of seeing things (Jenkins, 1997).

Chung and Bemak (2002) offer three specific things counselors can do to foster cultural and relational empathy:

1. Have a genuine interest in learning more about the client's cultural affiliations
2. Have a genuine appreciation for cultural differences between the counselor and the client
3. Incorporate culturally appropriate help-seeking behaviors and treatment outcomes and expectations into the helping process as needed (p. 157)

■ ■ ■ ■ ■ ▬▬▬▬▬▬▬▬▬▬▬▬▬▬▬▬▬▬▬▬▬▬▬▬▬▬▬▬▬▬▬▬▬▬▬▬▬

APPLICATION EXERCISE 2.1
ACCURATE EMPATHY AND CULTURAL EMPATHY

A. HEARING AND VERBALIZING CLIENT CONCERNS

Using triads with one person as speaker, a second as respondent, and the third as observer, complete the following tasks. Then rotate roles until each person has had an opportunity to react in all three ways.

1. The speaker should begin by sharing a concern or issue with the listener.
2. The respondent should
   a. listen to the speaker and
   b. verbalize to the speaker what he or she heard.
3. The observer should note the extent to which the others accomplished their tasks and whether any understanding or misunderstanding occurred.

Following a brief (five-minute) interaction, respond verbally to the following questions:

Speaker: Do you think the respondent heard what you had to say? Did you think he or she understood you? Did the listener seem to understand your culture? Discuss this with the respondent.

Respondent: Did you let the speaker know you understood or attempted to understand? How did you do this? What blocks within yourself interfered with doing so? Did you struggle with the person's cultural affiliations?

Observer: Discuss what you saw taking place between the speaker and the respondent.

Now reverse roles and complete the same process.

B. UNDERSTANDING CLIENT CONCERNS

This exercise should be completed with a group of 3 to 10 people sitting in a circle.

1. Each participant is given a piece of paper and a pencil.
2. Each participant should complete, in writing and anonymously, the following sentence: *My primary concern about becoming a counselor is*

_____

_____

_____

3. Papers are folded and placed in the center of the circle.
4. Each participant draws a paper. (If one person receives his or her own, all should draw again.)
5. Each participant reads aloud the concern listed, then talks several minutes about what it would be like to have this concern. Other participants can then add to this.

This process continues until each participant has read and discussed a concern. When discussing the concern, attempt to reflect only your *understanding* of the world of the person with this concern. Do *not* attempt to give a solution or advice.

After the exercise, members should give each other feedback about the level of empathic understanding that was displayed during the discussion. Feedback should be specific so participants can use it for behavior change.

C. CULTURAL AND RELATIONAL EMPATHY

Consider your capacity to relate to clients who are both similar to and different from yourself along cultural dimensions. Explore and discuss the following three questions, adapted from Hardy and Laszloffy (1995, p. 234):

1. What are your family's beliefs and feelings about the group(s) that comprise your culture of origin? What parts of the group(s) do they embrace or reject? How has this influenced your feelings about your cultural identity?
2. What aspects of your culture of origin do you have the most comfort "owning"? The most difficulty "owning"?
3. What groups will you have the easiest time understanding and relating to? The most difficult?

Shame and the Empathy Bond

Another factor that is increasingly recognized as having a substantial impact on the helping relationship is shame. Shame is viewed as a central component or main regulator of a person's affective life. Normal shame is about values and limits; it is recognized, spoken about, and acknowledged. The shame that is considered problematic and a primary contributor to aggression, addictions, obsessions, narcissism, and depression is hidden shame—shame that is unacknowledged, repressed, or defended against that seems to result in either an attack on others or an incredible self-loathing (Karen, 1992).

According to Lewis (1971), shame is inescapable in the counselor-client relationship and has major implications for the empathic bonding of the counselor to the client. Karen (1992) quoted Lewis as follows: "However good your reasons for going into treatment, so long as you are an adult speaking to another adult to whom you are telling the most intimate things, there is an undercurrent of shame in every session" (p. 50). Lewis (1971) asserted that not only do counselors overlook shame in clients and bypass dealing with it but they inadvertently add to a client's "shame tank" through judgmental interpretations. Value judgments about the client's culture can also contribute to a sense of shame. Lewis stated that when this happens, the client becomes enraged at the counselor, but, because he or she cannot accept feeling angry toward someone who is a "helper," it is turned inward and becomes depression and self-denigration. Lewis cautioned counselors to be alert to client states of shame so that they can help clients work through and discharge the feeling. In this way, clients can move ahead. Otherwise, they are likely to continue to move in and out of shame attacks or shame spirals, both within and outside of the counseling sessions.

A major precursor to shame appears to be the lack of parental empathy. According to Miller (1985), a child's sense of self-esteem comes largely from the parents' capacity to tune in empathically with the child, to mirror and reflect the child as she or he develops. As Karen (1992) pointed out, in therapy, "the same phenomenon requires a special sensitivity on the part of the therapist. The patient is hypersensitive about acceptance and abandonment and uncertain of whether he can trust the therapist with his wound—a wound that, he no doubt senses, the therapy session has great potential to exacerbate. The therapist must win over the hiding, shameful side of the personality and gradually help it to heal" (p. 65). The counselor does this by creating an empathic bond with the client—that is, an emotional connection, a genuine feeling for the client. Although empathy can be conveyed by certain techniques (such as the verbal expressions we noted earlier), ultimately there is no substitute for the counselor's ability to genuinely care for and feel with the client. Empathy appears to be the critical variable in the healing of pathological shame (Jordan, 1997).

Shame can also be culture bound. Hardy and Laszloffy (1995) pointed out that every cultural group has pride and shame issues—that is, "aspects of a culture that are sanctioned as distinctively negative or positive" (p. 229). These are important issues to identify about a client's cultural group because they help to define appropriate and inappropriate behavior within a cultural context.

POSITIVE REGARD

In his early writings, Carl Rogers (1957) described positive regard as unconditional. More recent writers have relabeled positive regard as *nonpossessive warmth.* The effectiveness of positive regard appears to lie "in its ability to facilitate a long-term working relationship" (Farber & Lane, 2002, p. 185). Positive regard is associated with clients' perceptions of improvement in issues and it sets the stage for the use of various helping strategies and interventions (such as those we describe in later chapters). Lack of positive regard often produces and contributes to ruptures in the helping relationship (Farber & Lane, 2002, p. 192).

Positive regard, or nonpossessive warmth, is often misconstrued as agreement or lack of disagreement with the client. Instead, it is an attitude of valuing the client. To show positive regard is to express appreciation of the client as a unique and worthwhile person. It is also to be noncritical, to provide an "overall sense of protection, support, or acceptance, no matter what is divulged" (Karasu, 1992, p. 36). In this context, it is important for counselors not just to *feel* positively about clients, but also to *convey* these positive feelings to clients. As Farber and Lane (2002) noted, "This does not have to translate to a stream of compliments nor to a gushing of positive sentiment that, in fact, may overwhelm or even terrify some clients; rather, it speaks to the need for therapists to communicate a caring, respectful, positive attitude that serves to affirm a client's basic sense of worth" (p. 192).

■ ■ ■ ■ ■ ▬▬▬▬▬▬▬▬▬▬▬▬▬▬▬▬▬▬▬▬▬▬▬▬▬▬▬▬

APPLICATION EXERCISE 2.2
POSITIVE REGARD

A. OVERCOMING BARRIERS TO POSITIVE REGARD

Think of expressing to the client (1) those limitations that may be blocking your sense of liking for the client and (2) those strengths that increase your appreciation for the client. The following steps may assist you in expressing this:

1. Picture the other person in your mind. Begin a dialogue in which you express what it is that is interfering with your sense of positive regard. Now, reverse the roles. Become the other person. What does the person say in response? Then what do you say?
2. Complete this process again. This time, express the strengths you see in the other person—what you appreciate about that person. Again, reverse the roles. Become the other person. What does he or she say in response? Then what do you say?

This exercise can be used with any client toward whom you have difficulty experiencing positive regard.

(continued)

APPLICATION EXERCISE 2.2   CONTINUED

B. EXPRESSING POSITIVE REGARD
Take a few minutes to think of a person with whom you currently have a relationship and for whom you experience positive regard. What kinds of things do you do to express your feelings of positive regard for this person? Jot them down.

_____

_____

_____

There is no set answer to the preceding exercise because each person has a different style of communicating good feelings for another person. The first step, though, is positive regard—to feel comfortable enough to *express* warm feelings to someone else. Being free enough to spontaneously share feelings of regard for another human being is a process that can be learned.

Think again for a moment about several of your existing relationships with a few people close to you—perhaps your spouse, parent, child, neighbor, or friend. Then respond, in writing, to the following questions:

What is your level of expression of positive regard to these people?

How often do you say things like "I like you"; "It's nice to be with you"; "You're good for me"; "I enjoy you"; and so forth?

What is your feeling when you do?

What is the effect on the other person?

If your expression of these kinds of statements is infrequent, what might be holding you back?

Either now or later, seek out someone you like and try to express these kinds of feelings to that person. Then think again about the previous questions. Share your reactions with your partner. In doing this, you will probably note that warmth and positive regard are expressed both nonverbally and verbally.

CONGRUENCE

Neither empathy nor positive regard can be conveyed in helping relationships unless the counselor is seen by the client as *genuine*. The notion that the counselor should project genuineness is difficult to define. Rogers called it *congruence*, a condition reflecting honesty, transparency, and openness to the client. Congruence implies that therapists are real in their interactions with clients. As Corey (2001) noted, this means counselors are "without a false front, their inner and outer expression of that experience match, and they can openly express feelings and attitudes that are present in the relationship with the client" (p. 197).

Through being genuine and congruent, counselors model for clients not only the experience of being real but also the process of claiming one's truths and speaking about them. When this happens, there is usually more vitality and a greater "connection" in the counseling relationship. As Jordan (1997) noted, "We all know the deadened, bored, or anxious feelings that occur in interactions in which people cannot risk being in their truth. . . . Inauthenticity takes us out of real mutuality" (p. 350). Take a moment to think about the fact that most clients come into the helping process in a state of *incongruence*. In this respect, the *congruence* of the counselor is even more important. It helps clients become more congruent, making it easier for them to own their feelings and express them without excessive fear (Klein, Kolden, Michels, & Chisholm-Stockard, 2002, p. 196).

The beginning counselor may find this condition easier to apply in theory than in practice. Questions such as What if I really don't like my client? Should I let that be known? Wouldn't it destroy the relationship? inevitably rise when genuineness and congruence are examined. The appropriate answer to these questions may not be entirely satisfying. Congruence dictates that the counselor be honest, but in helpful, rather than destructive, ways.

Expression of your feelings should not take precedence over understanding the client's feelings. The counseling relationship does not have all the mutuality that is present in many other relationships, such as friend to friend, partner to partner, and so forth. Corey (2001) cautioned that congruence does not mean, however, that the counselor impulsively shares all thoughts and feelings with clients in a nonselective way. A general rule is to share your feelings when they are persistent and if they block your acceptance of the client.

Before you can express your feelings, you must become aware of them. For example, ask yourself what it means to be genuine. Can you tell when you are being yourself or when you are presenting an image that is different from the way you actually feel? In order to communicate congruence to the client, you must first learn to get in touch with yourself and your own truth—to become aware of who you are as an individual and what kinds of thoughts and feelings you have. This involves learning to discriminate between your various feelings and allowing them to come into your awareness without denial or distortion; it means, for example, that when you are happy, you can acknowledge that you are happy and when you are angry, you can be aware of your anger. It also means that you can speak about these "truths." Congruent responses involve both self-disclosure and feedback statements by counselors to clients.

■ ■ ■ ■ ■ ▬▬

APPLICATION EXERCISE 2.3
DYADIC ENCOUNTER: CONGRUENCE

To assist you in becoming aware of your own thoughts and feelings, select a partner and spend a few minutes with this dyadic encounter experience (Banikiotes, Kubinski, & Pursell, 1981). It is designed to facilitate getting to know yourself and another person on

(continued)

APPLICATION EXERCISE 2.3   CONTINUED

a fairly close level. All you need to do is respond to the open-ended questions as honestly and directly as possible. Both of you should respond to one question at a time. The discussion statements can be completed at whatever level of self-disclosure you wish.

My name is _____ .

The reason I'm here is _____ .

One of the most important skills in getting to know another person is listening. In order to check on your ability to understand what your partner is communicating, the two of you should go through the following steps one at a time.

Decide which one of you is to speak first in this unit. The first speaker is to complete the following item in two or three sentences:

When I think about the future. I see myself . . .

The second speaker repeats in his or her own words what the first speaker has just said. The first speaker must be satisfied that he or she has been heard accurately.

The second speaker then completes the item in two or three sentences. The first speaker paraphrases what the second speaker just said, to the satisfaction of the second speaker.

Share what you may have learned about yourself as a listener with your partner. To check your listening accuracy, the two of you may find yourselves later saying to each other, "Do you mean that . . . ?" or "You're saying that . . . ." Don't respond to any sentence you don't want to.

When I am new in a group, I . . .
When I am feeling anxious in a new situation, I usually . . .
You're saying that . . . (listening check)
Right now, I'm feeling . . .
The thing that turns me off the most is . . .
When I am alone, I usually . . .
I feel angry about . . .
Do you mean that . . . ? (listening check)

CHECKUP

Have a short discussion about this experience so far. Keep eye contact as much as you can and try to cover the following points:

How well are you listening?
How open and honest have you been?
How eager are you to continue this interchange?
Do you feel that you are getting to know each other?

Then continue with the following:

I love . . .
I feel jealous about . . .

Right now, I'm feeling . . .
I am afraid of . . .
The thing I like best about you is . . .
You are . . .
Right now, I am responding most to . . .

SELF-DISCLOSURE

Expression of your thoughts, ideas, and feelings follows after your awareness of them. This process might also be called *self-expression* or *self-disclosure*. Hill and Knox (2002) defined self-disclosure as statements that reveal something about yourself (p. 255). Self-expression and disclosure are important ways of letting the client know that you are a person and not just a role; however, self-disclosure should be used appropriately and not indiscriminately in the counseling sessions. Hepworth, Rooney, and Larsen (2002) cautioned against self-disclosure of hostility in particular.

It is important not to interpret self-disclosure to mean that you ought to talk about yourself, since the primary focus of the interview is on the client. Thus, congruence does not mean that you reveal your own experiences and values. It does mean, however, that occasionally it is appropriate and helpful for you to reveal or disclose a particular feeling you may have about the counseling session or about the client. The clue to appropriateness is often determined by the question: Whose needs am I meeting when I disclose this idea or feeling—the client's or mine? Clearly, the former is the much more appropriate instance of the two. There are several different kinds of self-disclosure:

1. The counselor's own issues
2. Facts about the counselor's role
3. The counselor's reactions to the client (feedback)
4. The counselor's reactions to the counselor-client relationship

Usually, disclosure in the latter two areas is more productive. Many times, counselors are tempted to share their problems and concerns when encountering a client with similar problems. In a few instances, this may be done as a reassurance to clients that their concerns are not catastrophic. But, in most other instances, a role reversal occurs—the counselor is gaining something by this sharing with the client. Some research indicates that the counselor who discloses at a *moderate* level may be perceived by the client more positively than the counselor who discloses at a high or low level (Edwards & Murdock, 1994). Thus, too much or too little self-disclosure may limit the client's confidence in you as an effective helper. Further, self-disclosure that occurs too frequently may blur the boundaries between counselor and client and can be a precursor to problematic dual relationships. On the other hand, lack of self-disclosure can turn clients away. Self-disclosure is an important way to build trust with adolescent clients, with clients who have substance abuse issues, and in multicultural counseling situations (Egan, 2002; Sue & Sue, 2003).

Often, clients may ask questions concerning information about the counselor: Are you married? Why did you become a counselor? Are you in school? These are common types of questions clients ask in seeking facts about the counselor. In this case, it is usually best just to give a direct, brief answer and then return the interview focus to the client. However, if this is a common occurrence with the same client, there are other ways of responding. Continual client questioning of this sort often indicates that the client is anxious and is attempting to get off the "hot seat" by turning the focus onto you. There are better ways to handle this than by spending the interview disclosing facts about yourself! Alternative ways of responding include:

1. Reflect on the client's feelings of anxiety: "You seem anxious about talking about yourself now."
2. Reflect on the process: "You seem to be asking a lot of questions now."
3. Make a statement about what you see happening: "I think you feel as if you're on the 'hot seat' and asking me questions is a good way for you to get off it."

■ ■ ■ ■ ■ ▬▬▬▬▬▬▬▬▬▬▬▬▬▬▬▬▬▬▬▬▬▬▬▬▬▬▬▬▬▬▬

APPLICATION EXERCISE 2.4
SELF-DISCLOSURE

Think about yourself in the following instances:

1. You have a client who describes herself as shy and retiring. During the third interview, she says, "I'd like to be like you—you seem so outgoing and comfortable with people. Why don't you just tell me how you got that way?" Do you then consider it appropriate to share some of your experiences with her? Do you think your response to this might vary, depending on the client's cultural affiliations? If so, how?
2. You have had one particular client for about seven individual sessions. After the first session, the client has been at least several minutes late for each session and waits until almost the end of the interview to bring up something important to discuss. You feel that he is infringing on your time. This is preventing you from giving your full attention and understanding to the client. You have acknowledged to yourself that this is bothering you. Is it appropriate to go ahead and express this to him?

Take a few minutes to think about yourself as the counselor in these two examples. Now write in the following space what you would do in each example to communicate congruence.

_____

_____

_____

_____

There are no right or wrong answers to these two examples; each counseling interaction is somewhat different. Ultimately, you, as the counselor, will have to make a decision like this for yourself in each instance. Based on the preceding written material, perhaps you did indicate that it would be more appropriate to express your irritation (the second example) than to disclose your experiences (the first). In the first instance, rather than sharing facts about yourself, there are more productive ways of helping that client reach her goals. For example, she would be more involved if you suggest role reversal. You become the client; have her be the outgoing and comfortable counselor she sees. In the second instance, the client, by being late, is not fulfilling his share of the responsibility or he is indirectly communicating something about his feelings that needs to be discussed.

Some counselors are able to acknowledge their feelings and determine when these can best be expressed in the interview but are not sure how to express these kinds of thoughts and feelings to the client. Self-disclosure or expressions of congruence are often characterized by sharing and feedback statements—statements that convey to the client your sense of what is going on and your feelings about it. These kinds of statements are illustrated by the following examples:

"I am glad you shared that with me."
"If that happened to me, I think I'd feel pretty angry."
"I don't feel that we're getting anywhere right now."

Other examples of sharing kinds of responses are:

Client: "It's hard for me to say so but I really do get a lot out of these sessions."
Counselor: "That makes me feel good to hear you say that."
    or:
"I'm glad to know you feel that way."

Note that in the counselor's sharing statements, the communication is *direct*—it focuses on the counselor's feelings and on the client. It is a better statement than a generalized comment like "I hope most clients would feel the same way." A sharing and feedback statement should avoid the trap of "counselor language." To begin a sharing and/or feedback statement with "I hear you saying," "It seems that you feel," or "I feel that you feel" gets wordy, repetitive, and even phony. Say *exactly* what you mean.

■ ■ ■ ■ ■ ▬▬▬▬▬▬▬▬▬▬

APPLICATION EXERCISE 2.5
EXPRESSING COUNSELOR FEELINGS

Sharing and feedback communicate to the client that you have heard or seen something going on and that you have certain thoughts or feelings about it that you want to communicate. Sometimes you will want to say not only what you feel about a specific instance or experience but also how you feel about the client. This will be more effective if your feelings are expressed as immediate ones—that is, expressed in the *present* rather than in

(continued)

APPLICATION EXERCISE 2.5   CONTINUED

the past or future. This is the meaning of keeping the process of relationship in the *here and now*, using what is going on from moment to moment in each session to build the relationship. It is represented by the type of statement that communicates, "Right now, I'm feeling . . . " or "Right now, we are . . . "

To experience this here-and-now kind of communication, try to get in touch with yourself this instant. What are you feeling *this very moment* as you are reading and thinking about this page, this paragraph, this sentence? Write down four or five adjectives that express your present feelings. Tune in to your nonverbal cues as well (body position, rate of breathing, tension spots, etc.).

_____

_____

_____

APPLICATION EXERCISE 2.6
USING SHARING STATEMENTS

With a partner, engage in some sharing-type statements that are direct, specific, and immediate. Can you tune in to your feelings as you engage in this kind of communication? What does it do for you and what effect does it have on the other person? Jot down some of these reactions here. List the sharing statements you have made to your partner.

_____

_____

_____

_____

_____

POSITIVE FEEDBACK STATEMENTS

Positive feedback statements are also related to counselor congruence. Like self-disclosure, these kinds of statements help clients see their counselor as a real human being. Johnson (2003) has pointed out that both self-disclosure and feedback statements can reveal things to clients they do not know about themselves. Like self-disclosure, feedback statements should never be made *against* the client (Claiborn, Goodyear, & Horner, 2002, p. 229).

In a review of related research about feedback, Claiborn, Goodyear, and Horner (2002) concluded that positive feedback is more acceptable than negative feedback and that this is especially true early in the helping relationship. Hepworth, Rooney, and Larsen (2002) noted that positive feedback statements can focus on client strengths and effective coping and can empower clients. According to the authors, tapes of sessions between workers and clients reveal a dearth of responses that underscore client strengths, successes, assets, coping behaviors, and areas of growth (p. 126).

Positive feedback statements are useful when you have warm and supportive feelings for clients that are truly genuine. Consider the following examples offered by Hepworth, Rooney, and Larsen (2002, p. 125):

> Counselor to individual client: "I'm pleased you have what I consider exceptional ability to 'self-observe' your own behavior and to analyze the part you play in relationships. I think this strength will serve you well in solving the problems you've identified."

> Counselor to client who is a member of a counseling group: "I've been touched several times in the group when I've noticed that, despite your grief over the loss of your husband, you've reached out to other members who needed support."

In making positive feedback statements, there are some guidelines to consider that are fundamental to effective feedback processes. Such statements express a feeling of acknowledgment and *ownership* by the counselor, as in "When something happens, I feel thus and so" or "When I see you _____, I think _____."

Note that these statements use the personal pronoun or "I messages." They avoid judgment and evaluation. Most of all, they do not accuse or blame, as in the following statement: "You are a real problem to work with because you are always late." In other words, they preserve the dignity and self-respect of the other person involved in the relationship. Furthermore, an effective feedback statement does not contain advice; it is not a "parenting" or scolding statement. It also should concern a behavior or attitude the other person has the capacity to change or modify. It would not be helpful, for instance, to use the following kind of feedback statement: "I just don't like the way you look. Why don't you do something about your complexion?" Focus your feedback statements on behavior rather than personality traits, and be specific rather than general.

Feedback is usually more effective when it is solicited. Thus, feedback statements that relate to clients' goals or to aspects of the counseling relationship may be better received by clients because of their involvement in this. In any case, though, you can determine the effects of your feedback by the clients' reactions. If your clients are defensive, give detailed explanation or justification, or make strong denials, this is a clue that your feedback was not solicited and that perhaps you have touched on an issue too soon. At this point in the relationship, clients need an indication of your support and acceptance. It is also important to give clients a chance to explore their feelings about and reactions to these feedback statements.

■ ■ ■ ■ ■

APPLICATION EXERCISE 2.7
USING FEEDBACK STATEMENTS

A. CHARACTERISTICS OF FEEDBACK

With a partner, try some feedback-type statements that meet the characteristics described in the preceding section. Be sure your responses include a description of your partner's behavior as well as your reactions to it. For example, you might say something like "I appreciate (your feeling) your taking the time to talk with me (partner's behavior)."

List the feedback statements you make to your partner. What are the effects on you? On the other person? On the relationship?

_____

_____

_____

B. POSITIVE FEEDBACK STATEMENTS

In a small group, construct a positive feedback statement that focuses on a positive ingredient or strength that each member brings to the group. This may refer to a specific behavior you have seen each person demonstrate in the group or it may refer to something you appreciate about that person. Share your statements verbally in the group. Make sure there is time for the group member to respond to your positive feedback statements.

A CLIMATE OF SAFETY

The primary reason why the conditions of a therapeutic relationship are so important is to help clients feel safe. When clients feel safe, they feel trusting and free to be open and disclosive. When clients do not feel safe, they often feel self-protective, guarded, and subdued. It is the counselor's responsibility to offer the kind of climate in which clients feel the sense of safety they need in order to ask for and accept help. If a client has come from a particular kind of family or relationship in which there was a lot of stress, such as abuse or incest, then the counselor's effort to provide a safe environment will need to be even more intentional and more intensive.

Clients, particularly those who have had their trust broken in the past, will often test the counselor. They will likely not believe that the therapist's initial efforts to be understanding, sincere, accepting, and warm are really true. They may want to find out if they really mean something to the counselor—if they really are valued as the therapist says they are. This reason may account for all kinds of client feelings and behaviors that are projected or reflected in or outside a session, including acting out, calling the counselor on the phone, being late to a session, becoming angry, and so on. It is as if clients long for a warm, caring empathic helper but, due to their history, fear this and in their fear, resist, attack, or retreat (Karasu, 1992, p. 21). Efforts to provide a safe therapeutic environment for clients need to be ongoing and persistent. This is also especially true in working with clients who do not have privileges and power from the mainstream culture and who have a history of discrimination and oppression.

SUMMARY

Although the counseling relationship has some marked differences from other interpersonal relationships, it does serve as a model that the client can use to improve the quality of relationships outside the counseling room. You must assume responsibility at the outset of counseling for those qualities that generate and maintain the relationship process. Later, as the client's comfort and social skills get stronger, the relationship becomes more of a mutually responsible process.

Clearly, the counseling relationship cannot succeed without the presence of accurate empathy or understanding of the client's world. When you assume that you understand, but you do not, you and your client detour from a constructive and helpful course and risk the dangers of false conclusions and failure. In a similar manner, if you do not value your client or if you do not consider the client's problems and concerns to be real, you are denying the most reliable information about your client's perceptions. Lacking this information, you cannot help your client develop in more constructive directions. Finally, and underlying both accurate empathy and positive regard, the degree to which you can be honestly and consistently yourself, knowing yourself, and sharing yourself with your client in congruent ways will establish the ultimate parameters of the helping relationship.

Although the behaviors presented in this chapter can be learned and incorporated into your style and repertoire, there is a dimension yet to be acknowledged. The integral human element of the counseling relationship cannot exist by mechanical manipulation of certain behaviors at given moments. Your relationship with each client contains its own uniqueness and spontaneity that cannot, without the loss of both genuineness and sincerity, be systematically controlled prior to its occurrence. Your spontaneity, however, will increase rather than decrease once you have become comfortable with a variety of counseling techniques. While you are learning counselor responses, this ease may not be quite as apparent because you will need to overlearn them. However, once the responses suggested in this book have become second nature to you, your spontaneity as a counselor will begin to emerge. You will be on your way to becoming the helper you hope to be.

REFLECTIVE QUESTIONS

1. How do you approach a new relationship? What conditions do you require to be met before you open yourself to a closer relationship?

2. What were the "unwritten rules" in your family and in your culture about interactions with nonfamily members? How might these rules affect the kind of relationship you are able to offer clients?

3. If you were a client, what conditions would you look for in your counselor?

4. Under what conditions do you feel safe? Open and disclosive? Trusting? Does this vary with persons of different ages, gender, values, and ethnic origins?

RECOMMENDED READINGS

Bohart, A., & Greenberg, L. (Eds.). (1997). *Empathy reconsidered*. Washington, DC: American Psychological Association.

Brammer, L. M., & MacDonald, G. (1999). *The helping relationship* (7th ed.). Boston: Allyn and Bacon.

Breggin, P., Breggin, G., & Bemak, F. (Eds.). (2002). *Dimensions of empathic therapy*. New York: Springer.

Chi-Ying Chung, R., & Bemak, F. (2002). The relationship of culture and empathy in cross-cultural counseling. *Journal of Counseling and Development, 80*, 154–159.

Glauser, A. S., & Bozarth, J. D. (2001). Person centered counseling: The culture within. *Journal of Counseling and Development, 79*, 142–147.

Hepworth, D. H., Rooney, R. H., & Larsen, J. A. (2002). *Direct social work practice* (6th ed.). Belmont, CA: Brooks/Cole.

Johnson, D. W. (2003). *Reaching out: Interpersonal effectiveness and self-actualization* (5th ed.). Boston: Allyn and Bacon.

Jordan, J. (1997). Relational development through mutual empathy. In A. Bohart & L. Greenberg (Eds.), *Empathy reconsidered* (pp. 343–352). Washington, DC: American Psychological Association.

Kelly, E. W., Jr. (1997). Relationship-centered counseling: A humanistic model of integration. *Journal of Counseling and Development, 75*, 337–345.

Moursund, J. P., & Erskine, R. G. (2004). *Integrative psychotherapy: The art and science of relationship*. Pacific Grove, CA: Brooks/Cole.

Norcross, J. C. (Ed.). (2002). *Psychotherapy relationships that work*. New York: Oxford University Press.

CHAPTER THREE

ATTENDING TO CLIENTS

Thus far, we have identified several conditions that affect the development of the counseling relationship. Those conditions—accurate empathy, positive regard, and genuineness or congruence—are called *core conditions* because they are central to the therapeutic process. Although these core conditions are necessary, the counselor must also bring other skills and knowledge to the therapeutic process. Certainly the first of these skills is the ability to *listen* actively and attentively to the client. This objective is not as simple as it might appear. It involves more than an attentive ear.

Have you ever talked to someone who was fiddling with a pencil, staring around the room, or seemed otherwise distracted as he or she listened to you? If you have—and who has not?—you will recall how this felt. The listener may have heard all that you said, but you probably interpreted his or her behavior as a lack of interest, concentration, or attention. That seemingly to be the case, you probably found it difficult to continue the conversation. Clients exhibit this same sensitivity to whether the counselor is paying attention to what they say. Nonverbal behavior does influence the verbal message with which it is paired, particularly when inconsistencies exist between verbal and nonverbal messages.

This chapter is concerned with the behaviors that do or do not facilitate communication and the core conditions in counseling. In addition, attending skills used by the counselor to assure the client and to support or reinforce the client are examined. These skills are very important for the client who is feeling vulnerable, uncertain, nonconfident, or nontrusting.

One precondition for the existence of these reinforcing or supporting behaviors is an awareness of the client's communication. This awareness must then be communicated through your undistracted attentiveness to the client. Attentiveness is one way of saying, "I am following both your message and your metacommunication; I am experiencing as you are experiencing this moment; I am invested and involved in your story." Studies have indicated that attentiveness is related to other counselor attitudes, most notably empathy and involvement.

COMMUNICATION OF ATTENTIVENESS

Attentiveness is communicated primarily through four channels: facial expressions, eye contact, bodily positions and movement, and verbal responses (Cormier & Nurius,

2003). Although attending to clients on the surface appears relatively simple, it is easier said than done. Egan (2002, pp. 90–92) listed a number of obstacles to the attending process:

1. Being judgmental
2. Having biases
3. Pigeonholing clients
4. Attending to facts
5. Sympathizing
6. Interrupting

The meanings people attach to different gestures or words have been learned. Some of the meanings are fairly standardized; others have distinct regional or cultural variances. For example, do you prefer to have people look at you when you talk to them? Most Euro-Americans do, but some Native Americans do not, and studies suggest that some inner-city African American youths do not. It is important to remember that some cultural groups have sanctions on direct visual contact during some types of interpersonal interactions. When you are telling someone what you think, what would be your reaction if that person began to frown? If the frown was not consistent with your feelings, you probably would begin to question the inconsistency between your message and the listener's response. If you feel strongly about a topic and the other person does not seem to care about it, are you likely to continue telling the person about your feelings? No, since most of us want to know that our feelings are falling on concerned ears.

For these and many more reasons, your behavior can contribute to your client's feelings of security. This increased sense of security that occurs at the same time clients are talking about themselves can become a self-reinforcing phenomenon. Most of you have probably had the experience of entering a new activity and feeling nervous and unsure of yourselves. But as you stayed with the activity and nothing bad (perhaps even some good things) happened, before long, your self-confidence began to grow. So it is with counseling. As the client begins to experience your acceptance, your understanding, and your commitment, the feelings of vulnerability, uncertainty, caution, or lack of trust begin to dissipate. In the following sections of the chapter, we describe nonverbal and verbal ways to increase your attentiveness with clients.

FACIAL EXPRESSIONS

Knapp and Hall (1997) have observed that the face is the primary means by which people communicate information about their emotional states. Facial expressions convey basic emotions such as anger, disgust, fear, sadness, and happiness. Unlike most other aspects of nonverbal attending behavior, facial expressions do not seem to vary much among cultures. These basic emotions seem to be represented by the same facial expressions across cultures, although individual cultural norms may influence how much and how often such emotions are expressed (Mesquita & Frijda, 1992). For example, anger is often conveyed cross-culturally through the eyes and by changes in the area of the mouth and jaw. However, men and women both within and between the same and different cultures may express anger in different ways and at different times. For example, some persons may reject the idea of releasing anger because they have learned it is "unchristian" or "unladylike" (Kelley, 1979, p. 24).

Your facial expressions communicate messages to the client that are as meaningful as those you receive from the client's facial expressions. A primary, though often not intentional, way that counselors use their facial expressions is to reinforce client behavior. Perhaps it would be more accurate to say that the effect of your facial expressions is to reinforce, either positively or negatively, clients' verbal behavior. It is also important for your facial expressions to reflect those of the client—if the client expresses pleasure, you look happy; if the client conveys sadness, you show concern.

Animation

Animation in facial expression gives clients the feeling that you are alert and responding to ongoing communication. It may be that your facial expressions serve as a mirror for clients' feelings as well as an acceptance of them. Certainly, an absence of facial expressions (a deadpan look) will suggest a lack of interest, awareness, or mental presence to clients. The most noticeable expression is the smile. The appropriate use of smiles can have a powerful effect on clients, particularly when paired with occasional head nods. Continuous smiling, however, becomes a negative stimulus. Frequent frowns can communicate disapproval. Occasional frowns, on the other hand, communicate your failure to follow or understand a particular point and are therefore useful.

■ ■ ■ ■ ■ ▬▬▬▬▬▬▬▬▬▬▬▬▬▬▬▬▬▬▬▬▬▬▬▬▬▬▬▬▬▬▬▬

APPLICATION EXERCISE 3.1
FACIAL EXPRESSIONS

A. FACIAL ATTENTIVENESS
With a partner, designate one of you as the speaker and the other as the listener. While the speaker shares one of his or her concerns, the listener's tasks are:

1. Do not respond with *any* facial expression or animation whatsoever while the speaker is talking; maintain complete facial passivity.
2. After two or three minutes, respond with a facial reaction that is opposite of the feelings and concerns being expressed by the speaker. For example, if the speaker is talking seriously, smile and look happy.
3. After another three minutes or so, respond with facial animation and expression that mirror the kind and intensity of feelings being expressed by the speaker.

Discuss the different results produced by these three approaches. Reverse roles and repeat the exercise. What can you conclude about facial attentiveness as a result of this

(continued)

APPLICATION EXERCISE 3.1   CONTINUED

exercise? What have you learned about yourself and your facial gestures? What do you want to change about your facial gestures and how do you intend to bring this change about? If possible, repeat this activity with a person from a distinctly different culture than your own. Do your conclusions change in any way?

B. RECOGNIZING FACIAL CUES

Find two people with whom to work. Designate one of you as the speaker for round 1; the second as the listener, and the third as the observer. Roles are rotated for round 2 and round 3. For each round, the listener feeds each of the four incomplete sentences to the speaker. The speaker repeats the sentence and adds the first completion that comes to his or her mind. The observer watches for changes and cues in the speaker's facial expressions as he or she works with all of the incomplete sentences in the round. For this to be most effective, when you are in the role of the speaker, take your time, breathe deeply, and say whatever comes into your mind without thinking about it or censoring it. The observer shares the observations with the speaker after the round is over. When you are in the role of the speaker, only disclose what feels comfortable to you.

1. Anger
   a. When I get angry . . .
   b. I get angry when . . .
   c. I feel disgusted that . . .
   d. One thing that makes me mad is . . .
2. Sadness
   a. When I get sad . . .
   b. I get sad when . . .
   c. I feel "blue" that . . .
   d. One thing that makes me sad is . . .
3. Fear
   a. When I get afraid . . .
   b. I feel afraid that . . .
   c. I get afraid when . . .
   d. One thing that makes me afraid is . . .

EYE CONTACT

What is the effect of eye contact? Research into interpersonal interaction indicates that eye contact has more than one effect and that these effects do vary across cultures. It may signal a need for affiliation, involvement, or inclusion; it may reflect the quality of an existing relationship; or it may enhance the communication of a complex message. Eye contact can also produce anxiety in the other person. A gaze lasting longer than about 10 seconds can signal aggressiveness rather than acceptance. An averted gaze may hide shame over expressing something seen as culturally taboo.

In some cultures, client eye contact is appropriate when listening. In other cultures, an individual may look away as a sign of respect or may demonstrate more eye contact when talking and less eye contact while listening. Good eye contact—eye contact that reinforces clients and makes their communication easier—lies somewhere between the fixed gaze and "shifty eyes," or frequent breaks of eye contact. Look at clients when they are talking. Occasionally, permit your eyes to drift to an object away, *but not far away*, from the client. Then return your eyes to the client. Let yourself be natural. Do not be afraid to invite the client into the world of your vision. At the same time, avoid making stereotypical judgments about the client's eye contact or lack thereof. As Cormier and Nurius (2003) noted, "Unfortunately, helpers all too often equate avoidance of eye contact with disrespect, shyness, deception and/or depression, but for some clients of color, less frequent eye contact is typical of their culture and is not a sign of any of the above" (p. 48).

■ ■ ■ ■ ■ ▬▬▬▬▬

APPLICATION EXERCISE 3.2
EYE CONTACT

Perhaps you can better grasp the effects of eye contact by participating in the following dyadic exercise. With a partner, determine who will be the talker and who will be the listener. While the talker speaks, the listener should listen but avoid eye contact with the speaker. Then discuss the following questions: What are the effects on the speaker? How well did the speaker feel that he or she was able to communicate? Try the exercise again, but this time maintain eye contact with the speaker as described in the previous section. What effect does this have? Reverse roles and repeat the exercise. Discuss how the effects may vary, depending on the gender and culture of the participants.

BODY POSITIONS AND USE OF SPACE

Body positions serve important functions in a counseling session. Body positions and movement regulate space or distance between the counselor and a client, greeting of a client, termination of a session, and turn taking (that is, the exchange of speaker and listener roles within a conversation) (Cormier & Nurius, 2003). Body movement and comfort with physical space (closeness or distance) vary among cultures and with gender. Generally, among Euro-Americans, counselors and clients sit face to face. Even an intervening object such as a desk is often considered a distraction. Yet, as Ivey, D'Andrea, Ivey, and Simek-Morgan (2002, p. 63) noted, in some Eskimo and Inuit cultural groups, persons sit side by side when discussing a personal issue. Euro-Americans usually prefer several feet of distance between chairs; however, those from contact cultures may be more comfortable with closer distances (Watson, 1970). The effects of space also vary with a client's expression of feelings. A client who has just expressed a lot of anger often requires more personal space than someone who is feeling sad or experiencing a lot of pain. In short, the concept of space has no universals.

Gender also dictates what is considered appropriate space. Some females may be more comfortable with a closer distance to the counselor, especially if the counselor is female. However, many female clients may feel intruded upon if a male counselor positions himself too close for comfort. Clients with a history of severe physical and/or sexual abuse may require greater space, particularly at the beginning stage of counseling. To be respectful of all clients, it is important to allow *them* to choose the appropriate amount of distance from the therapist in the counseling interactions.

One important aspect to body communication involves the amount of tension conveyed by the body. Astute counselors will note the degree of tension or relaxation in a client's body. A body that is blocking or holding back a feeling may be tense, with shallow, fast breathing. A relaxed body posture indicates comfort, both with the counseling setting and with the topic being discussed. Selective body tension communicates action. It may reflect a "working" moment for you—involvement with the client, movement toward a goal, or preparation for something new. Body tension that is continuous will probably communicate discomfort with the client, the topic, or yourself. To be comfortable with yourself, it is important to begin from a base of relaxation. Exercise 3.3 may help you to achieve a desired state of relaxation.

■ ■ ■ ■ ■ ▬▬▬

APPLICATION EXERCISE 3.3
RELAXING

A. MUSCLE RELAXATION

While sitting down, raise your hand and arms three to four inches above the armrests of the chair and then let them drop. Feel the tension flow out of your arms. Repeat this and try to increase the relaxation. Let your back and buttocks be in contact with as much of the chair as possible. Feel the chair pressing against your body. Tense the muscles in your legs and then release the tension. Feel the surge of warmth in your muscles as your legs relax. Repeat this tensing and releasing of leg muscles several times, each time achieving a little more relaxation. Now take three or four deep breaths slowly. After each breath, slowly release the air from your lungs. Do you feel more relaxed than when you started?

Do this exercise again, this time without any interruptions between different body exercises. This is a good exercise to do just before seeing a client. It is one of the ways by which you can prepare yourself for the session. As you do the exercise more often, you will find it easier and quicker to achieve a surprisingly comfortable state of relaxation.

B. MASSAGE RELAXATION

As you engage in this activity, breathe in and out through your nose in an even, balanced way. Rub the palms of your hands together for several minutes or until they feel very warm. Then lightly rest each hand on your head with your thumbs touching each temple. Place your hands on your forehead and smooth out any tension. Then gently massage this part of your head. Lightly massage over and under your eyes, moving your fingers down your nose as you massage under your eyes. Close your eyes and rest the palms of your hands on your eyes. Massage the area around your mouth and cheekbones. Move over to your jawbones and as you massage them, open your mouth and move your jaws around. Next, take your fingertips and massage all around your ears, allowing sounds around you to soften as you do so. Work your hands around to the back of your neck and massage the tension accumulated in this area. When finished, take your hands and shake the tension out, away from your body. This activity can also be done with a partner.

Visible Behavior

Together, facial expressions, eye contact, and body messages constitute the counselor's visible behavior. The impact of visible behavior on communication is considerable, as the following exercise will prove.

APPLICATION EXERCISE 3.4
THE IMPACT OF VISIBLE BEHAVIOR

Egan (2002) has described an exercise that illustrates the importance of what you see in another person when you communicate. This exercise will give you an opportunity to measure the effect of your facial and body gestures on the person receiving your message. Select as your partner a person you have been wanting to involve in a conversation. Sit down facing each other. Each of you close your eyes and keep them closed throughout the conversation. Talk to each other for about five minutes. Then open your eyes, complete the conversation, and discuss the differences between visual and nonvisual communication. What compensations did you have to make while talking without sight? How successful do you believe you were in your communication attempts? What, in particular, were you missing in terms of visual feedback from your partner?

VERBAL BEHAVIOR AND
SELECTIVE ATTENTION

The things you say will have an immediate impact on your clients. Many studies have shown that the counselor's responses can mold and shape the direction of the client's responses. In other words, whatever topic you respond to with a verbal acknowledgment, the client will probably continue to talk about it. Topics that you do not respond to often get cut off or interrupted. This process is called *selective attention*. As Egan (2002, p. 86) noted, "If helpers think everything that their clients say is key, then nothing is key."

Ivey, Gluckstern, and Ivey (1993) noted that what the counselor chooses to focus on says more about the counselor than the client. These authors also stated that it is important to notice what topics the counselor selectively attends to so that the clients are not inadvertently or unconsciously steered away from topics they need to discuss just because they are uncomfortable to the counselor. If you become aware of this happening, it is useful to consult your supervisor (see also Chapter 10).

Several points should be considered in terms of your verbal impact. Fit your comments or questions into the context of the topic at hand. Do not interrupt clients or quickly change topics. Stay with the topics that clients introduce and help them develop and pursue them. This implies more than a technique; it is a highly conscious awareness of what is going on between you and your client. It is called *verbal following*.

Egan (2002, p. 85) proposed some useful questions that may help you listen and attend to clients, especially with the skill of verbal following:

1. What are the main points of the client's message?
2. What experiences and actions are most important as reflected in the client's messages?
3. What themes are apparent in the client's messages and story?
4. What is the client's point of view?
5. What is most important to the client?
6. What does the client want me to understand?

Of course, the counselor doesn't distract clients by asking these questions directly. Rather, these questions are part of the counselor's process in listening and attending to clients and they reflect the counselor's interest in the client's world (Egan, 2002, p. 86).

■ ■ ■ ■ ■ ▬▬▬▬▬▬▬▬▬▬▬▬▬▬▬▬▬▬▬▬▬▬▬▬▬▬▬▬▬▬▬▬▬▬

APPLICATION EXERCISE 3.5
VERBAL FOLLOWING

A. ROLEPLAY OF VERBAL FOLLOWING

In the roles of counselor and client, choose a partner and sit in pairs. Concentrate on using the verbal reinforcing behaviors discussed in this chapter. In your responses, react only to what the client has just said; do not add a new idea. Let your thinking be as close as possible to that of the client.

Prevent your facial gestures, body gestures, and verbal responses from distracting the client. After five minutes, stop the exercise and discuss the following with your client: What was your client most aware of in your behavior? How well did your client think you understood his or her communication? What, if any, behavior got in your client's way? Now reverse roles and repeat the exercise. What effect did your own gender and culture have on this activity? What about the client's gender and culture?

B. VERBAL FOLLOWING AND SHIFTS IN FOCUS

Shown here are some client statements followed by counselor responses. Describe each counselor response: Do you feel that it is a response to the client's statement? If not, describe the nature of the inappropriate response, such as *shift of topic*, *focus on others*, or *focus on past*.

> **Client A:** "I think I just have to go away for a while. The pressure is really build-ing up."
> **Counselor:** "What would Bob say to that?"

The counselor did/did not (circle one) respond to the client's statement. If the counselor did not respond to the client's statement, the nature of the inappropriate response was ———————————— .

> **Client B:** "She doesn't really care anymore, and I've got to learn to accept that."
> **Counselor:** "You are fairly sure that she doesn't care."

The counselor did/did not (circle one) respond to the client's statement. If the counselor did not respond to the client's statement, the nature of the inappropriate response was ———————————— .

> **Client C:** "Grades are the biggest problem I have in school. I can't get poor grades and bring shame to my family."
> **Counselor:** "What did you do last year?"

The counselor did/did not (circle one) respond to the client's statement. If the counselor did not respond to the client's statement, the nature of the inappropriate response was ———————————— .

> **Client D:** "The job I have isn't fun, but I'm afraid if I quit, I might not get another job."
> **Counselor:** "Jobs are really getting hard to find."

The counselor did/did not (circle one) respond to the client's statement. If the counselor did not respond to the client's statement, the nature of the inappropriate response was ———————————— .

These exchanges illustrate some of the common pitfalls that await the counselor. In the exchange with client A, the response was probably inappropriate. The counselor seems to have jumped topics by bringing up Bob. In addition, the counselor ignored the client's reference to the pressure and its effect on him. The response given to client B could be quite appropriate, though it is not the only possible appropriate response. The counselor is responding directly to what the client said. The inappropriateness of the response to client C is more obvious. The counselor really did not respond to any of the key ideas in the client's statement. Instead, the counselor decided, for some reason, to col-lect information about the client. Moreover, the counselor also ignored the social and cul-tural implications of the client's situation. Finally, the response to client D is also inappropriate. The client is talking about feelings ("isn't fun"; "afraid"). The counselor's response has nothing to do with the client. Instead, the counselor shifted the focus to a social commentary on the current economic scene.

■ ■ ■ ■ ■ ▬▬▬▬▬▬▬▬▬▬▬▬▬▬▬▬▬▬▬▬▬▬▬▬▬▬

APPLICATION EXERCISE 3.6
CULTURALLY APPROPRIATE BEHAVIOR
FOR COUNSELOR ATTENTIVENESS

Now that you are aware of behavioral descriptions of inappropriate social behaviors and attending behaviors in the counseling setting, can you deduce some appropriate behaviors? Be specific as to nonverbal components (face, eyes, tone of voice, rate of speech, etc.), body-language components (head, arms, body position, etc.), and verbal components (choice of words, types of responses, etc.). List them on a sheet of paper.

For the second part of this activity, go back over your list you just created. Consider instances where your list of counselor attentiveness behaviors may not be culturally appropriate for some clients. Discuss examples you can think of with a partner or in a small group.

Vocal Characteristics and Minimal Verbal Followers

The use of a well-modulated, calm, but energetic vocal tone and pitch will reassure clients of your own comfort with their problems. The use of intermittent one-word phrases (minimal verbal followers) serves much the same purposes as do head nods and eye contact. These are verbal signs that you are listening and following what the client is saying. The more common minimal verbal stimuli are "mm-hmm," "mmm," "ah," and so forth. There is one hazard that should be mentioned: Overuse of these vocal stimuli can produce a parrotlike effect that has negative results. Later chapters will describe how you can use minimal verbal stimuli and other types of reinforcing behaviors to assist clients in developing their thinking.

LISTENING FOR CONTEXT

Egan (2002, p. 86) observed that clients "are more than the sum of their verbal and nonverbal messages. Listening in its deepest sense means listening to clients themselves as influenced by the contexts in which they live, move, and have their being." Moreover, "Key elements of this context become part of the client's story whether they are mentioned directly or not." Many of the elements of context were discussed in Chapter 1. They have to do with such things as the client's religion or faith heritage, race, ethnicity, gender, sexual orientation, social and economic class, occupation, geography, age, able-bodiedness, and so on. Often these elements of context form a central part of the client's identity and not to attend to them is to render the client invisible. For example, for some clients, being Jewish may be a core aspect of their identity and being in the world, whereas for others, the core aspect may be race, sexual orientation, money, social class, or health status. Listening for context not only involves attending to and acknowledging these elements of context surrounding clients but it also involves attending to and clarifying the meaning that clients give to these contextual elements.

SUMMARY

One of the major goals in the counseling setting is to listen attentively and to communicate this attentiveness through the use of eye contact, intermittent head nods, a variety of facial expressions, relaxed posture, modulated voice, minimal verbal followers, and verbal responses that follow the client's topics. As we have seen in this chapter, many of these components of attentiveness vary, depending on the gender and culture of both counselor and client.

Because helpers cannot attend to everything, attentiveness is selective, and in counseling sessions, helpers make moment-by-moment decisions about what is most important. In addition to listening to client verbal and nonverbal messages, counselors also need to pay attention to the context surrounding client stories and lives. As Ivey, Gluckstern, and Ivey (1993) concluded, "Listening to another person and giving them your full attention is one of the greatest gifts you can give" (p. 5).

REFLECTIVE QUESTIONS

1. How much do you rely on reactions (gestures or verbal responses) from the other person when you are trying to communicate an important message?

2. What is your typical response when you feel that you are failing in your attempt to communicate with another person?

3. What goals or objectives have you set for yourself in terms of improving your ability to be a good listener? What do you plan to do to achieve these goals?

4. What are some additional examples for social behaviors that you would find distracting if you were involved in a sensitive discussion of your private life?

5. Recall an incident in which you were sharing a significant moment with another person and that person displayed some distracting behavior. What was the effect of that person's behavior on you? What did you decide was the reason for that person's behavior?

6. What do you notice about nonverbal behavior among persons from varying cultures?

7. What effect does your own culture have on the way you seem to attend and respond to clients?

RECOMMENDED READINGS

Cormier, L. S., & Nurius, P. S. (2003). *Interviewing strategies for helpers* (5th ed.). Belmont, CA: Brooks/Cole.

Egan, G. (2002). *The skilled helper* (7th ed.). Belmont, CA: Brooks/Cole.

Ivey, A., D'Andrea, M., Ivey, M. B., & Simek-Morgan, L. (2002). *Counseling and psychotherapy: A multicultural perspective* (5th ed.). Boston: Allyn and Bacon.

Ivey, A., Gluckstern, N., & Ivey, M. B. (1993). *Basic attending skills*. North Amherst, MA: Microtraining Associates.

Knapp, M. L., & Hall, J. (1997). *Nonverbal communication in human interaction* (5th ed.). Orlando: Holt, Rinehart and Winston.

CHAPTER FOUR

RECOGNIZING COMMUNICATION PATTERNS

As the counselor-client relationship develops, communication patterns emerge. Issues related to the locus of control and responsibility in the session, choice of topics, timing, and other therapeutic logistics are undefined at the outset of counseling. In the first few sessions, these issues are resolved, either openly or tacitly, and become apparent through understanding the communication patterns that evolve.

There are many ways to think about patterning in the counseling process. Some patterning takes the form of ritual, whereas other patterning is responsive. That is to say, some of the behaviors become ritualized as a function of routine; for example, the client always chooses the chair facing the window, or the counselor always begins by asking, "What is on your mind today?" and so forth. Other patterns are negotiations between counselor and client, the intent of which may be to settle such matters as "Are we really going to work today?" or "I want you to take charge because I'm feeling overwhelmed."

Frequent topic shifts made by the client in early sessions of counseling may be an expression of client anxiety and of a need to control something about the process. If the counselor is unaware of these shifts in communication and also of the client's underlying affect, progress may be impeded. However, as you will see later in this chapter, communication styles and patterns are greatly influenced by culture and gender, and particular communication patterns do not always have the same meaning.

RITUALIZED PATTERNS OF COMMUNICATION

Ritualized patterns may be either situation specific or idiosyncratic to the individuals involved. We have already mentioned examples of situation-specific patterning with the client who, for example, always chooses a certain chair to sit in. This act of repeated choice may arise out of a very simple condition. It was the chair selected by the client at the initial session, and its continued selection in subsequent sessions offers familiar ground and reflects that the client feels no need to make a different choice. However, if the client arrives for the fifth session and, with no explanation, chooses a different chair, the act of choice may contain unspecified meaning. In other words, through the act of choosing, something is communicated, but what is communicated is unclear until the counselor explores this with the client.

Ritualized Counselor Patterns

The same situation may apply to the counselor. Most experienced counselors develop a style of interaction with their clients. Although their style takes individuals into account, it is nonetheless patterned and, as such, is a kind of trademark of that counselor's work. For example, a counselor may use the first several minutes of the session as relationship time and may communicate this to clients. A different counselor may view the first few minutes as history-taking time. However, should a client arrive in a distraught state, that pattern may be suspended and therapeutic work may begin immediately.

Ritualized Client Patterns

Clients also become involved in ritualized patterns of communication. Often, these patterns evolve out of assumptions about what the counselor wants or expects from the client. For example, a client may assume that the counselor expects to hear an account of the week's worries. The fact that this happened in the second session led the client to think such an account is expected, and so he or she continues the practice in subsequent sessions. Thus, although the activity may have little to do with the ensuing process, it remains a part of the pattern.

INTERACTIVE COMMUNICATION PATTERNS: CULTURE AND GENDER

Most patterning, and certainly the most significant patterning that occurs in the counseling session, is interactive in nature. It has been suggested by Hackney and Cormier (2001) that most clients approach counseling with two conflicting motivations: (1) "I know I need help" and (2) "I wish I weren't here." Given this dual set of motivations, the client may be expected to convey conflicting and even contradictory communications at times. Similarly, counselors must resolve the potential conflict that was mentioned in Chapter 2 regarding unconditional positive regard and congruence. We mention these conflicting tendencies because they can confuse the communication process. It is essential that the counselor know his or her inner motivations and conflicts. In addition to these inner motivations, interactive communication patterns are also influenced by culture and gender.

Communication and Culture

Many communication patterns are affected by both cultural heritage and gender. Sue and Sue (2003) have noted that different racial/ethnic groups differ in their communication

styles. They further observed that communication styles have a great impact on counseling intentions:

> Whether our conversation proceeds with fits or starts, whether we interrupt one
> another continually or proceed smoothly, the topics we prefer to discuss or avoid, the
> depth of our involvement, the forms of interaction (ritual, repartee, argumentative, per-
> suasive, etc.) and the channel we use to communicate (verbal-nonverbal vs. nonverbal-
> verbal) are all aspects of communication style. Some refer to these factors as the *social
> rhythms* that underlie all our speech and actions. Communication styles are strongly
> correlated with race, culture, and ethnicity. (p. 126)

For example, "in traditional Japanese culture, children have been taught not to speak
until addressed. Patterns of communication tend to be vertical, flowing from those of
higher prestige and status to those of lower prestige and status. Likewise, there are many
cultural groups in which restraint of strong feelings is highly valued. It is equated with
wisdom and maturity" (Sue, 1992, p. 12). Sue and Sue (2003) have provided other examples of different communication patterns, such as the following: "Many Black clients
may use a communication style that is 'high-key, animated, confrontational and interpersonal' whereas for many traditional Asian clients more subtle and indirect forms of
communication are the rule" (pp. 124–125). Unfortunately, a culturally uninformed
counselor may view varying patterns of client communication in pejorative ways. For
example, a client practicing restraint may be viewed by a culturally uninformed counselor as being "repressed, inhibited, shy, or passive" (Sue & Sue, 2003, p. 111).

Pedersen and Ivey (1993, p. 14) have identified four possible communication
barriers in cross-cultural counseling, including verbal and nonverbal language problems, interference from preconceptions and stereotyping, erroneous evaluation, and
stress. For example, clients who are bilingual or trilingual or who do not speak standard English or who have not been exposed to standard English as a result of poverty,
social class, or ethnicity may be misunderstood by counselors. Sue and Sue (2003)
stated that "use of standard English to communicate may unfairly discriminate against
those from a bilingual or lower-class background. . . . [Also,] even African Americans
who come from a different cultural environment may use words and phrases (Black
Language or Ebonics) not entirely understandable to the therapist" (p. 118). Other
language barriers may exist with clients from different geographic locations. For
instance, a client from Russia may not understand certain English phrases and idioms,
or a Jewish client may use Yiddish phrases to describe certain things to the counselor.
Sue and Sue concluded that "the lack of bilingual therapists and the requirement that
the culturally different client communicate in English may limit the person's ability to
progress in counseling. . . . [Moreover,] a minority client's brief, different or 'poor'
verbal responses may lead many therapists to impute inaccurate characteristics or
motives" (pp. 118–119). As you can imagine, from the client's point of view, having a
helper who does not understand the way you talk and express yourself can seriously
dampen your desire to return for future sessions.

Generally speaking, clients belonging to different cultural groups will be more
receptive to counseling communication patterns that are similar to their own and that

are respectful of their values. For example, American Indians, Asian Americans, Black Americans, and Hispanic Americans tend to prefer more active and directive forms of helping rather than more passive, nondirective communication (Sue & Sue, 2003, p. 144). Misunderstandings and breakdowns in the communication process in cross-cultural counseling dyads are more likely to occur if counselors assume that certain rules and patterns of speaking "are universal and possess the same meaning" (Sue & Sue, 2003, p. 126). Communication patterns are also affected by the gender of counselor and client.

Implications for Practice

Sue and Sue (2003) observed that "there are personal limits to how much we [counselors] can change our communication styles to match those of our clients"—perhaps because of inadequate training and experience, unresolved personal biases, or inability to understand the clients' different worldviews (p. 148). In these instances what other options are available to helpers? Sue and Sue (pp. 148–149) recommended a variety of alternatives, including:

1. Become aware of and seek feedback about your own communication style and how it tends to impact others, especially clients.
2. Expand your repertoire of helping styles and roles.
3. Become knowledgeable about how race, culture, and gender impact communication styles.
4. Obtain additional training and education on a variety of theoretical approaches and orientations, particularly ones that consider not only individual characteristics, but cultural factors as well.
5. In instances where communication styles with clients mismatch, acknowledge any limitations in your communication style and anticipate any adverse effects of this.
6. Think *holistically* about clients, recognizing that people are not just a product of their thinking or behavior, for example, but are *"feeling, thinking, behaving, cultural, spiritual, and political"* beings.

Communication and Gender

Communication patterns are also influenced by gender (Tannen, 1993). Gender has been linked to such communication variables as amount of talk time, swearing, interrupting, and use of silence (Gilbert & Scher, 1999). New research reported in various magazines and newspapers in the last several years has noted differences in brain-wave patterns between the genders, resulting in differences in how women and men think. Gender roles, schemas, and the resulting communication patterns are learned in a social and cultural context and are affected by cultural affiliations.

Tannen has described patterns of communication among women as "rapport talk" and among men as "report talk" (Simpkinson & Simpkinson, 1992). In rapport talk, women talk easily about private, intimate topics and about feelings. They talk to create a connection. In report talk, men discuss facts and figures, and share information. They talk to make a point or establish a position. Women tend to be more non-confrontational in communication with others. They also are often more comfortable in disclosing concerns and troubles and asking for help. Men are often more reticent to request help and place more emphasis on solutions or "fixing" problems. Female clients may be less likely than their male counterparts to speak up in group counseling because they may be more worried about reactions to their "voice" and because they do not use "talk" to enhance their status (Tannen, 1993).

In a ground-breaking book on the effect of gender in couples therapy, Worden and Worden (1998) noted that the two genders differ on issues of autonomy and connection, as well as expression of anger and power, resulting in differences in communication in the counseling process. These kinds of learned gender roles and schemas are evident in gay, lesbian, and bisexual men and women, as well, since they are also "not immune from the social-psychological construction of gender" (p. 19). Gender and roles and schemata cannot help but spill over or infiltrate into the counseling process, so that both ritualized and responsive patterns between same-gender and different-gender counselor and client pairs are likely to vary somewhat.

Tannen (1990) has stated that observation of such gender differences in language and style of communication helps both genders to be more accepting and respectful of differences. Since style is a learned and somewhat automatic process, awareness of your own style also may help you develop greater flexibility in responding to clients. As Worden and Worden (1998) noted, it is important "to become aware of the context and power of gender roles to powerfully influence what we hear, what we say, and the purpose of communication" as therapists (p. 40).

In a comprehensive review of gender issues in counseling, Enns (2000) observed that "power differentials" are reflected in communication patterns (p. 613). For example, use of language that conveys standards and expectations based on male norms communicates a subtle but biased power differential between the genders. Similarly, heterosexist biases are conveyed when noninclusive language is used to refer to intimate partnerships and parenting. Scott and Robinson (2001) explained that "men (this word should be understood as applying to heterosexual men because in society's eyes 'real manhood' requires heterosexuality or the appearance of heterosexuality) have unearned yet normative advantage given to them by religious, educational, corporate, and family institutions" (p. 416). Enns (2000) concluded that "counselors must maintain awareness that language is central to conveying standards of normalcy . . . and seek to avoid comparisons that reinforce existing power differentials" (p. 613).

Part of the use of gender-sensitive language means that counselors are sensitive to the ways in which all people, including those who hold unearned privilege, may feel disempowered by the patriarchal norms and values. Brown (1994) noted that "while the wounds of patriarchy to women are more obvious, the stories of patriarchal power and control damage men as well" (p. 118). Further, she concluded that even the *separation* of linked cultural oppression into the descriptive categories people use, such as gender, race, sexual orientation, religion, age, social class, health status, and so on, are themselves artifacts "of patriarchal structures that promote disconnections and silences" (p. 70).

Fixed gender roles not only result in differing communication patterns between women and men but they may also produce gender-role stress and shame-proneness for both, impacting communication. As Efthim, Kenny, and Mahalik (2001) asserted, counselors need to be attentive to the links between gender, shame, guilt, and externalized communication patterns. They stated that "clients who seem rigidly committed to traditional gender role norms may be shame-prone, and so the counselor should exercise care when communication centers around feelings of not 'measuring up' as a woman or man" (p. 79). From their research, these authors also noted that "male clients who are stressed about being in contexts in which traditional male dominance is threatened or in which tender emotions are being expressed may rely on externalizing defenses . . . [that is,] they may speak in the language of threat and counterthreat, particularly regarding the danger of being perceived as 'feminine' or of being seen as failing to prove their masculinity. Female clients, on the other hand, may respond with either overt shame or externalization when coping with stress in domains where male power has a direct impact on them: concerns about body image, feeling vulnerable about victimization, and discomfort with situations calling for assertive behavior" (p. 436).

Implications for Practice

Both women and men are impacted by traditional gender-role situations (Gilbert & Scher, 1999). Hoffman (2001) has offered a number of suggestions for gender-sensitive communication:

1. Support clients' desires to break free from the oppression of traditional gender norms.
2. Communicate empathy for the plight of both genders.
3. Use gender inquiry questions to help understand messages clients have received about gender, such as, "Do you remember anything that happened when you were growing up that strengthened your sense of being a girl or boy?" or "What did you learn about how you should be acting as a girl or boy?" and "How do these messages affect you?"
4. Attend to ways in which other aspects of culture affect gender development in the clients' lives. For example, how have dimensions such as religious affiliation, ethnicity, geography, age, and so on impacted the client's sense of being a woman or a man? Have these other dimensions restricted or expanded the client's sense of gender?

■ ■ ■ ■ ■

APPLICATION EXERCISE 4.1
COMMUNICATION PATTERNS

A. CULTURAL DIFFERENCES
In a small group, discuss ways in which communication patterns may vary among cultures. Relate your observations to the counseling process.

(continued)

APPLICATION EXERCISE 4.1   CONTINUED

B. GENDER DIFFERENCES
Observe the way men and women talk, even in ordinary, noncounseling conversations. What similarities and differences do you note? How do you think these similarities and differences will affect the counseling situation?

SILENCE

For most beginning counselors, silence can be frightening. It seems to bring the total focus of attention on them, revealing their most glaring weaknesses as counselors—at least this is how many beginning counselors describe their experiences with silence. As a result, their tendency is to say something—anything—to prevent silence. Typically, a question is asked. Often, it is a bad question—one that can be answered by a minimal response from the client. The answer to the question is relatively unimportant, since the question was not well thought out by the counselor. The counselor may not even be listening to the answer. Such a state of affairs suggests that it is the counselor's responsibility to keep the client talking, that talking is the only evidence that the client is working, and that silence is probably nontherapeutic or a waste of time. None of these assumptions is valid. As Karasu (1992) has noted, the importance of silence is frequently overlooked, as "therapists tend to underestimate the power of listening and overestimate the power of speaking" (pp. 81–82).

Silence has a similar effect on clients. They also perceive silence as a demanding condition and feel a need to fill the gaps of silence with talking. Because clients react to silence in this way, you can use silence as a counseling technique and as a way of responding to clients. Silence has another meaning that is important to acknowledge. After a period of hard work in the session, or after a moment of significant insight, the client often needs time to absorb the experience, to fit it into his or her existing system. This results in an *integration silence*, one in which the client is experiencing fully the therapeutic moment. You may not encounter this in your first counseling sessions, but you will as you gain experience.

Types of Silence

Silence can be a therapeutic moment as well as a self-conscious moment. But what makes one silence different from another? What are the dimensions of silence in a counseling session? Silence can be categorized broadly as counselor induced or client induced. Counselor-induced silence occurs at a time when the focus of the interview is on the counselor. In other words, if the counselor, rather than the client, is feeling responsible for the moment and responds with silence, that is a counselor-induced silence. Conversely, if the client has been talking, assuming responsibility, and then stops, that is a client-induced silence.

Counselor-Induced Silence. Counselor-induced silence can be examined in two contexts: the counselor's intentions and the consequences of the silence. Counselor intentions can vary widely. The underparticipatory counselor gives very little verbally. It is a style of behavior that may reflect the counselor's interpersonal interactions with people in general. It does not reflect therapeutic intentions. Rather, it may indicate a generalized tendency to hide, to withhold, to protect oneself from other people. It arises out of fear.

A second form of silence is that which occurs unsystematically. It is like being at a loss for words. Its intention is probably to give the counselor time to absorb and comprehend all that is going on at the moment. Again, it is not intended by the counselor to be a therapeutic moment, though the effect is often therapeutic. Many times, a counselor will fail to respond to the moment, for personal reasons, and the effect is to encourage the client to continue more deeply into the topic or the feeling. When this happens, the counselor is more apt to feel lucky rather than competent.

The third form of counselor-induced silence is that which the counselor has deliberately presented. It may be that the counselor has been very active and has decided to reduce that activity, thus transferring more responsibility to the client. Or it may be that the counselor senses a momentum on the client's part that will lead to insight, commitment, or new relevant issues. In this case, the counselor chooses not to respond, in order not to interfere with or impede the client's psychological momentum.

Client-Induced Silence. Client-induced silence also has varied intentions and consequences. As noted with counselor silence, client silence is affected by the issue of responsibility and what to do with it. If the client is feeling irresponsible or under-responsible, the intention behind the silence may be antitherapeutic or antigrowth. For example, suppose Betty has developed a life pattern of avoiding some personal issues. When these issues arise, her natural response is to deny or ignore them by deflecting attention from herself. In the counseling setting, she may be aware that these personal issues are the source of her difficulties. Yet her natural reaction continues to be avoidance, deflection, or resistance. In this example, Betty's silence would reflect an attempt to transfer momentary responsibility over to the counselor and away from herself. If she is successful, the consequence would be yet another time when important issues are avoided and underresponsibility is rewarded.

Another reason clients lapse into silence is to try to catch up on the progress of the moment. Counseling sessions sometimes move very quickly, covering a lot of ground, incorporating and relating many issues to one another. There is a need to stop, catch one's breath, observe the progress, or comprehend the implications. This is a very therapeutic type of silence. It allows clients to fit the new growth or insight that has occurred into their existing system. In effect, the client alters the existing system to include what has just been learned. There are also times when client-induced silence results from a client opening some new door to his or her awareness. For instance, Robert, who, with his wife, Carolyn, had been in counseling for several weeks, lapsed into a silence during a discussion of "families of origin" (a technique used to identify styles, expectations, and rules of interpersonal living). After a silence of a minute or more, he stated to the therapist and his wife, "I've been living with Carolyn for six years and thinking that I was overcoming the life I had with my parents. Now I can see that I have been more a reflection of my parents' home than I realized. I wonder what I really do believe in and want from my own family."

Silence also has different meanings from one culture to another. Sue and Sue (2003) stated that there are "complex rules" regarding the cultural appropriateness of the use of silence:

> U.S. Americans frequently feel uncomfortable with a pause or silent stretch in the conversation, feeling obligated to fill it in with more talk. Silence is not always a sign for the listener to take up the conversation. While it may be viewed negatively by many, other cultures interpret the use of silence differently. The British and Arabs use silence for privacy, while the Russians, French and Spanish read it as agreement among the parties. In Asian culture, silence is traditionally a sign of respect for elders. Furthermore, silence by many Chinese and Japanese is not a floor-yielding signal inviting others to pick up the conversation. Rather, it may indicate a desire to continue speaking after making a particular point. Oftentimes silence is a sign of politeness and respect rather than a lack of desire to continue speaking. (p. 131)

Patterns of silence may also vary with gender. A woman may wait for a pause in the conversation to make a point; a man may interrupt a conversation to offer a fact. When expressing feelings, a woman may do so with great verbal facility; a man may pause frequently or present his feelings more hesitantly (Simpkinson & Simpkinson, 1992, p. 30).

How are you to know what kind of silence is occurring? The intention of a client-induced silence must always be inferred. By watching the client closely and by being sensitive to the themes, issues, and feelings being expressed, you will be gathering clues to what is happening. Is the client relaxed? Are the client's eyes fixed on something without being focused? This may mean the client is thinking about or pondering something or examining a new idea, or ruminating around in his or her mind. Or is the client tense, appearing nervous, looking from one object to another and avoiding eye contact? If so, this may mean that he or she is avoiding some topic or idea. Again, we remind you to be careful about assigning universal meanings to client pauses and silent periods, as these meanings do vary with culture, gender, and individuals.

Therapeutic Silence.   Skilled counselors often use silence as their best technique for specific situations. This does not suggest that they are inactive. There is always nonverbal behavior that adds meaning to the silence, thereby communicating a therapeutic message to the client. The messages that the counselor may seek to communicate include "I want us to move a bit more slowly"; "I want you to think more about what you just said"; "I don't accept the message you just presented"; or "I care very much about you and your feelings in this moment." Silence can also be soothing to clients. There are other therapeutic messages that can be communicated through silence, but these tend to be the most common.

Pacing the Interview

Counseling interviews can be compared to a musical score. They have variations in theme, timing, activity, and inactivity. As you acquire self-comfort and skills, you will become aware that the different times in an interview have very different qualities. The counselor is a conductor of sorts for this therapeutic score. There are times when the client is hyperactive, babbling, or overreacting, and the desired objective is to slow down the pace of the session. You can always verbally call attention to the client's activity; oftentimes, silence achieves the same objective. You may not respond with total silence. Occasional verbal responses let the client know that you are still a participant. But you may want to monitor your reactions and not respond to all that stimulates you.

The use of silence to pace the session is especially important in initial interviews when the conditions of trust and safety are being built. Especially in these sessions, it is important to let the client determine the pace. As Hutchins and Cole-Vaught (1997) noted, "The helping interview may be one of the few opportunities clients have to express their thoughts and feelings without being rushed or pressed to perform. This luxury of unhurried time allows more complete expression than is typical in most interactions" (p. 104). In using silence to pace a session, it is important to explain the purpose of silence to clients, especially those in beginning sessions, so that they are not scared away (Sommers-Flanagan & Sommers-Flanagan, 2003, p. 63).

Silent Focusing

One of the ways in which silence is most useful is to focus attention on the moment. It is like stopping to listen to an echo. Throughout the book, we will be suggesting ways in which you can help clients hear themselves. Silence is the first of these ways. Sometimes, clients make totally irrational statements. By not responding to the statement, you allow the clients' messages to remain present, to continue to be heard even by the clients themselves. Other times, clients may make a statement of such relevance that you want to give them time to absorb the impact of that relevance. This would be the case when a client has just acknowledged a significant insight and needs time to fit this insight into an existing system of meanings.

Responding to Defenses

Occasionally, clients come to the interview filled with emotions that belong to other people or situations, yet they spill them out on you or the counseling process. Or you may make a statement to which the client responds defensively. These situations often reflect a lack of client awareness, though they are moments when the potential for awareness is great. The temptation for you may be to give the client insight into the situation. Often, it is more meaningful to allow clients to give themselves that insight. This can be done by using silence as your response.

Silent Caring

Silent caring occurs in those moments when no words are an adequate response to the feelings that are present. It may be a moment of quiet weeping for the client, or it may be a moment of heavy melancholy. Whatever the feeling may be, it is one of those moments when experiencing the feeling fully is more important than making it go away. You can communicate your compassion and involvement very clearly with caring silence.

Guidelines for Using Silence

After all is said and done, there are specific therapeutic guidelines to follow in using silence effectively with clients. Sommers-Flanagan and Sommers-Flanagan (2003) have summarized these:

1. When a client pauses after making a statement or after hearing your paraphrase, let a few seconds pass rather than immediately jumping in with further verbal interaction. Given the opportunity, clients can move naturally into very significant material *without* your guidance or urging. Give them a chance to associate to new material.

2. As you're sitting silently and waiting for your client to resume speaking, tell yourself that this is the client's time to express himself or herself, not your time to prove you can be useful. If you assume the role of an "expert" interviewer, you will probably feel greater responsibility (i.e., as if you need to say the right thing or ask the right question).

3. Try not to get into a rut regarding your use of silence. When silence comes, sometimes wait for the client to speak next and other times break the silence yourself.

4. Avoid using silence if you believe your client is confused, experiencing an acute emotional crisis, or psychotic. Excessive silence, and the anxiety it provokes, tends to exacerbate these conditions.

5. If you feel uncomfortable during silent periods, relax. Use your attending skills to look expectantly toward clients. This will help them understand that it's their turn to talk.

6. If clients appear uncomfortable with silence, you may give them instructions to free associate (i.e., tell them "just say whatever comes to mind"). Or you may want to use an empathic reflection (say something like "it's hard to decide what to say next").

7. Remember that at times silence is the most therapeutic response available.

8. Remember to observe your body and face while communicating silence. This is important because there is a big difference between communicating a cold and a warm silence. (pp. 63–64)

■ ■ ■ ■ ■ ▬▬▬▬▬▬▬▬▬▬▬▬▬▬▬▬▬▬▬▬▬▬▬▬▬▬▬▬▬▬

APPLICATION EXERCISE 4.2
BEING COMFORTABLE WITH SILENCE

In the United States, some people often have to learn to be silent. Perhaps you find silence to be intense and uncomfortable. If so, this exercise will help you become more comfortable with silence. Team up with two other people. One person will be the talker, you be the listener, and the third person can be the timekeeper. Invite the talker to talk about anything he or she wishes. You will listen and respond. But, before you respond, allow a pause to occur. Begin with 5-second pauses. Gradually increase the duration of pauses until you are allowing 15 seconds to pass before responding. The timekeeper should sit in a position from which he or she can signal the number of seconds to you without distracting the talker. After a 10-minute discussion, rotate roles and repeat the exercise until all three of you have had a turn as listener.

As a variation on this exercise, consider your contacts with people you encounter every day. Become conscious of your interaction patterns. Do you interject your reactions as soon as the other person has completed a communication? Do you interrupt the other person, thus preventing the slightest possibility of a silence? During the next few days, monitor your response behavior. When someone speaks to you, pause and think about the message for a few seconds and then give your response. Record any feedback you receive from your friends or acquaintances regarding your communication behavior.

SUMMARY

The practice of professional counseling involves a compromise between personal authenticity and professional skills. Both authenticity and skills are maintained by patterns of behavior that emerge as the counselor matures and grows in experience. Similarly, clients evolve patterns of behavior that reflect both their personal qualities, their problems, and their culture. We have noted how these patterns affect and are affected by the counselor's interventions.

The beginning counselor's most noticeable patterns are those involving interactive qualities as well as cultural and gender factors. The use of another language as well as the use of nonstandard English can impact the communication between counselors and clients. Counselors must be careful to avoid imposing their communication styles and values on clients and must be sensitive to communication styles from culturally diverse clients. Gender expression of language affects the counseling process as well. Again, it is crucial for counselors to be sensitive to the ways in which gender roles are expressed through language and to be aware of the difficulties that patriarchal gender norms have created for both women and men. As the counselor's comfort level with the counseling setting improves, these patterns may be examined for their effect on the session. More subtle, and perhaps of greater concern, are the counselor patterns that become ritualized. Ritualized patterns exist for expediency's sake. They are the behavioral shorthand that allows more efficient functioning. The problem is that efficient functioning may not be effective functioning, particularly in the helping relationship. Consequently, it is professionally imperative that counselors examine their patterns of interaction with clients, not just early in their careers but throughout their careers.

REFLECTIVE QUESTIONS

1. If you are able to eliminate inappropriate social behavior from your counseling repertoire, what impression do you think this will make on your client?

2. What types of messages can be communicated with a silence? How many of these messages might occur in a counseling session? How can you tell one message from another?

3. What do you think your own tolerance/comfort level is with silence? Are you more comfortable with silence that is initiated by you or the client?

4. Provide examples that illustrate how the meaning and use of silence is affected by culture and gender.

5. Discuss some examples in which you have observed communication patterns being influenced by culture.

6. Describe your reactions to the idea that gender affects communications.

7. How do you think the communication styles and patterns discussed in this chapter relate to yourself?

RECOMMENDED READINGS

Enns, C. (2000). Gender issues in counseling. In S. D. Brown & R. W. Lent (Eds.), *Handbook of counseling psychology* (pp. 601–638). New York: Wiley.

Gilbert, L. A., & Scher, M. (1999). *Gender and sex in counseling and psychotherapy.* Boston: Allyn and Bacon.

Hoffman, R. M. (2001). The measurement of masculinity and femininity: Historical perspective and implications for counseling. *Journal of Counseling and Development, 79,* 472–485.

Sommers-Flanagan, J., & Sommers-Flanagan, R. (2003). *Clinical interviewing.* New York: Wiley.

Sue, D. W., & Sue, D. (2003). *Counseling the culturally diverse.* New York: Wiley.

Worden, M., & Worden, B. (1998). *The gender dance in couples therapy.* Pacific Grove, CA: Brooks/Cole.

CHAPTER FIVE

MANAGING THE COUNSELING SESSION

We have discussed the qualities of a therapeutic relationship and how effective counselors attend to and understand the client, but we have not yet discussed the *structure* within which all this occurs. Experienced counselors enter each session with a sense of who they are, what they wish to do and to be in the session, and how they will represent themselves to the client. This is true in the first session as well as in the twelfth session. As we mentioned in the previous chapter, experienced counselors develop a personal style that they carry into the relationship. That style provides the structure for how to begin the process, how to develop it, and how to end it.

In this chapter, we will consider some awkward and sensitive times in the counseling relationship that require structure. Many counselors and clients have difficulty with beginnings and endings, whether they be the beginning or ending of a counseling interview or the beginning or ending of a counseling relationship. As you read the chapter, you will find suggestions and thoughts that may help you make smoother transitions into and out of these moments. There are two types of beginnings that will be examined: beginning the first interview you have with a client and beginning subsequent interviews. Similarly, we examine the two types of termination: session termination and counseling termination.

THE FIRST INTERVIEW

Your first interview with a client will have a special set of dynamics operating. It is the beginning of a potentially significant relationship. As such, there are hopes and expectations, fears and reservations, acute awareness of some conditions and an amazing lack of awareness of other conditions—all of which have a bearing on the session. With so many emotional issues operating, you might be wondering how you can possibly have a successful first interview. Counselors deal with this issue in one of two ways. Some counselors choose to work with the relationship dynamics that are operating. Others choose to make the first session an intake interview and collect needed information about the client. Whichever choice you make, you must still attend to the other issue later. If you focus on interpersonal dynamics in the first session, in the second or third interview you will want to collect information. If you use the first session as an intake session, soon afterward you will need to acknowledge relationship dynamics.

If you wish to focus on relationship dynamics, then the content of Chapter 2 is particularly relevant. Specifically, you will want to achieve an accurate sense of the client's world and communicate that understanding back to your client. Learning to understand means putting aside your own agenda long enough to allow the client's world to enter your awareness. It means not worrying about yourself (Am I doing the right thing? Am I looking nervous? etc.) and trying to avoid "analysis paralysis" (C. Helbok, personal communication, Nov. 20, 2002). Until you have had the experience of several beginning sessions, this will be a difficult task. Of course, you will have an underlying set of objectives in this session:

1. To reduce your client's initial anxieties to a level that permits him or her to begin talking
2. To refrain from excessive talking, since that takes time away from your client
3. To listen carefully to what your client is saying and attempt to reconstruct in your thinking the world that he or she is describing
4. To be aware that your client's choice of topics gives insight into his or her priorities for the moment

CULTURAL VARIABLES AND THE FIRST INTERVIEW

Whether you choose to focus primarily on establishing a relationship or on gathering information in an initial counseling session often depends somewhat on your setting as well as the client's cultural affiliation. Some settings specify that the initial session be an intake interview; this initial history-gathering session may even be conducted by an intake worker rather than the counselor assigned to work with the client.

The client's culture also influences your focus in an initial interview. Sue and Sue (2003) stated, "In multicultural counseling, the culturally diverse client is likely to approach the counselor with trepidation" and may not self-disclose "until you, the counselor, self-disclose first" (p. 147). This trepidation may be reinforced with white counselors whose sole focus in the initial session is individualistic rather than contextualistic—that is, viewing the client's problems as "residing within the individual rather than society" (Sue & Sue, 2003, p. 147). Moreover, some research reported by Sue and Sue (2003) has found that many Asian American and African American clients prefer a more structured and logical approach (e.g., an intake information session) to an affective and reflective one. In any initial session, regardless of approach, counselors need to exert caution and move slowly, as asking very personal questions in an initial session may be perceived as lacking in respect just as much as reflecting client feelings (Sue & Sue, 2003). It is important to be flexible enough in your counseling style to adapt your style in an initial session to meet the cultural diversity of your clients.

STRUCTURING OF INITIAL MOMENTS

In addition to these objectives, there are some logistics that require your attention. In opening the interview, be on time. This communicates respect. The beginning point can be as simple as a smile from you, along with a simple introduction and a motion to show the client where to sit—for example:

> "Hello, I'm Bill Janutolo. Please have a seat here, or in that chair, if you wish. I realize this is our first meeting together and I am interested in getting to know you and something about what brings you here today."

After introductions, you might allow for a brief pause. This gives your client a chance to talk if he or she is prepared to begin. Or you might proceed to give the first interview some structure. There are questions that must be resolved. How long will the interview be? (Often, the length of the interview depends on the age of the client, with shorter interviews for children and elderly clients.) How do you want your client to address you? What should your client expect the sessions to be like? What are your client's rights? What will be your role? Answers to these and other questions provide the structure for the relationship.

Structuring has been defined as the way the counselor defines the nature, limits, roles, and goals within the counseling relationship (Brammer, Abrego, & Shostrom, 1993). It includes comments about time limits, number of sessions, confidentiality, possibilities and expectations, as well as supervision, observation, and/or tape-recording procedures. Describing the counseling process and providing structure reduces the unknowns and thus reduces the anxiety of clients. It also permits clients the opportunity to check out their expectations. Kottler (1991) summarized the ingredients of effective structuring in initial sessions as follows:

1. Providing a general overview and preview of the counseling process
2. Assessing the client's expectations and promoting positive ones
3. Describing the counselor's expectations
4. Orienting the client to new language and new behaviors
5. Helping the client to increase tolerance for frustration and discomfort
6. Obtaining client commitment (pp. 141–144)

Not only does structuring provide a sense of safety for clients but it also fulfills the helper's ethical obligation to inform clients about the nature of counseling at the outset (American Counseling Association, 1995a; National Association of Social Workers, 1996). There are also aspects of structuring to consider in working with diverse clients. For example, with children, structuring is more limited and much of it occurs with the adult who is giving consent for the minor to be seen by a helper. With culturally diverse clients, structuring needs to occur in a way that generates "a mutually satisfying set of procedures that honor the cultures inherent to the therapy, the therapist, and the client" (Helms & Cook, 1999, p. 169). One of the most important aspects of providing structure to clients has to do with giving information and clarifying concerns about confidentiality.

Confidentiality

You will want to emphasize the issue of confidentiality to new clients. Does it mean you will talk to no one? What are the implications if you are being observed by a supervisor or if you are tape-recording the session? Will you keep a written record? If so, what are the client's guarantees that the record will be kept confidential? Some of these may not be relevant issues, in which case it would be better not to introduce them as issues. You can discuss this with a colleague or supervisor to determine which issues are relevant and which are not.

According to ethical guidelines for helping professions, the counselor is generally obligated to treat the client's communication in a confidential manner; that is, the counselor agrees not to share information given by the client with other persons. However, there are several exceptions to this general policy, such as when the client's condition indicates harm to self or others (American Counseling Association, 1995a). Some states also have legal statutes that require helpers to report instances of child and elder abuse or to testify under subpoena. Since these statutes vary from state to state, it is important to know the guidelines for your particular state. The important point is to discuss with clients both the protection and the limits of confidentiality as a part of the structuring process. Here is how one counselor begins a session with structuring:

> "Juanita, we have about an hour together. I'm not sure what brings you here, but I'm ready to answer any questions you have and also to listen to whatever you tell me. You can talk about whatever you wish—this is your time. And whatever you do talk about is kept between you and me. We call this confidentiality. It means that I keep what you say to me to myself. This is very important to me and to you. However, I do need to let you know there are a couple of exceptions to this that I need to share with you upfront so that you are aware of what they are. If you tell me about harming yourself or someone else, or about abusing a child or an elderly person, I have to break confidentiality. And the other exception would be if I was ordered by a court of law to provide information. Do you have any questions about what this might mean before we get started?"

(*Note:* If you are working under supervision, also add that you will be consulting with your supervisor who is also obligated to honor the confidentiality of the client's communication except in the instances you just noted to the client.)

Timing of Confidentiality. Most ethical codes for helping professions require that confidentialilty and its limitations be discussed as early as possible—usually at the beginning of the counseling process during the initial interview. This early timing is important for several reasons. First, this is intended to give clients enough "upfront" information to help them become informed about and consent to the conditions under which counseling occurs. Many clients are unaware that confidentiality is not always absolute. A number of state licensing and certification requirements require helpers to provide clients with a formalized written disclosure-consent statement at the beginning of the counseling process (Glosoff, Herlihy, & Spence, 2000). Second, should a disclosure by the counselor become necessary during the course of subsequent sessions, lack of information about it is not only unethical but it also contributes to a client's sense of betrayal.

Privacy Requirements. A recently enacted federal government rule called the Health Insurance Portability and Accountability Act (HIPAA) also affects helpers and confidentiality. The act involves regulations about electronic as well as traditional paper health-care related charts. Part of the HIPAA regulations are designed to protect client privacy in that they delineate the steps that providers have to take to secure client information. Perhaps the most controversial aspect of HIPAA has to do with the medical privacy regulations stipulating that for the "first time in the 227-year history of America, the federal government has granted itself the right to review *everyone's* medical record" (Freeny, 2003, p. 42). The medical record information includes the following: psychiatric diagnosis, symptoms, treatment plans, appointment times, and summaries of sessions. As Freeny (p. 44) pointed out, these items are now handled under HIPAA as routine medical information that "covered entities" may receive information about without explicit client consent. Fortunately, practitioners' notes are considered psychotherapy notes under HIPAA regulations and *do* require a specific client authorization for release. For additional information on HIPAA, we recommend the "Help on HIPAA" section of the American Counseling website at www.counseling.org/publications/hipaa.htm. Because issues around confidentiality and privacy are complex, when questions arise, it is wise to consult with your supervisor, a colleague, or a trusted attorney.

Encouraging the Client to Talk

After providing this initial structure, you and your client are ready to begin work. The obvious beginning is to get your client to talk, to indicate his or her reason for entering counseling, and perhaps to indicate in some form what he or she hopes to achieve as a result of counseling (the client's first statement of counseling goals). Your beginning will be an invitation to the client to talk. The nature of this invitation is important. A good invitation is one that encourages but does not specify what the client should talk about. This is called an *unstructured invitation* or an *open-ended lead*.

Unstructured Invitations. The unstructured invitation has two purposes: (1) it gives the client an opportunity to talk and (2) it prevents the counselor from identifying the topic the client should discuss. An unstructured invitation is a statement in which the counselor encourages clients to begin talking about whatever is of concern to them, such as:

> "Please feel free to go ahead and begin."
> "Where would you like to begin today?"

"You can talk about whatever you would like."
"Perhaps there is something particular you want to discuss."
"What brings you to counseling?"

By contrast, a structured invitation—one that specifies a topic—gives clients little room to reflect on the motives, goals, or needs that brought them to counseling. An example of a less desirable structured invitation to talk might be: "Tell me about what careers you are considering." The client is obviously tied down to a discussion of careers by this invitation, thus delaying or even negating a more relevant issue. (*Note:* If careers are what the client wants to discuss, an unstructured invitation allows this topic to emerge as well as a structured invitation would.) Other responses that solicit information include open, closed, and clarifying questions.

Open-Ended Questions.   Open-ended questions require more than a minimal or one-word response by the client. This type of question is introduced with either *what*, *where*, *when*, or *how*. You will find that it is very difficult to ask questions that clearly place the focus on your client. Fairly often, it happens that counselors ask questions that allow the client to respond with either a yes or a no. The result is that the client assumes no responsibility for the content of the interview. The purpose of the open question is to prevent this from happening. The following questions are examples of open-ended questions:

"What are you thinking when you are silent?"
"How do you plan to find employment?"
"When do you feel anxious?"

Closed Questions.   When your objective is to get the client to talk about anything, closed questions are not good responses. However, when you want the client to give a specific piece of information, a closed question can be the best response available, such as:

"How old were you when your parents died?"
"How many brothers and sisters do you have?"
"What medication are you taking now?"
"Have you ever received counseling or therapy?"

Clarifying Questions.   Requests for clarification can be used for soliciting information as well as for encouraging the client to elaborate about his or her feelings. It is important to keep in mind that such requests can be overused or underused. When overused, they can become distractors that repeatedly interrupt the client's train of thought. When they are underused, however, the counselor may have difficulty understanding what the client is saying. Sometimes, the counselor is reluctant to seek clarification because it might impede or distract the client from the topic. If you are simply unable to follow the client's train of thought, it is more important to seek clarification than it is to allow the client to proceed. Here are some examples:

"Could you go over that again for me?"

"Could you explain that relationship to me again?"

"What did you mean a while ago when you said your parents were pretty indifferent?"

The following exercise will help you develop the skills involved in initiating the interview.

■ ■ ■ ■ ■ ■

APPLICATION EXERCISE 5.1
INITIATING AN INTERVIEW

This is a class exercise that requires a videotape system. Have class members select partners. Each pair is to decide who is to be the counselor and who is to be the client. The exercise is to last for five minutes. The counselor is to work toward achieving the following goals:

1. Set the client at ease (body relaxed, voice without tension).
2. Help the client to start talking about anything (use unstructured invitation, silence).
3. Get the client to *identify* a current concern (acknowledge that the client came to counseling for a reason; ask about the reason).

Following each exercise, reverse roles and repeat the procedure. Then, when all pairs have had the opportunity to do the exercise, replay the tape and discuss the encounters, using the following format:

1. Ask the counselor for his or her reaction to the tape.
2. Describe those behaviors that were helpful in the exercise.
3. Identify and describe those elements in which there is need for further growth.

CLIENT REACTIONS TO INITIAL INTERVIEWS

Client reactions to initial interviews often depend on whether they have had any prior experience with counseling before, and, if so, whether that experience was a positive or negative one. Clients who have had positive experiences with counseling are not as likely to have the same fears and reservations as clients who have had negative or mixed experiences or who have never seen a counselor before. Still, *all clients need to feel a sense of safety* or they are unlikely to return for more sessions. It is the helper's task to provide safety and security and to recognize and address any client fears and reservations. Sommers-Flanagan and Sommers-Flanagan (2003) noted that common client fears at the beginning of the counseling process include the following sorts of questions:

> Is this professional competent?
> More important, can this person help me?
> Will this person understand me and my problems?
> Am I going crazy?
> Can I trust this person to be honest with me?
> Will this interviewer share or reject my values (or religious views)?
> Will I be pressured to say things I don't want to say?
> Will this interviewer think I am a bad person? (p. 142)

In addition, Sue and Sue (2003) have added that for some culturally diverse clients, their fears and trepidation are initially centered on concerns such as the following:

> What makes you any different from all the Whites out there who have oppressed me?
>
> What makes you immune from inheriting the racial biases of your forebears?
>
> Before I open up to you (self-disclose), I want to know where you are coming from.
>
> How open and honest are you about your own racism, and will it interfere with our relationship?
>
> How well will you, the helper, be able to understand my cultural status and affiliations? (p. 147)

These kinds of client concerns are likely to appear in initial interviews, regardless of whether you approach the initial interview as a time to establish the relationship or as a time to gather pertinent information, as in an intake interview, which we describe in the following section.

INTAKE-INTERVIEW CONTENT

We have described the intake as an information-gathering interview, but we have not indicated what that information should be. This section presents a suggested outline of topics to cover and the rationale for their importance. Morrison (1995) has written a helpful guide for the first interview.

An assumption behind the intake interview is that the client is coming to counseling for more than one interview and intends to address problems or concerns that involve other people, other settings, and the future, as well as the present. Most counselors try to limit intake interviews to an hour. In order to do this, you must assume responsibility and control over the interview. The following is a suggested outline.

Variations in this outline will occur, depending on the setting and on certain client variables such as age, gender, race, class, and ethnicity.

I. **Identifying Data**
   A. Client's name, address, and telephone number at which client can be reached. This information is important in the event the counselor needs to contact the client between sessions. The client's address also gives some hint about the conditions under which the client lives (large apartment complex, student dormitory, private home, etc.).
   B. Age, gender, ethnic origin, race, partnered status, occupational status, educational status, as well as languages, citizenship, and immigration status. Again, this is information that can be important. It lets you know if the client is still legally a minor and it provides a basis for understanding information that will come out in later sessions.

II. **Presenting Issues, Both Primary and Secondary**
   It is best when these are presented in exactly the way the client reported them. If the issue has behavioral components, these should be recorded, as well. The following questions can help reveal this type of information:
   A. How much does the concern interfere with the client's everyday functioning?
   B. How does the concern manifest itself? What are the thoughts, feelings, and so on that are associated with it? What observable behavior is associated with it?
   C. How often does the concern arise? How long has the concern existed?
   D. Can the client identify a pattern of events that surround the concern? When does it occur? With whom? What happens before and after its occurrence?
   E. What caused the client to decide to enter counseling at this time?

III. **Client's Current Life Setting**
   How does the client spend a typical day or week? What social, spiritual, and religious activities, recreational activities, and so on are present? What is the nature of the client's vocational and/or educational situation? What is the client's living environment like? What are the client's most important current relationships?

IV. **Family History**
   A. Father's and mother's ages, occupations, descriptions of their personalities, and relationships of each to the other and each to the client and other siblings.
   B. Names, ages, and order of brothers and sisters, and relationship between the client and siblings.
   C. Is there any history of emotional disturbance and/or substance abuse in the family?
   D. Descriptions of family stability, including number of jobs held, number of family moves, significant losses, and so on. This information provides insights in later sessions when issues related to client stability and/or relationships emerge.

V. Personal History

   A. Medical history: Has the client had any unusual or relevant illness or injury from prenatal period to present, including hospitalizations, surgeries, or substance use?

   B. Educational history: What is the client's academic progress through grade school, high school, and post–high school? This includes extracurricular interests and relationships with peers.

   C. Military service record.

   D. Vocational history: Where has the client worked, at what types of jobs, for what duration, and what were the relationships with fellow workers?

   E. Spiritual and religious history: What is the client's prior and current faith heritage, religious values and beliefs, and current spiritual practices?

   F. Legal history: Has the client had any "run-ins" with the law—such as speeding tickets, accidents, time in prison, bankruptcy, divorce and custody issues, fights, weapons, or violence?

   G. Substance use history: What is the client's past and current use of substances? Note the client's drug(s) of choice, including prescription medicines, frequency, the amount of substance use daily and weekly, and any particular consequences of substance use the client has experienced.

   H. Sexual relationship history: Where did the client receive sexual information? What was the client's dating history? Any engagements and/or marriages? Other serious emotional involvements prior to the present? Reasons that previous relationships terminated? What was the courtship like with the present partner? What were the reasons (partner's characteristics, personal thoughts) that led to marriage? What has been the relationship with the partner since marriage? Are there any children? Separations? Divorces? Be careful not to assume the client's sexual orientation.

   I. Counseling experience: What experience has the client had with counseling and what were the client's reactions? Who referred the client?

   J. Traumatic experiences: Has the client encountered neglect, or physical, emotional, or sexual abuse? Medical traumas or accidents? Natural disasters? Oppression? Discrimination?

VI. Description of the Client during the Interview

Here, you might want to indicate the client's physical appearance, including height and weight, dress, posture, gestures, facial expressions, voice quality, and tensions; how the client seemed to relate to you in the session; the client's readiness of response, motivation, warmth, distance, and passivity; and so on. Does there appear to be any perceptual or sensory functions that intrude on the interaction? (Document with your observations.) What was the general level of information, vocabulary, judgment, and abstraction abilities displayed by the client? What is the client's first language and second language? What is the stream of thought, regularity, and rate of talking? Are the client's remarks logical? Connected to one another? What information have you gathered about the client's race, ethnicity, and general cultural affiliations?

VII. **Summary and Recommendations**

Here, you will want to acknowledge any connections that appear to exist between the client's statement of a problem and other information collected in this session. What is your understanding of the problem? What are the anticipated outcomes of counseling for this person? What type of counseling do you think would best fit this client? If you are to be this client's counselor, which of your characteristics might be particularly helpful? Which might be particularly unhelpful? How realistic are the client's goals for counseling? How long do you think counseling might continue? Is there anything in the client's history that seems like a "red flag" to you?

In writing up the intake interview, there are a few cautions to be made. First, avoid psychological jargon. It is not as understandable as you might think! Second, be as concise as possible and avoid elaborate inferences. Remember, an inference is a guess—sometimes an educated guess. An inference can also be wrong. Try to prevent your own biases from entering the report. Third, the National Association of Social Workers (1996) ethical code gives two guidelines about a written intake report: "Social workers' documentation should protect clients' privacy to the extent that it is possible and appropriate, and should include only that information that is directly relevant to the delivery of services" (p. 13). It is your responsibility to take steps to safeguard client privacy and confidentiality of communication. Make sure that the word *confidentiality* is stamped on the report itself and on each page if it is more than one page in length. Don't leave drafts of the reports around on your desk or in your mailbox or opened up on your computer screen!

USING INTAKE-INTERVIEW INFORMATION

Following the intake interview, but preceding the second session, you will want to review the write-up of the intake interview. Counselors develop different approaches to using this information. Some counselors look primarily for patterns of behavior. For example, one counselor noted that her client had a pattern of incompletions in life; for instance, he received a general discharge from the army prior to completing his enlistment, dropped out of college twice, and had a long history of broken relationships. This observation provided food for thought. What happens to this person as he becomes involved in a commitment? What has he come to think of himself as a result of this history? How does he anticipate future commitments?

Another counselor uses the intake information to look for signals that suggest how this client might enter the counseling relationship. Is there anything to indicate how the client might relate to females? Is there something in his life at present that common sense would suggest is a potential area for counseling attention; for example, is the client in the midst of a divorce? Is the client at a critical developmental stage? The main caution is to avoid reading too much into the intake information. It is far too early for you to begin making interpretations about your client.

OPENING SUBSEQUENT INTERVIEWS

If your first interview was used to collect information about the client, it will be important to focus on developing a therapeutic relationship in subsequent sessions. We refer you to the beginning of this chapter and to Chapter 2 for ways to develop this goal. Once you have established a relationship or rapport with your client, subsequent interviews will require that you reinstate the relationship that has developed.

Reinstating the relationship usually amounts to acknowledging the client's absence since the last interview. This includes being sensitive to how your client's world may have changed since your last contact and your reactions in seeing the client again. This can be done with a few short statements, such as, "Hello, Marvel. It's nice to see you again." This might be followed by some observation about the client's appearance: "You look a little hassled today" or "You're looking more energetic today." Or you might begin by asking, "How are you feeling today?" These types of questions focus on the client's current or immediate condition and reduce the likelihood that the client will spend the major part of the session recounting how the week has gone. If your client needs a bit of small talk to get started, it probably means that he or she needs time to make the transition into the role of help seeker or help taker.

The important point is that you probably will not need to go to the same lengths in establishing rapport as was necessary when counseling was first initiated. Keep in mind, however, that some degree of relationship building occurs in each and every session.

TERMINATING THE INTERVIEW

The beginning counselor is often unsure about *when* to terminate the interview, and may feel ready to conclude either before or after the client is ready. A general rule of thumb is to limit the interview to a certain amount of time, such as 45 or 50 minutes. Rarely does a counseling interview need to exceed an hour in length, as both client and counselor have a saturation point. With children, sessions may only be 20 to 40 minutes in duration and some part of this time may be spent in play therapy.

There is also a minimal amount of time required for counseling to take place. Interviews that continue for no more than 10 or 15 minutes make it very difficult for the counselor to know enough about the client's concern to react appropriately. Indeed, counselors sometimes require 5 to 10 minutes just to reorient themselves and to change their frame of reference from their preceding attention-involving activity to the present activity of counseling.

Acceptance of time limits is especially important when the client has a series of interviews. Research has shown that clients, like everyone else, tend to postpone talking about their concerns as long as possible. Without time limits, the presumed one-hour interview may extend well beyond an hour as a result of this postponing tendency. It is the one instance in which the client can easily manipulate the counselor.

Sommers-Flanagan and Sommers-Flanagan (2003) have identified two factors basic to the closing process of the interview:

1. Both the client and the counselor need to be aware that the interview is "winding down."
2. Terminating a session involves what has already occurred, so no additional information should be sought or discussed during the last few minutes. (p. 157)

If the client introduces a new topic near the end of a session, the counselor can suggest discussing it at the outset of the next session. The rare exception to this would be when the client presents a truly urgent and immediate concern. Sommers-Flanagan and Sommers-Flanagan (2003) have summarized the main tasks necessary for terminating an interview effectively:

1. Leave enough time for closing the session so that you and the client do not feel rushed.
2. Reassure clients by validating their expressions of concerns and any self-disclosure that has occurred in the interview.
3. Instill hope about the helping process and try to solidify a followup appointment or any referral you make.
4. Empower the client by giving [him or her] an opportunity to ask questions or make comments as the session wraps up. (pp. 157–159)

Some ways to accomplish these tasks are discussed next.

Other Termination Strategies

Often, a brief and *to-the-point statement* by the counselor will suffice for closing the interview:

"It looks as if our time is up for today."
"Well, I think it's time to stop for today."

This type of statement may be preceded by a pause or by a concluding kind of remark made by the client.

Another effective way is to use *summarization*. Summarization provides continuity to the interview, is an active kind of counselor response, and often helps the client to hear what he or she has been saying. It is essentially a series of statements in which the counselor ties together the main points of the interview. It should be brief, to the point, and without interpretation. An example of a counselor's use of summarization at the end of an interview is the following:

"Essentially, you have indicated that your main concern is with your family— and we have discussed how you might handle your strivings for independence without their interpreting this as rejection."

Another possible termination strategy is to *ask the client to summarize* or to state how he or she understood what has been going on in the interview, as in the following example:

> "As we're ending the session today, I'm wondering what you're taking with you; if you could summarize this, I think it would be helpful to both of us."

Mutual feedback involving both the client and the counselor is another possible tool for termination of an interview. If plans and decisions have been made, it is often useful for both individuals to clarify and verify the progress of the interview, as in the following example:

> "I guess that's it for today; I'll also be thinking about the decision you're facing. As you understand it, what things do you want to do before our next session?"

Boundary Issues in Terminating an Interview

It is up to the counselor to set boundaries for terminating a session, but some clients for various reasons such as anxiety, dependence, or reactivity challenge these limits. For example, a client may abruptly end a session and say, "That's it for me today" before the allotted time has occurred. Other clients may wait until you initiate termination and then say something provocative, such as, "Well, actually the real reason I came today is because I had to file for bankruptcy yesterday" or "I have something I must tell you before I leave today."

In both of these situations, it is the counselor's responsibility to maintain time boundaries established at the beginning of the session—which, as we mentioned earlier, will vary with the age of the client and the setting in which you work. The rare exceptions to this would be with a client who is desperately anxious to leave early and with a client who brings up a recent traumatic event or a serious threat against oneself or someone else, such as, "Last night I got in the car with a loaded gun and drove over to the house of the man who is having an affair with my wife."

As Sommers-Flanagan and Sommers-Flanagan (2003) have noted, beginning interviewers often feel guilty about maintaining time boundaries. But, according to the authors, disregarding these boundaries usually doesn't serve clients well in the long run (p. 162). "Reality is not always easy, and neither is closing an interview or therapy session, but by doing so in a kind, timely, professional manner, the message you give your client is: 'I play by the rules, and I believe you can, too. I will be here next week. I hold you in positive regard and am interested in helping you, but I can't work magic or change reality for you.'" (p. 162).

APPLICATION EXERCISE 5.2
OPENING AND TERMINATING THE INTERVIEW

Use the following triadic exercise to review styles of opening and terminating the interview. With one class member as the speaker, another as the respondent, and the third as the observer, complete the following tasks by using the Observer Rating Charts (Figures 5.1 and 5.2).

FIGURE 5.1   Observer Rating Chart: Opening the Interview

COUNSELOR RESPONSE	ORDER
Unstructured invitation	
Open questions	
Closed questions	
Clarifying questions	

OPENING THE INTERVIEW

Speaker: Talk about yourself; share a concern with the listener.

Listener: Respond to the speaker as if you were opening an interview. Try out the responses mentioned in the chapter: unstructured invitation and open, closed, and clarifying questions.

Observer: Observe the kinds of responses made by the listener. Keep a frequency count of the types of responses made. Share your report with the listener.

Recycling: If, as the listener, you did not use at least two of the four response classes in your interaction with the speaker, complete the interaction again.

Role Reversal: Reverse the roles and follow the same process.

FIGURE 5.2   Observer Rating Chart: Terminating the Interview

COUNSELOR RESPONSE	ORDER
Time limits	
Summarization of feelings	
Mutual feedback	
Structuring next session (time, date, etc.)	

TERMINATING THE INTERVIEW

Speaker: Continue to explore the same topic you introduced in the preceding interaction.

(continued)

APPLICATION EXERCISE 5.2 CONTINUED

Listener: Respond to the speaker as if you were terminating an interview. Try out at least one of the procedures mentioned in the section as approaches for termination of the interview (acknowledgment of time limits, summarization, or mutual feedback).

Observer: Observe the procedure for termination used by the listener. Share your report with the listener.

Recycling: If, as the listener, you did not use any of the termination procedures, or if, for some reason, termination did not occur with your speaker, complete the interaction again.

Role Reversal: Reverse the roles and follow the same process.

Record the order and frequency of responses used. If the counselor's first response was an unstructured invitation, place a 1 in the space provided in the Observer Rating Charts. If the second counselor response was an open question, place a 2 in the appropriate space, and so forth.

TERMINATING THE COUNSELING RELATIONSHIP

The process of terminating a counseling relationship can evoke various and even conflicting reactions for the counselor. Some may think of it as a loss experience if the relationship has been highly meaningful, or certainly as a "letting go" (Murdin, 2000). Others may consider termination to be an index of the counselor's success or failure. From the client's point of view, termination may be a symbol of success or it may be a reenactment of many former good-byes in life. Whatever the interpretation, it is apparent that termination possesses an emotional dimension that can be intense. Often, it evokes an awareness of what the client means to us and vice versa. Through the process of termination, both counselor and client are usually changed (Murdin, 2000, p. 211).

Perhaps the most useful way to conceptualize termination is to think of it as a transition rather than an event (Hackney & Cormier, 1996). As the counseling relationship develops and as the client is able to address and resolve the issues that necessitated counseling, the prospect of termination becomes a therapeutic stage in the process. More often than not, the counselor becomes aware of the approaching termination first. Concerns related to the timing of termination, the preparation for termination, and the anticipation of therapeutic problems related to termination become dominant in the counselor's mind.

When Should Termination Occur?

Some counseling theories provide guidelines for the timing of termination. These include such possibilities as letting the client determine the timing or having the counselor establish the date of termination at the outset of counseling (Hackney & Cormier, 2001). Such issues will be dependent on your own theoretical orientation. However, there are some pragmatic factors that contribute to the question of timing. Hackney and Cormier (2001) have summarized these pragmatic considerations as follows:

1. When counseling has been predicated on a behavioral or other form of contract, progress toward the goals or conditions of the contract presents a clear picture of when counseling should end.
2. When clients feel that their goals have been accomplished, they may initiate termination.
3. When the relationship appears not to be helpful, either to the counselor or client, termination is appropriate.
4. When contextual conditions change—for example, the client or counselor moves to a new location—termination must occur.

Preparing Clients for Termination

Clients should be made aware throughout the process of counseling that there will come a time when counseling is no longer appropriate. This does not mean that they will have worked out all their issues, nor will it mean that they have acquired all the tools and awareness necessary for a happy life. It does mean that they have grown to the point at which they have more to gain from being independent of the counseling relationship than they would gain from continuing the relationship. Murdin (2000) noted that an important indicator of client readiness for termination is the client's ability and willingness to discuss reasons for wanting to terminate (p. 41). We believe that human beings are happier and more self-fulfilled when they are able to trust their own resources. Of course, healthy people rely on others, but they do so out of self-perceived choice rather than self-perceived necessity. As Kottler (1991) observed, "Effective therapists are skilled at trying to help their client end in a way, *any* way, that allows them to feel good about their work and continue to be their own therapist in the future" (p. 171).

Occasionally, you will know in the first session with your client that the relationship will last a certain length of time. For example, if your client is seeking premarital counseling and the wedding is to take place in two months, the time constraints are apparent. People going to university counseling centers may know that vacations dictate the amount of time allowed for counseling. In such cases, it is appropriate to acknowledge throughout the relationship that these time constraints exist.

When the relationship is more open ended and determined by the client's progress, the termination stage begins well before the final session. We believe that for any relationship that has existed more than three months, the topic should be raised three to four weeks prior to termination. This allows the client time to think about and discuss the ramifications of ending counseling with the counselor.

Cultural Variables and Termination

It is important to recognize that not all cultural groups share the same values and beliefs about the dimension of time, and this, too, can affect the termination process.

For example, Euro-Americans generally have a highly structured and future-oriented view of time, but some clients from other cultural groups have a much more casual view of time (Ivey, D'Andrea, Ivey, & Simek-Morgan, 2002, p. 63). In cross-cultural counseling situations, the time element of termination needs to be discussed, negotiated, and understood from the client's perspective, as well.

Also, many clients of color terminate counseling at a much earlier time than other clients. Often, these clients are the decision makers as to when to stop counseling, presumably because it is not relevant enough to them and their experiences, particularly their culturally linked experiences (Sue & Sue, 2003). Therefore, it is presumptuous to assume that in all situations the "control" of the termination process is in the counselor's hands.

Introducing Termination

Introducing termination can be done by saying something on the order of:

> "We've been dealing with a lot of issues and I believe you've made a lot of progress. One of our goals all along has been to reach the point where counseling is no longer needed. I think we're reaching that point, and probably in about three or four weeks, we'll be stopping."

You can anticipate that your clients will have any of several reactions to this. They may feel good about their progress, nervous about the prospect of being on their own, or sad to see a significant relationship ending, to name but a few reactions. It is also important for the client to summarize both what has been achieved and what remains undone (Murdin, 2000, p. 150).

Occasionally, it is appropriate to terminate gradually. This can be done by spacing the time between interviews. If you have been seeing your client weekly, change the appointments to every other week or once a month. Or you may schedule a six-month check-in that gives your client the sense of an ongoing relationship, one that leaves the door open, should that be necessary. Even with these gradual transitions, you will still have as a major concern the transition of a significant relationship.

In all cases, it is important to emphasize the client's continued growth once counseling has ended. This includes summations of what the client has learned in counseling, discussions of other resources and support systems the client can make use of in her or his life, and the invitation for followup sessions as necessary. Kottler (1991) observed that "some people believe that therapy never ceases, that clients continue their dialogues with us (as they do with deceased parents) for the rest of their lives" (p. 173).

Finally, it occasionally happens that the ending of a counseling relationship has a character of finality. Perhaps you or your client is moving. Or you may be referring your client to another help provider. In such instances, there may be a grieving process connected with termination. It is appropriate to view this grieving process as necessary and therapeutic in its own right. It is as important for the counselor as for the client. Occasionally, a client may terminate simply by canceling the next appointment and there is no formal termination that occurs, yet the counselor may still feel some grief. It is a symbolic or ceremonious conclusion, an acknowledgment that the relationship had importance and that reality dictates that it end. In such cases, it is better not to hang on to it; that would only make the transition more difficult. If you are making a referral to another counselor, you must give up your role as helper for both ethical and practical reasons.

Challenges to Termination

Murdin (2000) summarized a number of possible and differing challenges to the termination of counseling and psychotherapy. She noted, for example, that sometimes clients leave counseling suddenly and/or prematurely for fear of losing their own power. She observed that "the whole ending process involves questions about who has the power and whether or not it can be given up or shared" (p. 38).

Some clients fight the termination process and have trouble saying good-bye for fear of losing the counselor and her or his compassion (Murdin, 2000, p. 37). Even in instances where the termination point has been decided at the outset of the helping process—such as in behavioral or time-limited counseling—challenges to the termination process can and do still occur. For instance, it is not uncommon for clients to have a crisis as the end of the contract approaches. Often, these clients may try to persuade the counselor to work beyond the agreed upon ending time. Murdin (2000) recommended that in most cases the counselor should keep faith in the client and abide by the agreed upon ending date (p. 151). She stated that "in time-limited work, the therapist must be prepared to work for an ending right from the beginning and must not waiver from the view that an ending is desirable" (p. 155). Before agreeing to any changes in the termination date, Murdin has recommended that counselors search themselves and their own motivations for extending the time (p. 153). For any exception that may be made to the original contract, she also believes it is better to initiate a new contract than to extend the existing one (p. 153).

Challenges to termination often occur because the attachment produces a fear of loss. The greatest difficulty in termination of counseling lies in "hidden anxieties" about this loss (Murdin, 2000, p. 37). The fear of loss can result in such emotions as anger and jealousy (in addition to the sadness we mentioned earlier). Occasionally, clients' fear of loss may be so great they even pursue counselors by stalking them. Obviously, there is a great deal that counselors can do to promote a *healthy* attachment with clients and to avoid an unhealthy attachment such as extreme dependence or adoration (Murdin, 2000).

Ethical Issues in Termination

In both the United States and the United Kingdom, numerous ethical complaints made by clients have to do with termination issues that clients felt were handled improperly (Murdin, 2000). Generally, it is important for counselors to avoid sudden endings. If a situation such as a severe illness requires a sudden termination, the counselor is responsible for facilitating a referral to another helper. And the counselor has certain ethical responsibilities in the referral process. These include protecting the client's privacy and confidentiality unless there is a written client release on file, providing the client with choices of several other professional helpers, and ensuring that these other helpers are regarded as competent and ethical professionals (Welfel, 2002).

When the counselor has been using some form of a contract, such as in behavioral counseling or time-limited counseling, it is important to adhere to the terms for termination that were set up and agreed to at the beginning of the counseling process, despite the challenges that were described in the previous section. Murdin (2000) has recommended that if there is any doubt in the counselor's mind about the appropriateness of termination, it is important to seek consultation or supervision. This is ethically acceptable to do as long as this was explained to the client at the outset of the counseling process in the contract, consent, or disclosure process.

SUMMARY

Beginnings and endings can present challenges for both counselors and clients. At the outset of counseling, both individuals might experience some anxiety and uncertainty. It is important for counselors to establish safety and trust from the beginning of the process, as many clients have both fears and reservations about counseling. This is especially true for many culturally diverse clients and for clients who have had either no prior experience or negative experience with counseling. Structuring and disclosure can ease client fears and insecurities about the process. Both rapport and information gathering are important tasks in the initial stage of the counseling process. One of the most important topics to address at the beginning of counseling is confidentiality and its limits.

Termination—both of counseling interviews and of the counseling process—evokes its own set of challenges and emotions. It is important for counselors to terminate an interview as well as the counseling process in a way that empowers clients. Clients who feel disempowered, such as some culturally diverse clients, might choose to terminate early or suddenly, often because the counseling does not feel relevant to them, or the counselor does not understand their worldviews, or aspects of oppression and discrimination are re-created in the counseling process for them.

Both the termination of interviews and the termination of the counseling process require the counselor to manage a transition effectively. This transition becomes more difficult if either the counselor or the client has any hidden anxieties about separation and/or loss. It is important for counselors to address feelings of loss, to prepare clients for termination over a period of time, and to help clients find ways to support their growth after counseling has ended.

REFLECTIVE QUESTIONS

1. Discuss what it might be like to be a client seeking help for the first time from an unknown counselor. Now discuss this as it applies to a cross-cultural dyad.

2. Discuss the positive and negative perceptions that a client might have after going through an intake interview.

3. What do you think are the most important elements, from a counselor's perspective, in terminating a significant relationship? From the client's perspective?

4. What are the ethical issues in beginning or continuing to help a client who is also receiving counseling from another therapist?

RECOMMENDED READINGS

Hackney, H., & Cormier, L. S. (2005). *The professional counselor* (5th ed.). Boston: Allyn and Bacon.

Morrison, J. (1995). *The first interview: A guide for clinicians.* New York: Guilford.

Murdin, L. (2000). *How much is enough: Endings in psychotherapy and counselling.* London: Routledge.

Sommers-Flanagan, J., & Sommers-Flanagan, R. (2003). *Foundations of therapeutic interviewing* (3rd ed.). Boston: Allyn and Bacon.

Sue, D. W., & Sue, D. (2003). *Counseling the culturally diverse* (4th ed.). New York: Wiley.

Welfel, E. (2002). *Ethics in counseling and psychotherapy.* Pacific Grove, CA: Brooks/Cole.

CHAPTER SIX

RESPONDING TO COGNITIVE CONTENT

In the last chapter, we talked about opening and closing an interview. As the interview ensues, the counselor responds to the client in many ways, both verbally and nonverbally. Since your responses will have an impact on clients and the topics they discuss, it is necessary to be aware of the effect your responses will have. One very important effect deals with the changing pattern of the client's verbal behavior. As the verbal interaction and communication begin, topics arise; some topics are developed, some are modified, and some are diverted into new topics. As an active participant in the helping process, you must be sure that your responses will influence the *direction* of topic development in such ways as choosing from among the topics that are to be discussed and the length of time allotted to the topics. Responding to client content suggests alternatives and conscious choices that you will have to make in the interview. Then, when one choice has been made, the effect of that choice will become the basis for further alternatives. The following example will illustrate the types of choices you, the counselor, will be making. Suppose your client says:

Client: "I've known what this operation would do to my plans for a long time."

Your choices for responding are several. You could (1) paraphrase the client's remark ("You have known about the impact of this operation for quite a while now"); (2) ask a question directly related to the client's statement ("What will it do?"); (3) say "mm-hmm"; (4) reflect the client's feelings about the operation ("You feel very certain about the consequences of the operation"); or (5) respond with silence and simply wait to see what the client does or says next. Obviously, these five responses will produce different effects with clients. The client in this example may proceed to talk about the operation, about plans, or about how she anticipates events. In any case, your response would shape or mold the topic development, and, as a result, influence the future matters the client discusses.

Since your responses greatly influence the nature of topic development, you will be faced with the decision of which kind of content to respond to and, thus, emphasize. Very often, the client's particular response contains *both* a cognitive message and an affect message. *Cognitive messages* usually deal with people, places, and things, whereas *affect messages* primarily reflect feelings and emotions. Typically, in early interviews the affect message is disguised. The disguises may be thin but nonetheless necessary to the clients. It is their way of protecting themselves until they can determine what kinds of things to which you are willing to listen. Once you are able to hear the affect message (and this comes with practice), you will have to make some decisions. It is important that you respond to that portion of the client's communication that you think is most significantly related to the client's concerns. The process of choosing between client cognitive and affective topics is called *differentiation*. Whether you choose to respond to the cognitive portion or the affect portion depends largely on what is happening in the interaction at that moment and on what the client needs. In other words, choosing to respond to the cognitive content serves one objective, whereas choosing to respond to the affect content serves another objective.

Some approaches (e.g., the phenomenological) favor almost an exclusive emphasis on affect, whereas others (e.g., rational-emotive, reality therapy) suggest that the primary emphasis should be on the cognitive process. Of course, there are many variables influencing this sort of emphasis. In working with one client who intellectualizes frequently, the counselor may focus primarily on affect in an effort to get the client to recognize and accept his or her feelings. However, the same counselor, with another client who intellectualizes, may choose to emphasize cognitive elements if the counseling time is too limited for the client to feel comfortable with emotions. There are certainly times when emphasis on the affective takes precedence over the cognitive area and vice versa. Generally, though, during the interview process it is important to respond to *both* affective and cognitive topics. This is because, for all clients, there are times when feelings govern thoughts and times when thoughts and their consequences govern or influence feelings. The important point is not which comes first, but which type of counselor intervention is likely to be the most effective for each particular client.

In this chapter, we will be working with content choices of a cognitive nature, as opposed to affective or feeling-type choices. (In Chapter 7, we will explore affective content and responses to it.) In other words, the emphasis now is on your recognition and demonstrated ability to identify and respond to client thoughts or ideas dealing with *problems*, *situations*, *people*, or *things*.

RECOGNIZING ALTERNATIVES

Each comment of the client presents alternatives to you in terms of content to which you may respond. How you respond to one alternative will shape the next remark of the client. Your task is to identify accurately the kinds of content presented by the client and the alternatives to which you, as the counselor, can respond.

APPLICATION EXERCISE 6.1
IDENTIFYING ALTERNATIVE TOPICS

To give you practice in identifying topic alternatives, read carefully the following client statements. Then identify and list all the different topics in each client response.

1. "I don't know just exactly how it does work, but you can take weekend trips in connection with the Air Force. It would be like duty because you have to qualify for it and you can travel all over the U.S."

   _____

   _____

   _____

   _____

2. "And I thought it was great. And I realize that some people have a bad opinion of women in the service but, uh, they shouldn't really, because a woman is going to be what she is, no matter where she is."

   _____

   _____

   _____

   _____

FEEDBACK
The correct answers to the exercises above are as follows:

1. a. I don't know just exactly how it does work.
   b. You can sign up to take weekend trips in connection with the Air Force.
   c. It would be like duty.
   d. You have to qualify for it.
   e. You can travel all over the U.S.
2. a. I thought it was great.
   b. I realize that some people have a bad opinion of women in the service.
   c. They shouldn't really.
   d. A woman is going to be what she is, no matter where she is.

RESPONDING TO ALTERNATIVES

The process of selecting alternatives can best be illustrated by excerpts from actual interviews:

Client: "I like this type of a setup where you can talk directly to people and talk with them. Uh, I don't like big crowds where I don't know anybody and they don't know me."

Counselor: "You'd rather not be in big crowds."

In this example, the client's response contained two basic communications: (1) I like to talk directly to people and (2) I don't like big crowds in which individuals get lost. The counselor chose to respond to the second communication in the client's response. Had the counselor responded by saying, "You prefer situations that permit you to get to know people," the topic focus would have been on getting to know people and the necessary conditions for this. As it was, the response led to a topic focus on the ambiguity of not knowing people. This does not necessarily mean that one response was more appropriate than the other; it is used only to point out the available alternatives.

A study of counseling typescripts suggests that when the counselor has alternative communications to which he or she may respond, the tendency is to respond to the *final* component of the response. Perhaps this is because of the immediacy of the final part of the response; but if so, that is a poor criterion. It is more logical that the counselor respond to the part of the client's communication that has *greatest bearing* on the client's concern and is therefore most important.

The counselor may also be tempted to respond to that portion of the client's communication that he or she finds most interesting. In this case, the interview tends to center on those topics that the counselor may identify with or be dealing with personally. Again, the counselor must ensure that the choice of alternative topics reflects a decision about the client's needs rather than the counselor's. This is especially true in instances of cross-cultural counseling. If the counselor chooses to respond to the portion of the client's communication that is most interesting to the counselor, this may be a reflection of the counselor's personal and cultural biases and cultural worldview, and may not be relevant to the client's culture. In cross-cultural counseling, there are often barriers or stumbling blocks to intercultural communication (Pedersen & Ivey, 1993). (They are not likely to be barriers for those *within* the same culture because of shared meaning.) Assuming similarities instead of differences in cross-cultural counseling is one such barrier. The counselor cannot safely assume that what he or she chooses to attend to is what is of most importance to the client from a different culture.

VERBAL RESPONSES TO COGNITIVE CONTENT

There are several types of responses you can use to focus on and elicit specific content expressed in the client's communication. The responses presented here can be used specifically to respond to the cognitive content of the client's communication—that is, ideas that deal with *problems, situations, people,* and *things.*

Although these are not the only possible ones, four verbal responses will be identified here for this purpose: silence, minimal verbal activity, paraphrase, and questions.

Emphasis will be directed toward the latter two. The use of silence and minimal verbal activity has already been noted in previous chapters. Their use as discriminator responses will be presented here briefly.

Silence

Silence affects the course of topic development by indicating that the counselor does not want to select or direct the topic at the given time it is used (see Chapter 4). Although the use of silence gives the counselor much less control over the direction that topic development takes, it serves to increase the power of other types of responses. Thus, after you have remained silent for several moments, your next verbal response will have more influence in shaping the direction of topic development.

Minimal Verbal Activity

Minimal verbal responses are those verbalizations and vocalizations that people use when they are listening to someone else. The most common are "mm-hmm," "mmm," "yes," "oh," and "I see." They are unobtrusive utterances, but have a significant reinforcing value. That is to say, when an utterance such as "mm-hmm" is used consistently following a particular topic or word, the future occurrence of that particular topic or word usually increases.

Paraphrase

The paraphrase is the rephrasing of all or a selected portion of the client's previous communication, and it neither adds to nor detracts from the basic communication. It confirms for the client that the counselor has heard the communication. Operationally, the paraphrase may be defined as a simple, compound, complex, or fragmentary sentence that mirrors the client's previous communication using your own words. It is dependent in its grammatical structure on the grammatical structure of the client's previous response. The paraphrase can be used effectively so long as it is interspersed with other types of counselor responses. Otherwise, it can produce a parrotlike effect that has an adverse effect on clients. When using a paraphrase response, it is helpful to use the most important words and ideas expressed in the content portion of the client's message. When you do this, your response lets clients know you have heard their message accurately and are able to respond to it in a way that does not simply copy or mimic their expression. Examples of paraphrases will help you understand this particular response:

> **Client:** "I'm hoping to get a good job this summer."
>
> **Counselor:** "You're counting on getting the job you need this summer." (Paraphrase)
>
> **Client:** "It doesn't look like we'll get a vacation this summer."
>
> **Counselor:** "It looks like a vacation is not going to happen for you this summer." (Paraphrase)

Client: "I like people but I sure get tired of them."

Counselor: "After a while, being around people can be fatiguing for you." (Paraphrase)

Now, try your hand with a few paraphrases:

Client: "This has been a really rough year for me."

You: "_____."

Client: "Probably the worst class I have is literature."

You: "_____."

Discuss your responses with someone.

Questions

In the last chapter, we discussed the use of questions as a tool to open an interview. Questions also can be a way to respond to content. Although most effective questions are usually the open-ended ones, which require more than minimal responses by the client, occasionally closed or clarifying questions are also useful for responding to client content messages. Recall that closed and clarifying questions usually focus on a specific piece of information. If you want to focus on one particular part of the client's content message, you may decide to use a closed question. For example, suppose the client says, "I seem to be having relationship problems with just about everyone in my life." You might want to focus on a specific piece of information related to the issues and could follow up with a closed question, such as, "Have these relationship problems started recently or have they been going on for a while now?" Similarly, a clarifying question may be used to help explore and clarify the meaning of the client's content message. In this same example, you could use a clarifying question, such as, "Can you elaborate on what you mean by 'relationship problems'?"

In contrast to closed and clarifying questions, open-ended questions require more than a minimal one-word answer by the client. They are introduced with *what, where, when,* or *how*. You will find that it is very difficult to ask questions that clearly place the focus on your client. Typically, when you start asking questions, the client will give a minimal answer and then wait for the next question. In other words, the client has not assumed responsibility for the content of the interview. One purpose of the open-ended question is to prevent the client from answering questions with a yes or no response. Open-ended questions also are useful for encouraging clients to elaborate and to give information. Some examples of open-ended questions include the following:

"What do you like about it?"
"What is keeping you from doing it?"
"How do you feel about it?"
"How is it helping you?"

"When do you feel that way?"

"Where does that occur for you?"

"How does your wife enable you to keep doing this?"

Why questions are usually avoided because clients rarely know the answer and because they appear intrusive.

Open-ended questions can easily be overused in an interview. A beginning counselor often tends to bombard initial clients with questions. Extensive use of questions gives a ping-pong effect; the counselor asks, the client answers, and so on, thus the counseling resembles little more than an interrogation process. Cournoyer (2000) suggested that one way to avoid this is "to intersperse your questions with active listening responses" such as paraphrasing (p. 186).

When counselors overuse questions, they may be acting more out of their own needs rather than trying to help the client in the form of structuring, clarifying, expecting, or soliciting information. Examples of situations in which questions are used to meet the *counselor's* needs include:

Voyeurism—wanting to know certain things about the client to satisfy our own curiosity,

Narcissism—wanting to make ourselves look good or look like the expert by the kinds of questions we ask,

Sadism—bombarding the client with frequent or painful questions so much as to constitute harassment. (Kottler, 1991, p. 160)

Murphy and Dillon (2003) recommended two issues a counselor can consider to use questions selectively and effectively: (1) What is the purpose of my question? and (2) How is this purpose therapeutic—how does it help the client? These authors believe that clients have a right to be informed about the purpose of your questions, to know how the information will be used and by whom, as well as to decline to answer any questions (p. 108).

Occasionally, beginning counselors resort to questions simply because they feel more comfortable with this type of lead. This is a good example in which silence may be used in lieu of another question. Ultimately, learning a variety of alternative verbal leads will help prevent overuse of questions.

It is also important to note that clients may have very different reactions to questions. Some clients may construe counselor questions as a sign of interest on the counselor's part. Other clients may view questions as intrusive and react by withdrawing. Questions can be culturally insensitive and offensive, particularly if they seek very personal information from clients in initial sessions or if they suggest a cause-effect orientation (Sue & Sue, 2003). Asking questions of a very personal nature may be perceived as lacking in respect by some Asian American clients. Also, the worldview of some clients from other cultural groups, such as American Indians, reflects an intuitive and harmonious approach rather than a cause-effect approach. As with all verbal responses, counselors need to monitor closely the effects of their verbal leads, particularly questions, on new clients.

Try a few open-ended questions for yourself:

Client: "It's hard to admit, but I really have wondered whether college is for me."

You: "_____."

Client: "I've gotten to the point where I can't do anything I'm supposed to do."

You: "_____."

Discuss your responses with someone.

Summarization of Content Response

A *summarization response* is one that ties together multiple elements or key points of a client's message—either perhaps a long-winded message or a series of messages that occur over time, such as during an entire session. A *summarization of content* is a rephrasing of at least two or more different content or cognitive messages expressed by the client. This response is used to give focus and direction to an interview and to identify possible themes, narratives, or key ideas expressed within the client's communication. (Recall from Chapter 5 that summarization can be used also at the end of an interview to tie together the session and provide an ending for it.) Consider the following examples of the summarization of content response:

Client: "I've been pretty tired for the last few months. I just don't seem to have my usual energy. I am sleeping OK, but by early afternoon, I just run out of steam. Maybe it's because so much has happened around me lately—my partner just lost his job and also my dog died about a year ago."

Counselor: "Wow—it seems like a lot of pretty significant things have been happening in your life and you have noticed these affecting your energy level." (Summarization of content)

Client (early in the session): "I don't think I have a big problem with pot. I mean I do smoke it every day but it doesn't seem to interfere with anything I need to do."

(later in the same session): "Well, sometimes I guess I do feel a little concerned because I like the feeling I get from it [pot] and so I don't want to give it up."

Counselor: "You have said a couple of things during this session about your smoking pot—that it doesn't interfere with anything you need to do and you don't want to give it up because of the effect it has on you." (Summarization of content)

In the next chapter we will explore how summarization can be used to respond to affective messages as well, in the summarization of feeling response. For now, try a few summarization of content responses on your own!

Client: "I find it easier to relate to my stepson than my own son. I think it is because we are not biologically related, if you know what I mean. There just seems to be so much less conflict between us."

You: "_____."

Client: "My partner confronted me about my drinking and got me to agree to come in here to see you, but I really don't want to be here. I don't think how much I drink is anyone else's business but my own."

You: "_____."

Discuss your responses with a colleague, supervisor, or instructor.

APPLICATION EXERCISE 6.2
IDENTIFYING AND RESPONDING TO COGNITIVE CONTENT

A. IDENTIFYING COGNITIVE CONTENT

To give further practice in identifying cognitive content—thoughts or ideas pertaining to problems, situations, people, or things—read carefully the following client statements. Then identify and list the different cognitive topics within each client response.

1. "I'm thinking about either going to graduate school or getting a job—whichever would be better experience is what I'll do."

   _____

   _____

   _____

2. "People can say whatever they want about it, but as far as I'm concerned, my place as a woman is in the home and it will not change."

   _____

   _____

   _____

FEEDBACK

The answers to the preceding exercises are as follows:

1. a. I'm thinking about going to graduate school.
    b. I'm also thinking about getting a job.
    c. I'll do whatever provides the best experience.
2. a. People can say whatever they want to about a woman's place.
    b. I think my place as a woman is in the home.
    c. My opinion about this will not change.

B. RESPONDING TO COGNITIVE CONTENT

The following exercise will give you practice in using paraphrase and open questions. Read each client statement and then respond with the type of response indicated in parentheses:

1. **Client:** "Yes, I think that the best way to learn a language is to actually live with the people and learn it that way. Um, the first year that I was going back to Germany, I didn't learn very much at all."

   You: *(Paraphrase)* "_____
   _____."

2. **Client:** "I'd like to know the language, but still I can't carry on a conversation because it isn't used that much in my classes."

   You: *(Open-ended question)* "_____
   _____."

3. **Client:** "I wish I had more friends here at school. People are in their own little cliques. I'd almost rather be alone than be in a clique and be a snob."

   You: *(Summarization of content)* "_____
   _____."

4. **Client:** "I wanted to go back to school mostly because of the fact that I thought that there would be someone to lead me because I just don't know which direction to go sometimes for a few things."

   You: *(Paraphrase)* "_____
   _____."

5. **Client:** "Well, I know you're supposed to study every night, which I don't do, but I'm not the only one who hasn't studied this semester. A lot of other kids have lost interest, too."

   You: *(Open-ended question)* "_____
   _____."

6. **Client:** "Taking tests is real hard for me. Maybe it's because I came here from Mexico when I was younger. My English isn't that good. I can speak OK but sometimes I don't always understand the meaning of all of the words, and that gets to be a problem on tests a lot."

   You: *(Summarization of content)* "_____
   _____."

Discuss your responses with someone.

DIFFERENTIATION AND
SELECTIVE RESPONDING

The emphasis in this chapter has been on the selective responding to some client messages as opposed to others. When the client presents you with a multiple message, you can respond to all the messages or to only part of them. If you respond to only part of the client's messages, that part to which you do not respond may be dropped by the client in future communication, unless it is very important to him or her. In this case, the client may attempt to initiate discussions of the topic once again.

Selective responding involves a covert process on the counselor's part known as *differentiation,* which is the process of identifying all the different parts of the client's communication and making an intentional decision about which part to respond to and how. It also involves paying attention to or monitoring the effects of your choices on subsequent client communication.

The effects of selective responding require you to be very attuned to yourself and your own issues, and ultimately to be comfortable with yourself, your issues, and your feelings. Effective responses to clients demand a sort of consciousness on your part about yourself. For example, if you are personally uncomfortable with issues such as sexuality, abortion, divorce, and so on, you may avoid responding to the mention of these topics by clients, or if the expression of anger scares you, you may avoid responding to anything that might indicate the client is feeling angry. A major way that counselors become and stay conscious of themselves and their impact on clients is through consultation with a supervisor. We discuss this in greater detail in Chapter 10.

Because clients vary along many dimensions, the effects of your responses with clients will also vary in impact—positive and negative. Thus, it is erroneous to assume that all of the responses and interventions presented in this book will work with all clients or will have the same meaning or results for all clients.

To summarize the discrimination process of selective responding, consider these two key points:

1. The counselor is able to generate a maximum number of ideas, words, and responses to communicate with a diverse group of clients.
2. The counselor is able to observe the effects of the responses implemented in the session with a diverse group of clients and is flexible enough to modify these responses when the observations suggest they are not working.

THE DIFFERENTIATION PROCESS
IN CROSS-CULTURAL COUNSELING

The differentiation process and selective responding is particularly challenging in cross-cultural counseling. The temptation is to respond to the content or the affect of client messages in a way that is consistent with your own culture and yet may be inconsistent with the client's culture. Although it is important for counselors to "keep track of the salient cultural perspective" of clients and the shifts in these perspectives over time, "the counselor and client are typically bound by different rules of behavior and

learned expectations in multicultural settings. . . . Culture-centered counselors not only need to focus on the client's salient culture, but also dare not
be distracted by their own contrasting (cultural) salience" (Pedersen &
Ivey, 1993, p. 188).

APPLICATION EXERCISE 6.3
SELECTIVE RESPONDING

A. ANTICIPATING CLIENT RESPONSES
Using your responses to the client in Part B of Exercise 6.2, write what you think would
be the client's response to what you said. For example, with response 1, if you had said,
"When were you in Germany?" the client might have responded, "I was there from 1989
through 1991."

1. Your response: _____

   _____

   Client's next response: _____

   _____

2. Your response: _____

   _____

   Client's next response: _____

   _____

3. Your response: _____

   _____

   Client's next response: _____

   _____

4. Discuss with another person the effects of each of your responses on the client.

B. OBSERVED PRACTICE
One of you, designated as the speaker, will share a concern with the listener. As the
speaker, make sure your initial statement contains several different ideas to which anyone
could respond. For example, "I'm really having trouble in school. There's just so much
work I can't keep up with it. I wonder if I can make good enough grades. I also need to
keep my job to have enough money to pay for tuition, but I don't know if I'll continue to
be able to work and study at the same time."

(continued)

APPLICATION EXERCISE 6.3   CONTINUED

1. The respondent's task is to select *one* of the ideas or topics and respond to it by using either a *paraphrase*, an *open question*, or a *summarization of content*. After your initial response, allow the speaker to continue, then respond with either *silence* or a *minimal verbal response*.
2. The observer's task is to track the way in which the speaker develops the topic and the course of future topics depending on which part of the communication the listener chose to respond.
3. After completing this in one triad, reverse the roles and complete the same process two more times.
4. At the end of three practices, discuss what you have noticed about how the listener's choice of responses and topics influences the path of the speaker's communication.

EFFECTS OF RESPONDING TO COGNITIVE CONTENT

Responding to cognitive content can be an anxiety-reduction tool for clients easily threatened by feelings. Thus, there are times when rapport with clients is established more quickly by discovering how they think before wondering how they feel.

It is also important to realize that behavior incorporates both feelings and thoughts. In order to solve problems and make decisions effectively, clients have to be able to think as well as to feel. Responding to cognitive content assists clients in developing and expressing those thought processes involved in problem solving and decision making.

Because behavior is governed by thoughts as well as feelings, clients need to examine not only what they feel but how they think. Behavior rigidity is often maintained by the kinds of thought patterns present in the clients' repertoires. These may need to be discussed and explored before any behavior change can occur.

Although exploration of feelings is useful to most clients, it is often not sufficient for goal achievement. Once the counseling goals have been established, action plans must be developed to produce goal attainment. Responding to cognitive content goes one step further than responding to affect in that it focuses directly on behavior change. On the other hand, responding primarily to cognitive content presents the following limitations:

1. It may reinforce the intellectualization process; that is, it may encourage the client to continue to abstract and deny feelings that are actually influencing his or her behavior.
2. It may not provide the opportunity that the client needs to share and express feelings in a nonjudgmental setting. The counseling relationship may be the only one in which a client can feel that his or her emotions (and consequently, the self) will not be misunderstood.

3. It may continue to repeat a pattern similar to the rules in the client's family of origin in which "feeling talk" is not allowed, encouraged, or explored.

Again, it must be stressed that the initial strategy in the differentiation process is an *exploratory* one. All clients will respond differently to your emphasis on feelings or on cognitive content. In the next chapter, we discuss client affective messages and possible counselor responses to them in the differentiation and selective responding process.

SUMMARY

In this chapter, we have shown that the counselor has numerous response choices, and each choice has a corresponding effect on the client's following statement. In this reciprocal arrangement, both the counselor and the client influence the path that counseling will take in the session. Most helpers would acknowledge the importance of the client's choices, which reflect how the client conceptualizes problems and solutions, self and others, success and failure, and responsibility and control. However, they do not always acknowledge that the counselor similarly influences the session by choosing to respond to some messages rather than others, and by exploring some issues rather than others—in short, by selecting what becomes the focus of the session.

These counselor choices are made in rather commonplace ways, including silence, minimal vocal responses, paraphrases of the clients' message, questions, and summarization of content. The highly experienced counselor makes these choices almost intuitively; the inexperienced counselor must make these choices deliberately. If the inexperienced counselor relies on intuition, the possibility of making bad choices is about equal to the possibility of making good choices. But what is more important, the inexperienced counselor who is unaware of, and thus is not making intentional choices, is very likely to lack a sense of what is happening in the process of counseling.

We also have indicated throughout this chapter that the effects of your responses will not only affect the focus and direction of each interview but will also vary among clients of various cultural groups. The client's worldview is an important determinant in this process.

REFLECTIVE QUESTIONS

1. What are some of the conditions that might work against you as you try to recognize the different messages in a client statement?

2. How can a counselor shape or influence the topical direction of a session without even being aware that he or she is doing so?

3. Under what counseling conditions might you want to have your clients talking about problems, events, situations, or people, as opposed to feelings?

4. With yourself or a partner, talk about ideas, beliefs, topics, or issues that are uncomfortable for you to discuss. How might this affect the way in which you respond to clients who present these issues and beliefs?

5. How might your own cultural affiliation and worldview affect what you focus on in an interview?

RECOMMENDED READINGS

Cournoyer, B. (2000). *The social work skills workbook* (3rd ed.). Belmont, CA: Wadsworth/Brooks/Cole.

Ivey, A. (2003). *Intentional interviewing and counseling* (5th ed.). Pacific Grove, CA: Brooks/Cole.

Ivey, A. E., D'Andrea, M., Ivey, M. B., & Simek-Morgan, L. (2002). *Theories of counseling and psychotherapy* (5th ed.). Boston: Allyn and Bacon.

Johnson, D. W. (2003). *Reaching out: Interpersonal effectiveness and self actualization* (8th ed.). Boston: Allyn and Bacon.

Murphy, B., & Dillon, C. (2003). *Interviewing in action* (2nd ed.). Pacific Grove, CA: Wadsworth.

CHAPTER SEVEN

RESPONDING TO AFFECTIVE CONTENT

What are some of the ways you communicate how you feel? When you are "down in the dumps," how does your voice sound? When you are angry, what is your face like? Your mouth? Your eyes? Your jaws? When you are afraid, what are some of the expressions you use to communicate this feeling? Human beings have many ways of communicating their internal states. The set jaw often is associated with determination. The glaring eyes speak for anger, even in the small child. The trembling voice, the soft voice, the downcast eyes—all have their meanings.

Clients use all of the verbal and nonverbal modes to tell the counselor their concerns. The emotions that accompany the narrative enrich and modify the message. They give the counselor the events of the clients' world *and* the clients' reactions to those events. These cues are not always easy to read and can vary across cultures. Clenched teeth can mean more than one thing. The trembling voice only suggests the presence of an intense emotion. A part of being a counselor is putting together the pieces or cues of clients' messages in such a way that you can make reasonably good guesses about the underlying emotion.

As indicated earlier, a client's communication presents alternatives. In addition to alternative cognitive topics, you will find that you are faced with choices between cognitive topics and affective topics. This chapter focuses on the affective message, how to recognize it, and how to reinforce its exploration by clients. As Teyber (2000) observed, "Painful feelings lie at the heart of enduring problems. Change in therapy is a process of affective relearning. . . . This affective unfolding is a pivotal point in therapy because it reveals the emotional basis of clients' problems" (p. 116).*

To review briefly, client communications that deal primarily with people, events, or objects may be described as *cognitive* details. Communications that reflect feelings or emotions may be described as *affective* details. Many messages contain both cognitive and affective components. When this occurs, the affective message may not be obvious in the words of the client. Instead, the feelings may be expressed through nonverbal modes, such as vocal pitch, rapidity of speech, body position, and/or gestures.

*This and all other material from this source are from *Interpersonal Process in Psychotherapy: A Relational Approach*, 4th edition by E. Teyber. © 2000. Reprinted with permission of Wadsworth, a division of Thompson Learning: www.thomsonrights.com. Fax 800-730-2215.

THE IMPORTANCE OF RESPONDING
TO AFFECTIVE CONTENT

Affective content represents feelings or emotions held by clients. Numerous clients are often either unaware of their feelings or afraid of them. Many people, including those who learn to be helpers, do not want to feel feelings because of the rules those individuals have made about feelings. In fact, a major rule in dysfunctional families is "Don't feel"—sometimes made more specific such as "Don't feel angry" or "Don't feel sad." Little boys may hear "Don't feel sad or cry—you'll be a sissy"; little girls may hear "Be nice—be a good girl—don't say anything angry." Often, these rules have the effect of masking or interfering with how people truly feel. Fosha (2000) noted that a good part of the alienation from and fraying of family and social life can be traced to the fear of affect: "People disconnect from their emotional experience, afraid of being overwhelmed, humiliated or revealed as inadequate by the force of feelings, only to pay the price later in depression, isolation, and anxiety" (p. 13). One of the most important functions in responding to client affect is to give clients permission to feel their feelings, to allow their feelings just to be, rather than stifling, controlling, or holding them back. Persons who, in fact, have held feelings for a long period of time may tend to hold the feeling in a particular musculature of the body, such as tight shoulders or neck, tense lower back, churning gut, and so on (Kelley, 1974).

When clients are given permission to reveal and release feelings, often their energy and well-being are also increased. This occurs because all of the deep primary feelings have a survival value (Kelley, 1979). For example, anger allows an individual to protect his or her rights and establish personal boundaries or limits (Kelley, 1979). The capacity to recognize and express anger is the basis for healthy assertiveness. As Kelley (1979) observed, "The person who cannot become angry, whose anger is deeply repressed, is severely handicapped. . . . These persons' assertions lack conviction and they are often at the mercy of or emotionally dependent on those who are capable of becoming angry" (p. 25). Moreover, the expression of anger is useful in close relationships to "clear the air" and prevent chronic boredom and resentment from building up. Anger and disgust that are expressed and released prompt subsequent expression of love; pain and sadness that are expressed promote later expression of joy and pleasure; and fear that is discharged allows for greater trust (Kelley, 1974). Fosha (2000) has elaborated on the healing power of affect: "To live a full and connected life in the face of difficulty and even tragedy requires the capacity to feel and make use of our emotional experience" (p. 13).

When a client's communication contains both cognitive and affective components, some therapists recommend that the first priority is to acknowledge the affective pattern of the message. Teyber (2000), for one, noted that in all of the indices a therapist has about how to respond to a client, as a general guideline, the most productive response is to *respond to the feeling as the client is currently experiencing it* (p. 118).

Teyber (2000) also noted that another important function of responding to affective content is to help clients *experience* rather than simply talk about feelings. "Little change occurs until clients are able to stop talking about their emotions in an intellectualized manner, and actually feel their feelings in the presence of the therapist"

(p. 122). One way to help clients experience their feelings involves modeling or reflecting the feelings, as we discuss later in this chapter. It is also important to do so when the clients are experiencing the full emotional impact of their issues, since change is most likely to occur at that time (Teyber, 2000).

VERBAL AND NONVERBAL CUES ASSOCIATED WITH EMOTIONS

You may have wondered how you can identify another person's feelings. Although you cannot feel the client's feelings, you can infer what those feelings are and experience very similar feelings. That is to say, you may be able to know what it is like to feel a certain way. How do you do this? You draw from your own emotional experiences and recall that you, too, have experienced pain, anger, and joy, and remember how they felt. You must first recognize the feeling in your client before you can reproduce a similar feeling in yourself.

To do this, you may need to become more aware of, and sensitive to, certain verbal and nonverbal cues that are elements of the client's communication. Some of these cues are referred to as *leakage*, since they communicate messages the client did not deliberately intend to have communicated (Ekman & Friesen, 1969). Other cues, primarily verbal, are more deliberately intended and are more easily recognized and identified. In the case of affective leakage, it is important to account for the inferences you draw. For example, when you say, "The client seems happy," that is an inference. If you say, instead, "The client is smiling, and that may mean that he is happy," then you have accounted for your inference.

The total impact of a client's message includes both verbal and nonverbal elements. The verbal impact means that there are certain nouns, adjectives, adverbs, and verbs that express the client's feelings about something or someone, as shown here:

"I am really *worried* about school."

The verbal element associated with the client's feelings in this example is the word *worried*. These kinds of words can be called *affect* words. They express some feeling that the client possesses. If an adverb such as *really* or *very* precedes the affect word, this indicates an even stronger intensity of emotion.

Nonverbal Cues to Affect

Not everything that follows an "I feel" client statement is necessarily an expression of affect. Usually, in one way or another, the *body* or some part of it is also involved in signaling and expressing affect. In other words, there is a "profoundly physical experience to the emotions (as in 'lump in my throat,' 'heavy heart,' or 'my blood is boiling')" (Fosha, 2000, p. 25). Nonverbal cues can be seen by observing the client's head and facial movement, position of body, quick movements and gestures, and voice quality.

Although no single nonverbal cue can be interpreted accurately alone, each does have meaning as part of a larger pattern, or *gestalt*. Thus, there are relationships between nonverbal and verbal aspects of speech. In addition to the relationship between nonverbal and verbal parts of the message, nonverbal cues may also communicate specific information about the relationship of the people involved in the communicative process—in this case, the counselor and the client. Nonverbal cues convey information about the nature and intensity of emotions, sometimes more accurately than verbal cues. The *nature* of the emotion is communicated nonverbally primarily by *head* cues; the *intensity* of an emotion is communicated both by *head* cues and *body* cues (Ekman & Friesen, 1967).

Close observation of the client's body, nonverbal behavior, and facial expressions in particular can offer important information to the counselor about the nature and intensity of blocked feelings as well as feelings that are starting to emerge. For example, one of us recently saw a client who had been coming in weekly for the last few months. On this particular occasion, the counselor noted that shortly after the client sat down, her face became contorted. She then began to describe a situation that had recently occurred involving a loss of an important relationship. The counselor commented on her facial expression—the tightness of it—and inquired about what she might be holding back. She then immediately cried, and upon release of tears, her face softened and relaxed.

Culture and Nonverbal Affect Cues

It is very important not to assume the meaning of a nonverbal affect cue without checking it out with the client. In part, this is because the meaning may vary among persons and also among cultures. For example, there seem to be differences in cultures between *contact* and *noncontact* nonverbal behaviors such as eye contact, touch, and physical distance between the counselor and client (Watson, 1970). The one area of nonverbal expression that does *not* seem to vary among cultural groups involves facial expressions. The primary or basic emotions of anger, fear, sadness, and happiness do seem to be depicted in the same facial expressions across cultures, although the various norms of each culture may affect how much and how often these emotions are expressed (Mesquita & Frijda, 1992).

It is important for you as a helper to be aware of your own stereotypes and values that may bias your interpretation of nonverbal affect cues, particularly with clients who are from culturally diverse groups. For example, western white helpers are accustomed to direct eye contact, but for some American Indian clients and for some Asian American clients, lack of eye contact may be consistent with their cultural norms and values and does not suggest lack of attention or disrespect (Sue & Sue, 2003). Similarly, some African American clients may be misperceived on the basis of their nonverbal behavior as well. Some white mental health practitioners may describe an African American client as hostile, angry, or resistant, simply because he or she is expressing oneself with nonverbal affect cues with which the white worker is unaccustomed, such as animated vocal expression, closer conversational distance, greater body movements, and prolonged eye contact when talking (Sue & Sue, 2003, p. 140).

■ ■ ■ ■ ■ ▬▬▬▬▬▬▬▬▬▬▬▬▬▬▬▬▬

APPLICATION EXERCISE 7.1
OBSERVING BEHAVIOR

Select a partner and interact with him or her for about five minutes. Then each of you, in turn, describe your partner, using the phrase:

"I'm observing that you are _____ ."

Be sure to describe what you *see*, not how you think the other person feels or what the nonverbal behavior means.

TYPES OF AFFECTIVE MESSAGES

Although there are many different kinds of feelings, most distinct, universal feelings that are identified by words fit into one of four categories: joy, anger, fear, or sadness. There are now many lists of affect words available, but we continue to use the one that we believe was the original of all such lists (shown on the next few pages).

Positive Affect—Joy

Feelings of joy reflect positive or good feelings about oneself and others and indicate positive feelings about interpersonal relationships. Many of them can be identified by certain affect words. Affect word cues that communicate the general feeling of joy, well-being, affection, or satisfaction may be subclassified into five general areas:

ENJOYMENT	COMPETENCE	LOVE	HAPPINESS	HOPE
beautiful	able	close	cheerful	luck
enjoy	can	friendly	content	optimism
good	fulfill	love	delighted	try
nice	great	like	excited	guess
pretty	wonderful	need	happy	wish
satisfy	smart	care	laugh(ed)	want
terrific	respect	want	thrill	
tremendous	worth	choose	dig	

Source: T. J. Crowley, *The Conditionability of Positive and Negative Self-Reference Emotional Affect Statements in a Counseling-Type Interview.* Unpublished doctoral dissertation. Amherst: University of Massachusetts, 1970. Reprinted by permission.

You can continue to add to this list of affect words related to positive affect. Can you begin to get the feeling for the message implicit in the usage of words such as these? Certain nonverbal cues often occur simultaneously with affection word cues.

The most obvious of these cues are facial ones. The corners of the mouth may turn up to produce the hint of a smile. The eyes may widen slightly. Facial wrinkles disappear. Often, there is an absence of body tension. The arms and hands may be moved in an open-palm gesture of acceptance, or the communicator may reach out and touch the object of the affection message. When the client is describing feelings about an object or event, there may be increased animation of the face and hands.

You might be wondering why we include positive affect, asking yourself, "Don't people who come to see helpers do so because of emotions such as anger, depression, anxiety, and so on?" Yes, that is partly the case. It is also true that intense positive affect can be as difficult or even more difficult for some clients to own and tolerate than negative or disruptive feelings. Positive affect can make some clients feel "embarrassed, self-conscious, out of control, and vulnerable" (Fosha, 2000, p. 70). Moreover, it is all too easy in the helping process to bypass any positive feelings in the course of the counseling sessions to focus solely on negative or problematic feelings (Fosha, 2000, p. 257). Finally, positive affect is important because clients can feel pride and joy in acknowledging and focusing on their ability to deal with and experience frightening or painful emotions. As Fosha has observed, "Joy, pride, self-confidence, and a new appreciation of one's abilities are some of the affective experiences that follow after the unbearable feelings become bearable," or, stated another way, "Joy can be the other side of fully faced and overcome fear" (p. 165).

Anger

Anger represents an obstruction to be relieved or removed in some way. Different kinds of stimuli often elicit anger, such as *frustration, threat,* and *fear.* Conditions such as competition, jealousy, and thwarted aspirations can become threats that elicit angry responses. Anger often represents negative feelings about oneself and/or others. Many times, fear is concealed by an outburst of anger. In such cases, the anger becomes a defensive reaction because the person does not feel safe enough to express fear. Anger is also a cover-up for hurt. Beneath strong aggressive outbursts are often deep feelings of vulnerability and pain. Verbal cues that suggest anger may be classified into four general categories:

ATTACK	GRIMNESS	DEFENSIVENESS	QUARRELSOMENESS
argue	dislike	against	angry
attack	hate	protect	fight
compete	nasty	resent	quarrel
criticize	disgust	guard	argue
fight	surly	prepared	take issue
hit	serious		reject
hurt			disagree
offend			

Source: T. J. Crowley, *The Conditionability of Positive and Negative Self-Reference Emotional Affect Statements in a Counseling-Type Interview.* Unpublished doctoral dissertation. Amherst: University of Massachusetts, 1970. Reprinted by permission.

You can continue to add to this list of affect words related to anger. Remember that anger covers a broad group of feelings and can be expressed in many ways. With the expression of anger, the body position may become rigid and tense, or it may be characterized by gross changes in body position or movement. Sometimes, anger toward another person or the self may be expressed by *hitting*, which consists of fault finding or petty remarks directed at the object of the anger. For example, in counseling a couple with relationship problems, one partner may express this sort of anger by continual verbal attacks on the other person or by incessant remarks of dissatisfaction with the partner. Hitting can also be expressed through nonverbal cues such as finger drumming or foot tapping.

Certain vocal qualities are also associated with anger. Many times, the voice will become much louder as the person becomes more rigid in what he or she is saying; if the anger is very intense, the person may even shout. In some instances of intense anger, the feeling may be accompanied by tears. Many times, the expression of anger will cause vocal pitch to become higher. With some people, however, the vocal pitch actually is lowered, becoming more controlled and measured. This often means that the person experiencing the anger is attempting to maintain a level of control over his or her feelings.

Fear

Fear represents a person's reaction to some kind of danger to be avoided. Often, this reaction is a withdrawal from a painful or stressful situation, from oneself or from other people and relationships. As such, the person experiencing the emotions of fear may also be isolated and sad or depressed. Fear can also be described as a negative set of feelings about something or someone that results in a need to protect oneself. Verbal cues that suggest fear may be classified into four general categories:

FEAR	DOUBT	PAIN	AVOIDANCE
anxious	failure	awful	flee
bothers	flunk	hurts	run from
concerns	undecided	intense	escape
lonely	mediocre	unpleasant	cut out
nervous	moody	uncomfortable	forget
scare	puzzled	aches	
tense	stupid	torn	
upset	unsure		

Source: T. J. Crowley, *The Conditionability of Positive and Negative Self-Reference Emotional Affect Statements in a Counseling-Type Interview.* Unpublished doctoral dissertation. Amherst: University of Massachusetts, 1970. Reprinted by permission.

You can continue to add to this list of affect words suggesting fear. Remember that fear is a broad category of feelings and can be expressed in a variety of ways.

Several facial cues are associated with fear. The mouth may hang wide open as in shock or startlement; the eyes may also dilate. Fear may cause a furrow to appear between the eyebrows. Fear of the counselor or of the topic at hand may be reflected by the client's avoidance of direct, eye contact, although remember that the meaning and use of eye contact varies among cultures.

Body positions and movements also are associated with the expression of fear. At first, the person experiencing fear may appear to be still in body position or may draw back. However, after this initial period, body movements usually become greater as anxiety increases, resulting in jerky and trembling motions. Although parts of the body may shake, often the hands are tightly clasped, as if giving protection. Tension also may be indicated through actions such as leg swinging, foot tapping, finger tapping, or playing with a ring or other piece of jewelry.

Voice qualities are also indicators of the level of anxiety the client is experiencing. As the level of anxiety increases, the breathing rate becomes faster and breathing becomes more shallow. As anxiety and tension increase, the number of speech disturbances increases. This yields a greater number of cues, such as errors, repetitions, stutterings, and omissions of parts of words or sentences. The rate of speech also increases as anxiety mounts.

Sadness

Some of the more common conditions expressed by clients are feelings of sadness, loneliness, or depression. These emotions may be a response to a variety of client conditions, including unsatisfying personal relationships, environmental conditions such as disempowerment and oppression, physiological imbalances, or even poor nutrition. Sometimes sadness can be a response to the helper's compassion and empathy. *Having the helper's care and understanding can make the client more aware of not having it or not having had it* in other life situations or with other people (Fosha, 2000, p. 227). Verbal cues that suggest sadness, loneliness, or depression include the following:

SADNESS	LONELINESS	DEPRESSION
unhappy	alone	depressing
adrift	abandoned	depressed
sorrowful	isolated	disillusioned
distressed	missing	weary
grieved	missed	listless
heartsick		discouraged
		despondent
		gloomy

Source: T. J. Crowley, *The Conditionability of Positive and Negative Self-Reference Emotional Affect Statements in a Counseling-Type Interview.* Unpublished doctoral dissertation. Amherst: University of Massachusetts, 1970. Reprinted by permission.

The intonation of a depressed person is also a departure from the normal intonation. The voice quality may become more subdued with less inflection, so that the voice takes on more of a monotonal quality.

It is important to recognize that sadness has different meanings among cultures. In fact, in some societies, depression is not even recognized as an illness or a sign of something being wrong but rather an indication of spiritual insight (Castillo, 1997). In another example, O'Neill (1993) found that among Native Americans living on reservations, sadness had positive connotations because "it signified maturity and recognition of the tremendous loss they experienced through domination by Anglo American society" (Castillo, 1997, p. 208). Grief is also a phenomenon that is embedded in sociocultural contexts. In Greece, for example, a widow grieves for five years after her partner's death (Kramer, 1993). Moreover, while sadness in Western society is often characterized by a *cognitive* feature such as self-talk, in many non-Western societies, it is represented more by *somatic* symptoms (Castillo, 1997).

■ ■ ■ ■ ■ ▬▬▬▬▬▬▬▬▬▬▬▬▬▬▬▬▬▬▬▬▬▬▬▬▬▬▬▬▬▬▬

APPLICATION EXERCISE 7.2
IDENTIFYING AFFECT CUES

To give you practice in identifying nonverbal and verbal affect cues, complete the following exercises:

A. IDENTIFYING NONVERBAL AFFECT CUES

Select a partner. One of you will be the speaker; the other will be the respondent. The speaker should select a feeling from the following list. (Note how any cultural affiliations affect this process.)

> Contentment or happiness
> Puzzlement or confusion
> Anger
> Discouragement
> Disgust
> Worry or anxiety
> Embarrassment and self-consciousness
> Excited or thrilled

Do not tell the respondent which feeling you have selected. Portray the feeling through nonverbal expressions only. The respondent must accurately identify the behaviors you use to communicate the feeling and should infer the feeling you are portraying. After he or she has done so, choose another and repeat the process. When you have portrayed each feeling, reverse roles and repeat the exercise.

An alternative way to do this activity is to do it in two small groups or teams. Each team picks one emotion to act out and the other team has to guess what it is just from the nonverbal affect cues. If the other team guesses correctly, they get one point. If they do not,

(continued)

APPLICATION EXERCISE 7.2   CONTINUED

the first team can continue to try to act it out, or can pick another emotion to act out. As soon as the second team guesses the emotion accurately, it will be their turn and they can pick an emotion to act out. If it is identified accurately by the other team, that team then gets one point. Try to continue until both teams have acted out all the different emotions on the list. Afterwards, you can process this activity with the following sorts of questions:

1. Which feelings were easiest to act out? Easiest to identify?
2. Which feelings were hardest to act out? Hardest to identify?
3. What have you taken away with you from this activity about nonverbal affect cues?

B. LINKING BODY CUES AND EMOTIONS

Many emotions are expressed graphically by descriptions about the body. Smith (1985) has provided an excellent list of some of these. We recommend his exercise, which is to enact each of them with your own body and note the feeling and body sensations that accompany each enactment.

He holds his head high.	He puts his best foot forward.
He has a tight jaw.	He drags his heels.
He does not hold his head straight.	He puts his finger on it.
His head is cocked.	He meets one with open arms.
He looks down his nose.	He is tight-fisted.
He keeps a stiff upper lip.	He waved me away.
He does not look one in the eye.	He is shady.
He is down in the mouth.	His shoulders are square.
He turns away.	He stoops low.
He has shifty eyes.	He sits tall.
He has a stiff neck.	He sits straight.
He sticks his chest out.	He is tied up in a knot.
His shoulders are stooped.	He is backward.
His arms are outstretched.	He is forward.
He is heavy-handed.	He leans on people.
He wants to sit on it.	He is weak in the knees.
He puts his foot down.	He is a high stepper. (pp. 60–61)*

C. IDENTIFYING VERBAL AFFECT CUES

The speaker should select a feeling from the following list:

Surprise
Elation or thrill
Anxiety or tension
Sadness or depression
Seriousness or intensity
Irritation or anger

*This and all other quotations from this source are from *The Body in Psychotherapy* by Edward W. L. Smith. Copyright © 1985 by McFarland & Co., Jefferson NC 28640. Reprinted by persmission.

Do not inform the respondent which feeling you have selected. Verbally express the feeling in one or two sentences. Be certain to include the word itself. The respondent should accurately identify the feeling in two ways:

1. Restate the feeling using the same affect word as the speaker.
2. Restate the feeling using a different affect word but one that reflects the same feeling.

Here is an example:

> **Speaker:** "I feel *good* about being here."
> **Respondent:** "You feel *good?*"
>
> or
>
> "You're *glad* to be here."

Choose another feeling and complete the same process. When you have expressed each feeling, reverse roles and repeat the exercise.

D. IDENTIFYING AFFECTIVE COMPONENTS

Read the following client statements taken from actual interview typescripts and identify the affective component(s) in each statement by writing first-person sentences and by underlining the affect word of each client's communication. Here is an example:

> **Client:** "I'm not the type that would like to do research or, uh, things that don't have any contact directly with people. I <u>like</u> to be with people, you know—I feel at home and secure with people."

In this statement the affect word *like* is identified and the following affective components are identified by written sentences using the first person:

1. I enjoy being with people.
2. People help me feel secure.

If there is more than one affective component within a given client communication, place an asterisk (*) next to the one that you feel has the greatest bearing on the client's concern. In the preceding example, asterisk either 1 or 2, depending on which has the greater bearing in your opinion.

CLIENT STATEMENTS

1. "Well, uh, I'm happy just being with people and having them know me."
2. "And, and, uh, you know, they always say that you know some people don't like to be called by a number; well I don't either."
3. "In speech I'm, uh, well, in speech I'm not doing good because I'm afraid to talk in front of a bunch of people."
4. "I can't afford to lose my place on the honor roll and bring shame to my family."

AFFECTIVE COMPETENCE

It is too simplistic to say that the counselor communicates understanding of client feelings through attitudes such as empathy and positive regard. Although empathy and positive regard are necessary to the counseling relationship, the means for communicating these conditions also must be identified. Two primary reasons why the counselor may not respond to client feelings are (1) the counselor does not know appropriate ways of responding and/or (2) the counselor "blocks" upon recognizing the client's feelings. Knowing how to respond to client feelings with empathy and positive regard takes more than the possession of these attitudes. The counselor must make sure that these attitudes are communicated through words, statements, and timing that convey affective competence to clients.

Teyber (2000) has observed how important it is for clients to receive from counselors a more satisfying response to their feelings than they have gotten from other persons in their past. In order to do so, when working with affective content from clients, counselors must be able to provide a safe and supportive atmosphere, often referred to as a *holding environment*. A holding environment simply means that the counselor is able to allow and stay with or "hold" the client's feelings instead of moving away or distancing from the feelings or the client. In doing this, the counselor acts as a container; that is, the counselor's comfort in exploring and allowing the emergence of client feelings provides the support to help the client contain or hold various feelings that are often viewed by the client as unsafe.

This holding environment is usually dramatically different from what either the young client is experiencing or what an adult client experienced while growing up. If the child was sad or hurt, often the parent responded by withdrawing from the child, shaming the child for feeling that way, or denying the client's feeling (Teyber, 2000, p. 134). In all of these parental reactions, the child's feeling was not heard, validated, or "contained"; as a result, the child learned, over time, to deny or avoid these feelings, or, even worse, to regard his or her feelings as bad and "deserving of shame, guilt, and punishment" (Fosha, 2000, p. 79). Children are developmentally unable to experience and manage feelings on their own without the presence of another person who can be emotionally present for them and receive and even welcome their feelings. If the parent was unable to help the child "hold" feelings in this manner, it will be up to the counselor to do so. Counselors do this by verbal responses that convey understanding of the client's feelings and by nonverbal responses that convey support and compassion. In this way, the counselor allows clients to know that he or she is not overwhelmed or threatened by their feelings, is not judgmental or rejecting of them, does not need to move away from them in any way, and is still fully committed to the relationship (Teyber, 2000, p. 137). This corrective or reparative emotional experience helps clients to own their feelings so they do not have to deny them or push them aside. It also helps clients to tolerate and regulate their emotions without being overwhelmed by them.

Blocking refers to the counselor's reaction to client feelings in ways that reduce or restrict his or her helpfulness. For example, the counselor may accurately identify the client's feelings of anger but avoid responding to these feelings for several reasons. The counselor might be afraid that the client will leave if the interaction gets too intense, or the counselor might not trust his or her own judgment and be afraid of turning the client off with an inaccurate response, or the counselor might fear that acknowledging the feeling would produce a flood of more intense feelings in the client that would be difficult to handle, or the counselor might have similar feelings that might be aroused. Client feelings related to sex, self-worth, and achievement are also potential blocks.

As mentioned earlier, the primary problem with blocking is that the counselor does not respond to the client's feelings in a more helpful way than the client received in the past. Blocking by the counselor repeats the same aloneness that clients had to endure with their feelings as a child. As Fosha (2000, p. 83) noted, aloneness and lone-liness, frightening and painful in themselves, only strengthen the painful experiencing of anything else a client may be going through or witnessing. Teyber (2000) has listed a variety of ways in which counselors may block dealing with client affect appropriately:

Become anxious and change the topic

Fall silent and emotionally withdraw

Become directive and tell the client what to do

Interpret what the feelings mean and intellectually distance themselves

Self-disclose or move into their own feelings

Reassure and explain that everything will be all right

Diminish the client by trying to rescue him or her

Become overidentified with the client and insist that the client make some decision or take some action to manage the feelings (p. 135)

When you find yourself responding in one of these ways, note what is happening to you and how you are feeling. This is another example of useful topics to talk over with your supervisor (see also Chapter 10).

VERBAL RESPONSES TO AFFECTIVE MESSAGES

It is possible to identify certain counselor responses that will assist you in discriminating among affective messages and communicating your understanding of the client's feelings at the same time. Two such responses are *reflection* of feelings and *summarization* of feeling. The most effective verbal responses to client affect messages are those that reflect the client's feelings and experiences in a spirit of empathy, compassion, authenticity, and helpfulness. This does not mean helpers will always be able to be perfectly empathic or make perfect reflective responses. It does mean, however, that clients will know they exist not only in the "mind" of the counselor but in the "heart" of the counselor as well (Fosha, 2000, p. 58).

Reflection of Feelings

The reflection-of-feelings response is distinctly different from the paraphrase response, but the two are often confused. As indicated earlier, the paraphrase is a rephrasal of all or a portion of the *cognitive* content in a client's response, whereas the reflection is a rephrasal of the *affective* portion. When the client's response contains both cognitive and affective components, the counselor must differentiate between the two in order to reflect the affective content.

Reflection of feelings accomplishes precisely what its name indicates: a mirroring of the feeling or emotion present in the client's message. This response helps clients to own and express feelings. The value in this is helping clients to recognize their feelings and to accept those feelings rather than fear them. Initially, clients may defend against feelings because they seem dangerous. People who feel sad may do everything in their power to avoid feeling sad or blue. Ultimately, the client needs to learn to trust his or her feelings; it is the experiencing and expressing the sadness rather than the blocking or numbing out of it that is healing (Brammer, Abrego, & Shostrom, 1993).

The reflection-of-feelings response can occur at different levels. At the most obvious level, the counselor may reflect only the surface feeling of the client. At a deeper level, the counselor may reflect an implied feeling with greater intensity than that originally expressed by the client. The more obvious level occurs when the counselor reflects an affect message that is *overtly* present in the client's message by using a *different* affect word but one that captures the same feeling and intensity expressed by the client, as in the following example:

Client: "I feel really mad that you interrupted me."
Counselor: "You're very angry about being interrupted."

The second kind of reflection occurs at a deeper level. This one mirrors an affect message that is only *covertly* expressed or implied in the client's message. Consider, for instance, the implied affect message in "I think we have a really neat relationship." The feeling inherent in the words refers to a positive affect message of *like, enjoy, pleased,* and so forth. Thus, a reflection that picks up on the implied feeling in this communication might be among the following:

"Our relationship is important to you."
"Some good things are in it for you."
"You're *pleased* with the relationship."

This reflection that occurs at a deeper level not only mirrors the *covert* feeling but also must at least match the intensity of the client's feeling and perhaps even reflect greater intensity of feeling. Furthermore, the most effective reflection is one that emphasizes what it is the client *anticipates*—in other words, one that acknowledges the *implied admission* of the client's message. Consider this sort of reflection in the following example. Note that the counselor reflects back the covertly implied feeling with a greater intensity of affect and acknowledges the implied admission—that is, what the client would *like* to do or feel, as shown here:

Client: "I feel like I have to be so responsible all the time."
Counselor: "Sometimes you'd feel relieved just to forget all that responsibility— to say 'to hell with it'—and really let go."

Although empathy and understanding of feelings are not themselves a panacea, they do serve some useful functions in the counseling process. For one thing, empathy enhances emotional proximity, creating an atmosphere of closeness and generating warmth. Also, empathy contributes to a sense of self-acceptance. When one person feels really understood by another, there is often a feeling of relief—"Gee, I'm not so confused and/or mixed up after all"—and a sense of acceptance about oneself—"This other person has understood me without condemning the way I think or feel."

Summarization of Feelings

Summarization of feelings is very similar to reflection of feelings in that it is a response that discriminates between different affective components of the client's communication and communicates understanding of the client's feelings by the counselor. The basic difference in the two responses is one of *number*, or quantity. The reflection of feelings responds to only *one* portion of the client's communication, whereas the summarization of feelings is an integration of several affective components of the client's communication. Thus, summarization of feelings is really an extension of reflection of feelings. In this response, the counselor is attending to a broader class of client responses and must have the skill to bring together seemingly diverse elements into a meaningful gestalt (Ivey, D'Andrea, Ivey, & Simek-Morgan, 2002).

Like the reflection of feelings, summarization of feelings involves reflecting the feelings of the client in your own words. Again, this encompasses not just one feeling but a bringing together of several feelings into a significant pattern.

Although there are some instances in which clients present one predominant feeling, there are other instances in which clients have several feelings going on at the same time. Teyber (2000) noted that two common affective constructions with mixed components include anger-sadness-shame and sadness-anger-guilt. In the first sequence, the primary feeling is often anger but it is a negative response to hurt or sadness. Often, the experiencing of the anger and sadness provokes shame. In the second sequence, the predominant feeling is sadness but it is often connected to anger that has been denied because the expression of it produces guilt. These affective sequences are typically acquired in childhood and are a result of both family of origin rules and culture. The summarization-of-feelings response can identify the various affective states the client describes or experiences. Consider the following examples:

    Client: "I'm so pissed off at my mother and my wife. They're always on my back, telling me what to do, where to go, how to think—planning my whole life for me. It's been this way for years. I wish I could do something different but I just feel hopeless about it. I wish for once I could be a man and stand up to them but I just keep giving in and giving in."

    Counselor: "You seem to be feeling several things in this situation—first, you're obviously *angry* about their behavior. Also, you feel *sad* and perhaps *ashamed* about your powerlessness to effect any change—is that accurate?"

    Client: "I'm really feeling down and out about my job. It's so hard to find the energy to keep going in day after day. I don't really mind the work but over the years the people there have been so nasty that I don't want to be around them. I know if I weren't the nice person that I am I would probably really tell them a thing or two."

Counselor: "You're feeling *discouraged* about your job. It also sounds like you're feeling pretty *angry* and *fed up* with your co-workers but, because of your own niceness, you feel a little *guilty* or *reluctant* to express your irritation with them."

Summarization of feelings is often used instead of reflection of feelings when a client's communication contains many different affective elements rather than just one or two. It can also be used effectively when the interview appears to be bogged down. For example, when one topic has been covered repeatedly or when a dead silence occurs during an interview, summarization can increase the interview pace. By tying together various feelings, summarization can identify a central theme. It also provides direction for the interview, and may thus furnish the needed initiative to get the interview going again.

In using both the reflection-of-feelings and the summarization-of-feelings responses, be careful to heed our earlier caution about the suitability of these two responses for diverse groups of clients, especially in initial sessions. Ivey, Gluckstern, and Ivey (1993) noted:

> In White, North American and other cultures, men are expected to hold back their feelings. You aren't a "real man" if you allow yourself to feel emotion. While many men can and do express their feelings in the helping interview, some should not be pushed too hard in this area in the first phases of counseling. Later, with trust, exploration of feelings becomes more acceptable.
>
> In general, women in all cultures are more in touch with and more willing to share feelings than men. Nonetheless, this will vary with the cultural group. Some cultures (for example, Asian, Native Americans) at times pride themselves on their ability to control emotions. However, this may also be true with those of British and Irish extraction.
>
> African Americans and other minorities have learned over time that it may not be safe to share themselves openly with White Americans. In cross-cultural counseling situations, trust needs to be built before you can expect in-depth discussion of emotions. (pp. 73–74)

■ ■ ■ ■ ■ ▬▬▬▬▬▬▬▬▬▬▬▬▬▬▬▬▬▬

APPLICATION EXERCISE 7.3
RESPONSES TO AFFECTIVE COMPONENTS

A. RESPONSES TO CLIENT STATEMENTS
For the following counselor-client interactions, please observe the following directions:

1. Read each interaction carefully.
2. For each client statement, identify, by writing sentences, the various affective components of the communication.

3. For each client statement, write your own response to the affective portion(s). Use both a reflection of feelings and a summarization of feelings for each client statement.

Client: "Uh, I'm unsure why I'm having such a hard time letting my family and friends know I'm gay. I mean I watch TV now and I see a whole sort of cultural revolution going on there. But when it comes to me, I feel very hesitant."

Affective components: _____

_____

_____

Reflection of feelings: _____

_____

Summarization of feelings: _____

_____

Client: "My daddy won't want to meet you because you're black and I'm half black. And he treats my mom and me like dirt. And he thinks only white people deserve to be treated well. I just wish I had a dad who was good to me and my mom. I miss that."

Affective components: _____

_____

_____

Reflection of feelings: _____

_____

Summarization of feelings: _____

_____

B. OBSERVED PRACTICE

Complete the following exercise with two other people:

1. One of you, designated as the speaker, should share a personal concern with the respondent.
2. The respondent's task is to respond *only* to affective topics using only the two responses covered in the chapter: reflection of feelings and summarization of feelings.
3. The observer will use the Observer Rating Chart (Figure 7.1, page 112) to keep track of the number and kinds of responses used by the listener. This feedback should then be given to the listener.
4. After interacting for approximately 10 minutes, reverse the roles.

FIGURE 7.1   Observer Rating Chart

COUNSELOR RESPONSE	TYPE OF COUNSELOR RESPONSE	
	Reflection of Feelings	Summarization of Feelings
1.		
2.		
3.		
4.		
5.		
6.		
7.		
8.		
9.		
10.		
11.		
12.		
13.		
14.		
15.		
16.		
17.		
18.		
19.		
20.		

EFFECTS OF RESPONDING TO AFFECTIVE CONTENT

The importance of responding to client feelings as an anxiety-reduction tool has already been mentioned. Generally speaking, responding to affect diminishes the intensity of feelings. For instance, responding to (accepting) strong feelings of anger expressed by the client will reduce the intensity of the feelings and assist the client in gaining control of them so that the client is not overwhelmed by feelings.

The expression of feelings may be an important goal for some clients. Some people have had so little opportunity to express their feelings openly that to find an acceptant listener provides highly beneficial relief.

Responding to affect with acceptance and understanding can also assist clients in incorporating personal feelings and perceptions into their self-image. In other words, the counselor's acceptance of feelings that have been previously denied and labeled as "bad" by the clients suggests that they may have mislabeled these feelings, and thus themselves. In this way, helpers model affective competence for clients. They help clients learn how to manage their feelings instead of denying them or shutting down and not functioning.

Finally, responding to affect often is the best way to communicate your warmth and involvement with clients. That is, responding to client feelings establishes a high level of trust between you and your clients. It is precisely this kind of trust that enables clients to own their feelings, behaviors, and commitment to behavior change. Fosha (2000) describes this process in a very clear way:

> Why is it more effective to say something to somebody than merely to think it and feel it, even if the other does little more than listen? Why should it make such an enormous difference to communicate something to another person? In expression—*and reception by the other*—the full cycle of processing core affect is complete. . . . The difference between aloneness and the sense of being integrated in the mainstream of mutuality—community—is created by the act of affective communication with one other person, who is open and interested. (p. 28)

Although responding to affect early in the counseling process can be the best strategy for reducing client anxiety, with some clients, your response to their affect message may only induce greater anxiety. With this kind of client, you will have to modify the strategy and respond to cognitive topics in order to find out how the client thinks and what kind of ideas he or she has.

Counselors who always emphasize feelings to the exclusion of cognitive content impose certain limitations on the counseling process. Some of the limitations of responding only to feelings include the following:

1. Responding *only* to feelings is unrealistic and therefore reduces the possibility of the client's ability to generalize aspects of the counseling relationship to other relationships. For most clients, it is highly unlikely that any of their friends or family would take only their feelings into account.
2. Responding *only* to feelings fosters an internal focus to the exclusion of the world around the client. Clients may become so preoccupied with themselves that the level of their other relationships deteriorates even more. Also, responding to an internal focus reflects a Euro-American worldview that will not be compatible with the worldview of some clients from other cultural groups.
3. Responding to affect induces catharsis—the ventilation of pent-up feelings and concerns. For some clients, this may be all that is necessary. For other clients, this is not a sufficient goal. With catharsis, there is a greater possibility of reinforcing

"victim mythology"; that is, the counselor's responses to feelings may only generate more client negative self-referent statements.

In this chapter, we introduced the process by which the counselor makes discriminations—sometimes subtle discriminations—that affect the outcome of a session. Choosing to respond to the cognitive dimension of a client's problems leads the session in one direction. Choosing, instead, to respond to the affective dimension leads in a quite different direction. The cultural affiliations of both counselor and client help to shape this process.

SUMMARY

The expression and development of affect is naturally assumed to be part of the process of counseling. However, this does not mean that the beginning counselor will be either comfortable with or sensitive to affective messages. Nor are clients always comfortable with affective messages and experiences either! Sometimes, affect is implicitly expressed in the client's communication. At other times, one type of affect masks a different and perhaps more significant affect, such as anger masking fear. When these conditions exist, it is easy to miss the affective message. When client affective messages are missed, clients may feel as though the counselor has blocked their emotional experience in the same way a caregiver did. Counselors need to be attuned not only to client affect, but also to ways in which their own experience makes them more likely to block the expression of affect by clients.

In this chapter, we introduced verbal and nonverbal cues that suggest the presence of affect, the nature of affect, and how to respond selectively to affect. We also emphasized that the meaning of affect cues varies among clients and cultures. The development of these counseling responses is closely related to the client's perception of counselor empathy. In other words, as you become more accomplished at recognizing affect accurately and responding to it, your behavior will be perceived as increasingly empathic. According to Fosha (2000, p. 58), clients experience the counselor's empathy when they know they exist not only in the *mind* of the counselor but in the counselor's *heart* as well. Reflecting and summarizing client feelings are two particularly helpful counseling responses in communicating your understanding to clients and in promoting affective competence in clients. This is not to suggest that you would want to respond to every perceived feeling. In Chapters 6 and 7 we considered the process of selective responding to affective or cognitive messages and the effect of your choices on the progress of the interview.

Once your exploratory objective has been achieved and you have chosen when to emphasize affective content and when to emphasize cognitive content, it is time to develop and implement strategies for each of these areas. There are some strategies that are more effectively used in working with affective material. Other strategies are best implemented when the focus is on behavior and cognitions rather than feelings. These strategies are presented in the following chapters.

REFLECTIVE QUESTIONS

1. When a client's message contains both cognitive and affective components, what conditions might lead you to respond to the affective element? How might this be affected by the client's culture?

2. If you were a client, would you prefer a counselor whose natural inclinations were toward feelings or toward rational thinking? What would be the advantages for you if you had the counselor you preferred? What would be the disadvantages for you with such a counselor?

3. Often, clients are less aware of their feelings than of their thoughts. How might you assist clients to become more aware of their feelings by the way you choose to respond?

4. One of the things we discussed in this chapter is the issue of *counselor blocks*—that is, ways in which a counselor may deliberately or inadvertently avoid responding to client affect. Considering the primary emotions of anger, fear, sadness, and happiness, what affect area do you think you would be most likely to block? How does your history contribute to this?

RECOMMENDED READINGS

Castillo, R. J. (1997). *Culture and mental illness.* Pacific Grove, CA: Brooks/Cole.

Fosha, D. (2000). *The transforming power of affect.* New York: Basic Books.

Knapp, M. L., & Hall, J. (1997). *Nonverbal communication in human interaction* (5th ed.). Orlando, FL: Holt, Rinehart and Winston.

Mesquita, B., & Frijda, N. (1992). Cultural variations in emotions: A review. *Psychological Bulletin, 112,* 179–204.

Smith, E. (1985). *The body in psychotherapy.* Jefferson, NC: McFarland.

Teyber, E. (2000). *Interpersonal process in psychotherapy* (4th ed.). Belmont, CA: Wadsworth.

CHAPTER EIGHT

CONCEPTUALIZING ISSUES AND SETTING GOALS

It is appropriate now to consider some of the larger issues of counseling—namely, the nature of client concerns and the establishment of goals that are realistic antecedents to the solution of those problems. There are philosophical questions that underlie these issues, since there is no one way of conceptualizing human problems. We will not be able to resolve the philosophical problems for you. In fact, it may require the greater part of your career to do that. But we will present a viewpoint that represents our stand at this time. We find it useful because it focuses not only on our clients but also on the world that they return to after each counseling session—a world in which the problems are real.

THE CLIENT'S WORLD

What brings clients to counseling? The answer to this, more than any other question, will reveal your role as counselor. It is a disarmingly simple question, but not one to be taken lightly. We begin with this response: Clients enter counseling when they experience issues and needs that they, alone, are unable to understand or to meet, or when their particular coping strategies to meet needs or resolve issues no longer work.

All human beings share certain basic needs. These include the need for security, nourishment, survival, affiliation, love, and self-esteem. In a classic article, Jourard (1963, pp. 33–38) has conceptualized these needs in a way that is useful for counseling. They include the following:

1. *Survival needs:* All people are concerned with self-preservation and safety. This includes psychological safety as well as physical safety. Although people may not always recognize threats to their psychological safety, they do recognize their responses to those threats—namely, increased anxiety, inaccurate or restricted perceptions of the world, and increasingly inappropriate behavior.

2. *Physical needs:* These include the need for nourishment, shelter, income, freedom from pain, rest, and replenishment of energy. When these needs go unmet or become distorted (e.g., overeating or migraine headaches), people's responses may inhibit the satisfaction of still other needs (e.g., the migraine sufferer finds it difficult to achieve love and sex needs).

3. *Love and sex needs:* These are the needs to become involved in a close personal way with another human being. People grow in their development of these needs and often recognize their intensity only when they have suddenly experienced the loss of a close personal relationship. When these needs are unmet, people question their potential to love and be loved, to be in an extended relationship, or to be able to give to or take from another person.

4. *Status, success, and self-esteem needs:* These are the needs that motivate people to achieve in the eyes of their peers and to gain respect, confidence, or admiration. When these needs are unmet, people lack self-respect and self-confidence, or overreact with excessive and manufactured self-respect and self-confidence.

5. *Mental health needs:* When these needs are met, people feel like functional human beings. When they are unmet, people are incongruent, disillusioned, disoriented, and vulnerable to despair.

6. *Freedom needs:* These are the needs to feel autonomous, free to make personal choices, or free not to choose. When these needs go unmet, people feel restricted, undervalued, or unappreciated.

7. *Challenge needs:* These are the needs for activity, future orientation, and opportunity. When they are missing, people are vulnerable to boredom, meaninglessness, or emptiness.

8. *Cognitive-clarity needs:* These needs reflect the drive to resolve the conflicts in values, ideas, and commitments that exist in people's lives and the need to live one's life with honor and integrity.

Perhaps you would add to or take away from this list, according to your view of human beings. The point, however, is that all human beings experience needs as a part of living. To experience a need does not set a person apart as unusual, inadequate, or in some other way lacking. On the other hand, human beings are not always adept at recognizing (comprehending) experienced needs, nor do they necessarily possess the skills required to meet needs once the needs are recognized. To recognize and meet one's needs is not necessarily a natural part of the process of living; it must be learned.

The place where people learn or do not learn what their needs are and how to get them met is in their family of origin. This is where needs are either affirmed and met or shamed and rejected. Teyber (2000) noted:

> Many enduring psychological problems begin when basic childhood developmental needs are not met . . . and once the need gets consistently or repetitively blocked, the child in growing up will either block the need in the same way his or her environment blocked it to avoid reexperiencing the need or will to try to rise above the need to have it met indirectly or to partially gratify it by a particular style of coping. . . .

> Childrens' unmet childhood needs do not dissipate or go away as they grow up. The need may be repressed or defended against, but it continues to seek expression. As a result, clients do not give up trying to have the need met. At the same time, the unmet need remains too anxiety-arousing to be expressed directly. So clients try to rise above the unmet need and indirectly, fulfill it by adopting . . . a particular interpersonal coping style. (pp. 181–186)

For example, an adult client whose early needs for affection were shamed may block current needs for affection and claim, "I don't need anybody's love. I can make it on my own." Yet, at some level, the unmet need for affection will still try to seek expression, and when it does, the client will try to cope with it in a particular way, but usually in an unsatisfying or troublesome way.

In addition to this intrapsychic view of needs, we also need to recognize the role of external stressors and environmental events in creating needs. For example, clients also experience needs in terms of current life events and may enter therapy when various life stressors or developmental issues become too hard to handle. Consider, for instance, an adult woman is coping well with her marriage and her job. But as her aging father unexpectedly develops Alzheimer's disease, her world starts to fall apart and she experiences needs now that were either not there or not apparent to her before this event.

Current life events and environmental stressors are particularly important in shaping needs of clients who feel marginalized because of race, gender, sexual orientation, religion, health status, ethnicity, or socioeconomic status and who experience the effects of stereotyping, discrimination, and oppression on a frequent and repetitive basis. In these situations, emotional distress resulting from current needs often is more the result of a lack of both real and perceived power in a client's everyday, current life rather than unmet developmental childhood needs (Brown & Ballou, 1992). For example, consider the situation of a financially challenged African American woman who is raising her three children single-handedly. She has no living parents to help her in child rearing and her two brothers were shot and killed in an urban gang fight. She has a part-time job with no benefits and is in danger of losing it because she has needed to take days off to care for her sick children. Furthermore, in riding the subway to her place of work, she is met with racial taunts. Clearly, the context of her current world is a major factor in her presenting needs.

Thus far, we have drawn a picture of the client as a person who is (1) continually experiencing issues and needs, (2) not always understanding or even recognizing some of those issues and needs, and (3) seeking your assistance when unrecognized and/or unmet issues and needs become the bigger issue of living. Though this may be an adequate description of the person entering counseling, it fails to embrace the total situation of the client. Any description of clients must also include the world in which they live, including significant others, employment or the setting in which they spend the major portion of the day, expectations for self and others, habits and routines, dreams and fantasies of the future, attitudes toward the past, values and the meanings of life, and methods developed for survival (survival of responsibilities, tensions, disappointments, expectations of others, dashed hopes, etc.). You might wish to refer to our discussion of the initial interview in Chapter 5 for a review of all of these components, as conceptualizing client problems begins in the initial session. In addition to this review, consider the following issue-oriented questions posed by Sperry, Carlson, and Kjos (2003):

What concerns brought you here?
Why now?
Have you (or any relatives) ever experienced this or other issues like this before?
How has this been affecting your daily functioning? (p. 67)

THE ROLE OF THE COUNSELOR IN ASSESSING CLIENT CONCERNS

Based on what we have said about the client who is entering counseling, it follows that you would have some fairly clear responsibilities. These responsibilities are above and beyond creating a favorable climate for counseling—even beyond being a good and caring listener. It is your role to hear the issues as clients describe their concerns and to help them hear those needs and issues as well. Next, it is your role to help clients formulate goals that will help meet the needs or resolve the issues. From these goals, plans of action may be constructed, implemented, and evaluated. Finally, you must help clients recognize that they are making progress. When clients have lived with problems too long, it is difficult to trust any progress.

The counseling process may often be viewed as an unfolding process in which the outer, more obvious issues precede the more subtle, less obvious concerns. As an example, consider an Asian American man who comes to counseling with an obvious dilemma: He cannot fall asleep at night. He has a *physical need* to sleep. After the insomnia problem has been addressed and the goals and strategies have been formulated to help with this, focus is then directed toward those pressures that led to the insomnia in the first place. This could be the result of old wounds or unmet needs that have become recently reactivated. For instance, he recently lost his job as a result of layoffs; he may now feel lacking in self-respect and self-confidence and have *esteem needs*, wanting to be respected, valued, and appreciated by himself and by others. He does not want to "lose face" among his family and culture. These may be carry-over needs from family and culture that are now being felt again because of a major loss. He may also have *survival* needs related to loss of income in his current life.

As you attempt to conceptualize or understand client issues, it is important that you keep in mind that client issues and needs are complex and multidimensional, consisting of multiple elements. In other words, it is the *exception rather than the rule* for a client to come in and say, "I am just having one problem with my best friend, that's it." And even in the case of children, an issue with a best friend is likely to be more than it appears to be at first. The child may be angry with the friend or may feel betrayed by the friend. The child may have concluded that he or she is unlikeable. The child may be acting in ways that put barriers between the friendship. The child may have a learning disability that contributes to misperceptions about or miscommunications with the friend or to troubles in the classroom. Or the child may be reacting to a breach in the friendship as a result of something that happened at home, school, or in the larger community or cultural network.

The primary dimensions of client issues involve the following five:

1. *Contextual factors:* Time, place, concurrent events, and cultural and sociopolitical issues
2. *Beliefs:* The client may already have beliefs that contribute to the problem, impede the solution, or become the problem
3. *Feelings:* The emotional responses to the problem that often exaggerate the problem, impede the comprehension of the problem, or become the problem
4. *Behavior:* The habits and routines that are inappropriate responses, and perhaps contributors to the problem
5. *Interaction and relational patterns:* Those established ways of reacting to familiar others, including the miscommunication channels, expectations, self-fulfilling prophesies, coping styles, and so on

Conceptualization of client issues does not come quickly. It comes progressively. After your first session with clients, you will begin to have some hunches about them, their world (and how they view it), and their concerns (and how they view them). In subsequent sessions, these initial hunches will be modified as you understand your clients better and as your clients understand and report their world to you. There will be mistaken hunches along the way. These are to be accepted as part of the process, too. Acknowledge and discard them. The remainder of this chapter is an extension of the conceptualizing process—that is, conceptualizing the client's goals.

These five dimensions of client issues derive from orientations to counseling that we call *theoretical approaches* or *counseling theories*. (Note that we summarize the major theoretical approaches in Chapter 9.) Some of these approaches emphasize the role of feelings or beliefs and cognitions in the development and maintenance of client issues, whereas others emphasize the role of behaviors, systems, and cultural factors. We take an integrative position that emphasizes the importance of all five dimensions. We will return to this five-component formulation again in Chapter 9 in which we discuss the use of counseling strategies to promote change in these five dimensions.

PROCESS AND OUTCOME GOALS

The counseling process involves two types of goals: process goals and outcome goals. *Process goals* are related to the establishment of therapeutic conditions necessary for client change. These are general goals, such as establishing rapport, providing a non-threatening setting, and possessing and communicating accurate empathy and unconditional regard. They can be generalized to all client relationships and can be considered universal goals. Process goals are your primary responsibility; you cannot expect your clients to help you establish and communicate something like unconditional regard.

Unlike process goals, *outcome goals* will be different for each client. They are the goals directly related to your clients' changes, to be made as a result of counseling. As you are able to help your clients understand their concerns, you will want to help them understand how counseling can be used to respond to these concerns. The two of you will begin to formulate tentative outcome goals together. As counseling continues, the original goals may be modified through better understanding of the issues and through the development of new attitudes and behaviors that will resolve them. Goal setting should be viewed as a flexible process, always subject to modification and refinement. Most importantly, outcome goals are *shared goals*, goals that *both you and your clients* agree to work toward achieving.

Outcome goals that are *visible* or *observable* are more useful, since they allow you to know when they have been achieved. Not all outcome goals are stated as visible goals, however. For example, consider these two outcome goals:

1. To help your client develop more fully his or her self-actualizing potential
2. To increase the frequency of positive self-statements at home and at work by 50 percent over the next six weeks

Both of these could be considered to be outcome goals. They might even be so closely related as to be the same in terms of outcomes. Your clients may be much more attracted to such goals as developing their self-actualizing potential. You may want to view the development of self-actualizing potential as a composite of many smaller and more specific goals. To state it a little differently, self-actualizing is a hypothetical state that cannot be observed. It can only be inferred through certain visible and audible behaviors. Using this goal, you have no way of knowing the types of activity that your clients will enter into while proceeding toward the goals. As a result, you and your clients will know very little about what they could be doing in the relationship, and you will have no way of assessing progress toward the desired results. Consequently, the first goal listed is not as satisfactory as the second, in that it does not provide you or your clients with specific guidelines for change.

When outcome goals are stated precisely, both you and your clients have a better understanding of what is to be accomplished. This better understanding permits you to work more directly with your clients' problems or concerns, and reduces tangential efforts. Equally important are the benefits you are able to realize in working with specific behavioral goals. You are able to enlist the cooperation of your clients more directly, since they are more likely to understand what is to be done. In addition, you are in a better position to select viable techniques and strategies when your clients have specific objectives. Finally, both you and your clients are in a better position to recognize progress—a rewarding experience in its own right. It is also important to realize that specific observable statements of outcome are required now as part of treatment planning by almost all counseling agencies that receive both state and federal funding because they are clues to client progress and effectiveness of the counselor's strategies and interventions.

CULTURALLY APPROPRIATE
COUNSELING GOALS

Counselors who expect clients who feel marginalized from the mainstream culture to develop long-range goals based on a variety of mental health needs may find that their services are irrelevant. Clients faced with financial challenges, discrimination, and disempowerment may be far more concerned with survival and physical needs and short-term goals that are oriented toward resolution of current life issues (Rosado & Elias, 1993).

Sue and Sue (2003) noted that "culturally diverse clients do not share many of the values and characteristics seen in both the goals and the processes of therapy" (p. 102). It is important for counselors to identify their own cultural biases and values and to ensure that they do not steer clients in a direction that disavows the beliefs and values of the *client's* culture. To do so is to enact a form of racism, sexism, ageism, and so on, because it suggests the counselor is in a superior position while the client is in an inferior position (Sue & Sue, 2003). Many clients from culturally diverse backgrounds do not return to counseling or end counseling early because they feel the counselor is committed only to the pursuit of long-term counseling goals. Long-term goals are often less suitable for some diverse clients, such as those with lower socioeconomic levels (Sue & Lam, 2002; Sue & Sue, 2003).

■ ■ ■ ■ ■ ▬▬▬▬▬▬▬▬▬▬▬▬▬▬▬▬▬▬▬▬▬▬▬▬▬▬▬▬▬▬▬

APPLICATION EXERCISE 8.1
GOAL SETTING

Maria is a young Latina woman who is a junior in college. She initially comes to the student counseling center for career counseling, but after the fourth session, she discloses that when she was 11 years old, she was sexually molested on one occasion at a family gathering by her 21-year-old cousin. She breaks down and cries when describing this situation. She has never told anyone about this before. She would like to tell her mother but her cousin is adored and revered within her family structure and she is not sure her mother will believe her.

Identify a few goals that you think might be appropriate in working with Maria, given that you know very little about her, so far.

_____

_____

_____

_____

Are your goals specific or vague? How would you and Maria know when you had achieved these goals? Are your goals process or outcome goals? If they are outcome goals, how would achieving them affect Maria? Are your goals consistent with Maria's cultural affiliation?

THREE ELEMENTS OF GOOD OUTCOME GOALS

Perhaps you have noticed from our previous examples that outcome goals are different from process goals in several respects. A well-stated outcome goal includes the following elements: the *behavior* to be changed, the *conditions* under which the change will occur, and the *level* or amount of change. These elements apply to any outcome goal, whether it is to modify eating patterns, reduce negative self-appraisal, or increase saying no to unreasonable requests.

The first element of an outcome goal specifies in behavioral terms what the client will do differently as a result of counseling. In other words, determine what unmet needs will become the targets of change and in what specific ways.

The second element of an outcome goal indicates the conditions under which the desired change will occur. It is important to weigh carefully the situations or settings in which the client will attempt a new behavior. You would not want to set your client up to fail by identifying settings in which there was little hope for success. The client might agree to modify eating habits at home during the evening, but not to attempt to modify eating habits at the company dinner on Saturday night.

The third element of outcome goals involves the choice of a suitable and realistic level or amount of the new behavior. That is to say, *how much* of the new behavior will the client attempt? Some clients enter diets with the expectation that they will reduce their consumption from 3,000 calories per day to 900 calories per day. A more realistic goal might be to reduce to 1,500 calories. This brings us to another thought about goals. As you modify goals, you come increasingly closer to the ultimate goals of the client. Each time you set a goal, it is a closer approximation of the results. Successive approximations are very important. They allow the client to set more attainable goals, experience success more often, and make what might be dramatic changes in lifestyle.

■ ■ ■ ■ ■ ▬▬▬▬▬▬▬▬▬▬▬▬▬▬▬▬▬▬▬▬▬▬▬▬▬▬▬▬▬▬▬▬▬▬▬▬

APPLICATION EXERCISE 8.2
OUTCOME GOALS

In the following exercise, examples of client outcome goals are presented. Determine which of the three elements of an outcome goal—behavior, condition, or level—may be missing. After each example, list the missing parts, using *B* for behavior, *C* for condition, and *L* for level. Feedback will be provided to you at the end of the exercise.

The following example is provided as an illustration: to increase job placement (behavior) of clients with physical challenges seen in a rehabilitation agency (condition) by 30 percent in a one-year time period (level).

Identify the missing parts in the following six outcome goals:

1. To decrease temper tantrums
2. To increase exercise to two times a week over a six-week period
3. To decrease the number of nightly arguments at home with your (the client's) partner
4. To decrease tardiness

(continued)

APPLICATION EXERCISE 8.2   CONTINUED

5. To reduce aggressive behavior with a sibling by 50 percent
6. To make three positive comments about the strengths of each member of your (the client's) family during a one-week period

FEEDBACK

1. The missing elements are the condition (C) and level (L) of the goal.
2. This goal specifies the behavior and the level; the condition (C) is missing.
3. The level (L) of the goal is missing.
4. This goal specifies the behavior; the condition (C) and level (L) are missing.
5. The behavior (B) is missing; "aggressive behavior" is a label and does not specify what the person would reduce.
6. This is a complete outcome goal! "Making positive comments" is the behavior; "three of them in one week" is the level; "to each family member" is the condition.

TRANSLATING VAGUE CONCERNS INTO SPECIFIC GOALS

Rarely does a client begin by requesting assistance in achieving specific behavior changes. Instead of saying, "I want to be able to talk to people without getting nervous," the client is likely to say, "I am shy." In other words, a personal characteristic has been described rather than the ways in which the characteristic is experienced. It then becomes the counselor's job to help the client describe the ways in which the characteristic could be changed.

Taking nonspecific concerns and translating them into specific goal statements is no easy task for the counselor. You must understand the nature of the client's problem and the conditions under which it occurs before the translation can begin. Even then, there are difficulties. Egan (2002) has suggested the use of certain future-oriented questions to help guide clients in the goal-setting process:

> What would this problem situation look like if I were managing it better?
> What changes in my present lifestyle would make sense?
> What would I be doing differently with the people in my life?
> What patterns of behavior would make life better?
> What current patterns of behavior would be eliminated?
> What would I have that I don't have now?
> What accomplishments would I have that I don't have now?
> What would this opportunity look like if I developed it? (pp. 268–269)

What can you expect of yourself and your clients in terms of setting specific goals? First, the goals that are set can never be more specific than your understanding and the client's understanding of the problem. This means that at the outset of counseling, goals are likely to be nonspecific and nonbehavioral. *But nonspecific goals are better than no goals at all.*

As you and your client explore the nature of a particular problem, the type of goal(s) appropriate to the problem should become increasingly clear. This clarification will permit both of you to move in the direction of identifying specific behaviors that, if changed, would alter the problem in a positive way. These specific behaviors can then be formulated into goal statements; as you discuss the client's problems in more detail, you can gradually add the circumstances in which to perform the behaviors and how much or how often the target behaviors might be altered.

After you and your client have established the desired outcome goal together, you can identify some action steps that might help the client achieve the overall goal or target. These action steps can be thought of as *subgoals*. Subgoals consist of a series of smaller or intermediate steps or tasks that help the client perform the desired behaviors gradually. When several subgoals are identified, these are usually arranged in a sequence or hierarchy. The client completes one subgoal successfully before moving on to another one. By gradually completing the activities represented by subgoals in a successful manner, the client's motivation and energy to change may be reinforced and maintained. Successful completion of subgoals also may reduce potential failure experiences by giving the client a greater sense of control and empowerment.

■ ■ ■ ■ ■ ▬▬▬▬▬▬▬▬▬▬▬▬▬▬▬▬▬▬▬▬▬▬▬▬▬▬▬▬▬▬▬▬▬▬▬▬▬▬

APPLICATION EXERCISE 8.3
OUTLINING GOALS

Assume that Brent has come to you for counseling, complaining of insomnia. As you and Brent probe the facets of his concerns, you can consider the specific changes Brent would like to make. Gradually, these changes can be developed into an outline of desired goals. We refer to this as an *outline* because the major headings (I and II) represent the two overall or primary outcome goals for Brent; the subheadings reflect the subgoals or activities Brent might perform to achieve the overall goal gradually. Remember that goal setting is a flexible process, and that the goals listed in this outline might change as counseling with Brent progresses.

Outcome Goal I: To be able to go to sleep within an hour of going to bed at least four nights of the week at home.

    A. To identify in writing all of his prior solutions for trying to go to sleep (counting sheep, daydreaming, eating a snack, etc.).
    B. To substitute these "trying to go to sleep" activities with "trying to stay awake" activities.

Outcome Goal II: To double (50 percent increase) Brent's positive feelings and thoughts about himself over the time in which he receives counseling.

    Complete the goal outline for this second outcome goal listed above. You might begin by establishing the criteria that Brent would consider important. You might also consider having Brent describe some of the situations in which he feels good about himself. You may also want to explore how he felt about growing up as a young boy in his family and

(continued)

APPLICATION EXERCISE 8.3 CONTINUED

his cultural referent group. What could Brent do to achieve his short- and long-term directions? From this kind of information and using your own imagination, construct the specific types of subgoals that would help Brent implement this second outcome goal. Continue this process for outcome goals II and III for Brent.

Outcome Goal II: _____

A. _____

_____

B. _____

_____

C. _____

_____

D. _____

_____

Outcome Goal III: To acquire another job at a higher salary range within the next year.

A. _____

_____

B. _____

_____

C. _____

_____

D. _____

_____

Notice the process by which outcome goals are established:

1. They begin as overall goals that are directly related to the client's specific or general concerns or descriptions of a set of problems and that are consistent with the client's culture.
2. Specific and observable subgoals are established which, if achieved, permit the realization of the overall goals.

Thus, goal setting moves from general to specific goals; the specific goals are directly related to the general goal, and the general goal is a reflection of the problems and needs presented to the counselor.

CLIENT RESISTANCE TO GOAL SETTING
AND THE STAGES OF CHANGE MODEL

Occasionally, a client may be hesitant about setting goals or reluctant to work toward change. For instance, after completing a counseling session with her client, a counselor said, "This was the fourth interview, and I still cannot get him to talk about goals." When this happens, the counselor must deal with the question, What is the client resisting?

In working with clients who are resistant to goals, it is helpful to realize that such behavior is purposeful. That is, what the client does or avoids doing achieves some desirable result for the client. Consequently, you may find that the client who resists setting goals may be protecting the behavior that is in need of modification because that behavior is doing something desirable. An example is the chronic smoker. Although an individual may recognize the negative consequences of smoking, he or she also clings to the habit, believing that it is a helpful way to deal with a tense situation, that it is relaxing, that it increases enjoyment of a good meal, and so forth.

It becomes your task to get clients to identify what they gain from their current behavior. In so doing, you may determine whether that gain or outcome can be achieved in more desirable ways. For example, a young student may throw paper airplanes out the school window in order to receive attention from peers. Gaining attention may be a desirable outcome. It is the method that is the problem. Therefore, you and your client may consider more appropriate means for gaining increased attention, other than throwing paper airplanes out the school window.

A useful way to think about client resistance to goal setting is to reflect on how resistant most people are to change itself. Outcome goals request clients to change! Prochaska, DiClemente, and Norcross (1992) developed a well-tested model of change called the *stages of change model* that helps to explain client resistance to change. In their model, there are five stages of change a person progresses through:

Precontemplation: The client is either not aware of a need to change or does not want to change; he or she often views the "problem" as belonging to someone else.

Contemplation: The client becomes aware of a need to change and thinks about it but has not decided to do anything about it. Some people can stay "stuck" in contemplation for years!

Preparation: The client has decided to take some action in the near future, perhaps as soon as the next month or two. Also, the client has tried some action in the past but it was unsuccessful.

Action: The client is ready to change and has usually begun to take some action toward the desired outcome, although the issue has not yet been successfully resolved.

Maintenance: The client reaches his or her goals through various action plans. Now the focus is on consolidating the gains that have been made and on preventing relapses.

As an example of this model, consider a person who has felt consistently anxious for the last few years. This anxiety is chronically debilitating in that it prevents her from doing certain things that are anxiety arousing. She comes to a college or mental health practitioner and reveals that she has been feeling this way for several years. During this time, she has sought out a lot of information on the web and from books about anxiety. But it has taken her two years to decide to seek out the help of a counselor and to inquire about the use of medication. When this client was in *precontemplation*, she was not aware of having an issue with anxiety, nor was she aware of the consequences it resulted in for her. When she did become aware of this, but did not yet do anything about it, she moved into the *contemplation* stage. As she sought information from books and the web and as she thought about what the information meant to her, she moved into the *preparation* stage. When she visited the practitioner and sought help and wondered about using medication, she had moved into the *action* stage. When, through the assistance of the counselor, she engages in behaviors to resolve the anxiety, she will move into the *maintenance* stage, where her task will be to continue her action plans to reduce the anxiety.

Research on the stages of change model has the following implications with respect to client resistance to change (Prochaska & Norcross, 2002):

1. The stages of change model can predict client dropout from counseling across a variety of client issues.
2. The amount of progress clients make during counseling depends on the particular stage of change they are in at the beginning of the helping process. Clients in precontemplation and contemplation have not yet made a commitment to change. Clients in the preparation stage have made a tentative commitment to change but are only ready for small steps toward the desired goal.

Unfortunately, although people in the action stage are ready to work quickly toward an outcome goal, they represent a minority of those clients actually seeking help! As a result, to work effectively with clients in the precontemplation, contemplation, and preparation stages, helpers must be more proactive in the change intervention strategies they use, and they also need to match their change strategies to each clients' stage of change (Prochaska & Norcross, 2002) (see also Chapter 9). It is also useful to help clients set goals that are both realistic and feasible in which they may simply be able to move from one stage of change to the next (Prochaska & Norcross, 2002, p. 311).

■ ■ ■ ■ ■ ▬▬▬

APPLICATION EXERCISE 8.4
STAGES OF CHANGE

Review the stages of change model we presented in the prior section. Select two or three current issues in your own life. Apply the stages of change model to each of these issues. What do you notice about the stages of change with respect to these two or three issues? What conclusions can you draw from this activity? You may want to complete this activity by yourself, with a partner, or in a small discussion group in your class.

Sometimes, clients resist attempts to establish goals because they feel that the counselor (either overtly or subtly) is pushing them in a certain direction. As we mentioned earlier, this may be a particular issue with clients who feel marginalized. Unless clients can determine some *personal* goals of counseling, the probability of any change is minimal. You can avoid creating client resistance to goals by encouraging active participation by clients in the goal-setting process.

CLIENT PARTICIPATION IN GOAL SETTING

Often, goal setting is construed to mean that you listen to the client, make a mental assessment of the problem, and prescribe a solution or goal. In fact, such a procedure is doomed to failure. The nature of counseling is such that the client must be involved in the establishment of goals. Otherwise, the client's participation is directionless at best and interferes with counseling at worst.

An example will illustrate this idea. A beginning counselor was seeing a client who was overweight, self-conscious about her appearance, reluctant to enter into social relationships with others because of this self-consciousness, and very lonely. The counselor informed the client that one goal would be for her (the client) to lose one to three pounds per week, under a doctor's supervision. With this, the client became highly defensive and rejected the counselor's goal, saying, "You sound just like my mother."

Goal setting is highly personal. It requires a great deal of effort and commitment on the client's part. Therefore, the client must select goals that are important to the client. In the preceding example, the client's resistance could have been prevented if the counselor had moved more slowly, permitting the client to identify for herself the significance of her weight and the importance of potential weight loss for herself. At this point, both the counselor and client could then work together to determine the specific goals and subgoals that, when achieved, might alleviate the client's concerns.

Sperry, Carlson, and Kjos (2003) suggest some useful questions to elicit client participation in the goal-setting process:

How have you tried to make things better—and with what results?

How do you think the issue is best handled—what do you see as your part in this change process? As my part in this process?

When will things begin to change and get better for you?

What will your life look like when things get resolved for you—and how does this feel? (p. 68)

Finally, we stress again the importance of the client's cultural beliefs and values in deciding what goals to pursue for counseling. In the preceding example, consider the fact that most Euro-American girls and women in the United States are preoccupied with weight and body image in a way that many men and girls and women of color are not. It is up to the client, not the counselor in the mainstream culture, to decide what goals are relevant and appropriate.

SUMMARY

In this chapter, we entered into the therapeutically active portion of the counseling process. In addition to the interactive process that takes place between counselor and client, the counselor begins to establish an internal conceptualization process in which the client's world is studied. That *study* is both within the client's context and in the larger context of the family, the culture, and the society in which the client lives. Clients will become involved in this study, often quite naturally, as they unfold their experiences, feelings, and thoughts about themselves, others, and their current world. Interwoven in this process is an emerging awareness of a different or perhaps better set of conditions, which become translated into *goals*. Some of these goals are related to the counseling relationship. Others are more related to the client's world. Through the recognition and establishment of these goals, the counselor begins to understand the direction counseling will take and can begin to help the client reach that same awareness.

In conceptualizing client issues and goals, it is useful to remember the stages of change model (Prochaska, DiClemente, & Norcross, 1992). Not all clients are ready for change or for change in big ways! We continue this exploration of the process of change in the following chapter, where our focus turns to the use of counseling change intervention strategies.

REFLECTIVE QUESTIONS

1. Both the client and the counselor bring their worlds into the counseling session. We indicated that goal setting evolves out of an understanding of the client's world. How might the counselor's world affect that process of goal setting? Should the counselor be concerned about this issue? Why?

2. With yourself or with a roleplaying partner, identify a current problem in your life. Consider the list of Egan's nine questions found on page 124. How do these questions help you (or your partner) develop goals and future scenarios for this concern?

3. In the beginning of this chapter, we discussed how unmet childhood needs can be reactivated in adult life. As an exercise, first for yourself and then with a client, consider completing the following questions posed by Steinem (1992): "Write down on [a piece of paper] . . . the things you wish you had received in your childhood and did not" (pp. 104–105). When you have completed this exercise, you have discovered what your needs for yourself are now.

4. How might the needs of a financially challenged low-income client differ from the needs of a client with a high-paying and secure job? What about the needs of a company manager who was recently laid off due to downsizing? How would these needs affect the goals for counseling?

5. Discuss the stages of change model with respect to several different client issues. For example, consider this model with a child who is afraid to come to school, an adolescent who became pregnant after a night of intoxication and doesn't know what to do, an

adult who is addicted to painkillers after suffering a severe back injury at work, and an elderly person who is starting to suffer from dementia and does not want to move out of his home.

RECOMMENDED READINGS

Egan, G. (2002). *The skilled helper* (7th ed.). Pacific Grove, CA: Brooks/Cole.

Prochaska, J. O., DiClemente, C., & Norcross, J. (1992). In search of how people change. *American Psychologist, 47,* 1102–1114.

Prochaska, J., & Norcross, J. C. (2002). Stages of change. In J. C. Norcross (Ed.), *Psychotherapy relationships that work* (pp. 303–314). Oxford: Oxford University Press.

Rosado, J. W., Jr., & Elias, M. J. (1993). Ecological and psychocultural mediators in the delivery of ser-vices for urban, culturally diverse Hispanic clients. *Professional Psychology, 24,* 450–459.

Sperry, L., Carlson, J., & Kjos, D. (2003). *Becoming an effective therapist.* Boston: Allyn and Bacon.

Sue, D. W., & Sue, D. (2003). *Counseling the culturally diverse.* New York: Wiley.

Sue, S., & Lam, A. (2002). Cultural and demographic diversity. In J. C. Norcross (Ed.), *Psychotherapy relationships that work* (pp. 401–422). Oxford: Oxford University Press.

CHAPTER NINE

USING INTEGRATIVE COUNSELING STRATEGIES AND INTERVENTIONS

In the previous chapter, we mentioned a variety of factors that contribute to the issues that clients bring to counseling, including feelings, beliefs, behaviors, interactional patterns, and cultural factors. To deal effectively with such complex issues, counselors need to equip themselves with a variety of strategies and interventions designed to work with all the various ways in which the concern is manifested. Nelson (2002) concluded that "interventions that are based on specific client needs and problems, rather than on the preferred strategy of the counselor, tend to lead to better outcomes" in counseling (p. 416).

In this chapter, we examine a number of helping strategies or interventions. Those that are presented here have been selected because they are used by counselors of varying theoretical orientations and because, when used in conjunction with each other, they treat the *whole* person. The strategies we describe are used to help clients (1) work through feelings, (2) work with belief systems and attitudes, (3) work with behaviors, (4) work with interactional patterns and relationships, and (5) work with cultural and social systems. As Morgan and MacMillan (1999) have suggested, successful counseling "assists clients in developing insight, exploring and validating affective and cognitive processes, and promoting behavioral modification in response to insight, affect, and cognitions related to the person's difficulties (p. 153).

Table 9.1 illustrates a variety of counseling strategies that are based on various theoretical orientations to helping. This table also shows manifestations, or "markers," of five dimensions of client issues. The theoretical orientations reflected in Table 9.1 constitute the major approaches to counseling practices and interventions. Although these theoretical orientations have different views regarding the helping process, the helping relationship, and specific helping interventions, each theoretical orientation has "useful dimensions" (Corey, 2001, p. 3).

Sharf (2000) has concluded that in this day and age, practitioners use different parts of various theories in actual practice and have become much more integrative in their work (p. 18). James and Gilliland (2003) also have endorsed an integrative model by noting that "different theories have strengths and weaknesses not only in dealing with different problems, but also in dealing with different populations" (p. 10). Although we touch briefly on varied theoretical approaches in this chapter because they are linked

TABLE 9.1   Treatment Strategies and Corresponding Manifestations of Client Problems

AFFECTIVE	COGNITIVE	BEHAVIORAL	SYSTEMIC	CULTURAL
Person-centered therapy; Gestalt therapy; body awareness therapies; psychodynamic therapies, experiential therapies: Active listening: empathy; positive regard; genuineness; awareness techniques; empty chair; fantasy; dreamwork; bioenergetics; biofeedback; core energetics; radix therapy; free association; transference analysis; dream analysis; focusing techniques.	**Rational-emotive therapy; Beck's cognitive therapy; transactional analysis; reality therapy:** A-B-C-D-E analysis; homework assignments; counter-conditioning; bibliotherapy; media-tapes; brainstorming; identifying alternatives; reframing; egograms; script analysis; problem definition; clarifying interactional sequences; coaching; defining boundaries; shifting triangulation patterns; prescribing the problem (paradox).	**Skinner's operant conditioning; Wolpe's counter-conditioning; Bandura's social learning; Lazarus's multimodal therapy:** Guided imagery; role-playing; self-monitoring; physiological recording; behavioral contracting; assertiveness training; social skills training; systematic desensitization; contingency contracting; action planning; counter-conditioning.	**Structural therapy; strategic family therapy; intergenerational systems:** Instructing about subsystems; enmeshment and differentiation; addressing triangulation, alliances, and coalitions; role restructuring; clarifying interactional systems; reframing; prescribing the problem (paradox); altering interactional sequences; genogram analysis; coaching; defining boundaries; shifting triangulation patterns.	**Multicultural counseling; cross-cultural counseling:** Meta-theoretical, multimodal, culturally based interventions; focus on world views, cultural orientation, cultural identity; liberation and empowerment perspectives; culturally sensitive language, metaphors, rituals, practices, and resources; collaboration; networking; consciousness raising; advocacy.
Manifestations Emotional expressiveness and impulsivity; instability of emotions; use of emotions in problem solving and decision making; sensitivity to self and others; receptive to feelings of others.	*Manifestations* Intellectualizing; logical rational, systematic behavior; reasoned; computer-like approach to problem solving and decision making; receptive to logic, ideas, theories, concepts, analysis, and synthesis.	*Manifestations* Involvement in activities; strong; goal orientation, need to be constantly doing something; receptive to activity, action, getting something done; perhaps at expense of others.	*Manifestations* Enmeshed or disengaged relationships; rigid relationship boundaries and rules; dysfunctional interaction patterns.	*Manifestations* Level of acculturation; type of worldview; level of cultural identity; bi- or trilingual; presenting problems are, to some degree, culturally based.

intrinsically to counseling interventions, for thorough explorations of the major theoretical approaches to helping, we urge you to consult a number of useful texts (see Corey, 2001; Corsini & Wedding, 2000; Ivey et al., 2002; James & Gilliland, 2003; Prochaska & Norcross, 2002; Sharf, 2000).

WORKING WITH CLIENT FEELINGS

Greenberg (2002) asked, Why do people have feelings and what are their value to well-being? He concluded that feelings or emotions (also referred to as *affect* in Chapter 7) are "not a nuisance to be gotten rid of or ignored," but rather "are crucial to survival, communication, and problem solving. . . . Emotions are signals, ones worth listening to" (p. 11).* Greenberg observed that unfortunately the complex task of "handling our emotions is usually given little attention and, as a result, too many people flounder in this task. . . . Without the skills for dealing with emotional storms, some develop the belief that controlling their emotions is the best solution . . . still others embrace spontaneity and follow their feelings without deliberation . . . and some grow not to trust their own emotional signals, trying not to have emotions at all" (p. ix). Greenberg concluded that practitioners are always "coaching people in how to cope with emotion more effectively" (p. x). Further, people worldwide understand the language of feelings. Greenberg stated that although "culture trains people to hide emotions or express them in a unique way, all people, regardless of where they are born, come into the world with the same emotional system that serves as the basis of a common humanity" (p. 19).

A big part of working with client feelings involves the recent concept of *emotional intelligence (EQ)*—that is, the art of learning when and how to express a feeling, and when expression of a feeling will not help (Greenberg, 2002, p. 14). Emotional intelligence forms the basis of the interventions we suggest here for working with client feelings. These interventions support clients' work with their feelings in three ways that specifically promote EQ:

1. To identify and assess feelings
2. To elicit and express feelings
3. To understand and regulate feelings (Greenberg, 2002; Mayer & Salovey, 1997)

The strategies we present are derived primarily from experiential theoretical approaches to helping, such as gestalt therapy, and from psychodynamic and interpersonal therapies.

Identifying and Assessing Feelings

Helping clients become aware of their feelings enables them to identify what they are really feeling, deep down, or at their "core," and helps them in problem solving

*This and all other material from this source are from *Emotion-Focused Therapy: Coaching Clients to Work through Their Feelings* by L. S. Greenberg. Copyright © 2002 by the American Psychological Association. Reprinted with permission.

(Greenberg, 2002, p. 86). We describe two strategies to help clients identify and assess their feelings: verbal leads and emotion logs.

Verbal Leads for Identifying Feelings.   One strategy to encourage clients to identify feelings is often and simply accomplished by using verbal leads or open-ended questions that focus on client feelings and that help clients elicit different facets of their emotions. The following examples are particularly helpful:

> Can you bring that feeling to life for me and help me understand what it is like for you when you are feeling that?
>
> Do you have an image that captures that feeling, or goes along with it?
>
> Is there a particular place in your body where you experience that feeling?
>
> Is this a familiar or old feeling? When is the first time you can remember having it? Where were you? Who were you with? How did the other person respond to you?
>
> How old do you feel that you are when you experience that emotion? Can you attach an age to it, such as 7 years old or 13 years old? (Teyber, 2000, p. 121)

Emotion Logs.   Greenberg (2002) has recommended the use of a daily emotional log to help clients identify feelings. (For an example of one of these, see Figure 9.1.) When the clients have identified and tracked their feelings on this log, they can bring the completed log to the next session. Together, the counselor and client can explore the following questions to assess the feelings recorded on the log as recommended by Greenberg:

1. What is your name for the emotion?
2. Was it a more sudden onset emotion or a more enduring mood?
3. Did you have body sensations with your emotion?
4. Did thoughts come into your mind?
5. Did you act, or feel like doing something or expressing something?
6. What brought on the emotion or mood?
7. What information is your emotion giving you? (pp. 128–129)

As Greenberg (2002) has pointed out, changing emotion requires experiencing it: "To change in therapy, clients cannot just talk intellectually about themselves and their feelings, they need to viscerally experience what they talk about . . . as total suppression of emotion is unhealthy" (pp. 8, 10). We describe three interventions to help clients elicit and express their emotional experience.

Eliciting and Expressing Feelings

Increasing Body Awareness of Feelings.   Clients can also learn to get in touch with their feelings through the use of strategies that encourage greater awareness of what is occurring within one's body. When a person feels tense, it is usually seen or experienced in the contraction of a muscle or group of muscles. Continued tension results in pain such as a headache or numbness, which occurs from nerve pressure accumulated

FIGURE 9.1 Emotion Log

TYPE OF EMOTION	MONDAY	TUESDAY	WEDNESDAY	THURSDAY	FRIDAY	SATURDAY	SUNDAY
Happy							
Interested							
Excited							
Caring							
Affection							
Love							
Loved							
Compassion							
Grateful							
Proud							
Confident							
Hurt							
Sad							
Regret							
Irritated							
Angry							
Resentful							
Disgust							
Contempt							
Ashamed							
Guilty							
Envious							
Jealous							
Anxious							
Afraid							
Other							

Source: Emotion-Focused Therapy: Coaching Clients to Work through Their Feelings by L. S. Greenberg (p. 130).
Copyright © 2002 by the American Psychological Association. Reprinted with permission.

from the tension. Smith (1985) has recommended the following invitation to help clients acquire body awareness:

> Close your eyes and just relax for a few moments. Breathe comfortably. (Pause.) (Repeat the directions to relax and the pauses until the client seems to be involved in the exercise.) Check out your body to see what you find. Note anything in your body which calls attention to itself. Just monitor your body, inch by inch, from the tips of your toes to the top of your head and down to the tips of your fingers. In particular, note any hot spots, cold spots, tight or tense muscles, pains, tingling, or anything happening in your body. Don't try to edit or change anything, just be aware and note what is happening. (Pause for a minute or two.) Take your time. When you are finished, open your eyes. (Wait until client opens her or his eyes.) (p. 107)

Following this, the counselor asks the client to describe whatever he or she noticed.

Perls (1973), a gestalt therapist, suggested that clients also can identify and express feelings by being asked to exaggerate a particular body action. This strategy is useful because people often make bodily movements that suggest an action that reflects a current and present emotion; it is considered a "slip of the body," much in the way a person says something unintended yet meaningful, as in a verbal "slip of the tongue." As Smith (1985) noted, by inviting the client to repeat the action in an exaggerated form, the meaning of the body action usually becomes apparent. Smith gave the following illustration:

> An example of this is the patient who, while talking about her ex-lover, begins slightly swinging her leg which is crossed over the other leg, knee on knee. The therapist asks her to be aware of her leg and she says, "Oh, I'm just nervous today." So the therapist asks her to exaggerate the movement. She swings her leg in a larger arc, with more force, and declares, "I must want to kick him. But I didn't know I was angry today. Oh, I just remembered what he said last week. I am mad at him!" (p. 110)

By asking the client to exaggerate the body movement, the counselor helps the client see that she has both repressed and inhibited a feeling of anger. When a client's movement is directed toward oneself—for instance, if she has been chewing her cheek—the exaggeration of this would also illustrate how she had taken the feeling of anger toward the ex-lover and directed it back toward herself.

Breathing.   Another way to help clients get in touch with and express feelings is through work on breathing. According to Lowen (1965), a bio-energetics therapist, every emotional problem is manifested in some sort of disturbance in breathing. Perls (1969), the founder of gestalt therapy, connected shallow breathing and sighing with depression, yawning with boredom, and restricted breath with anxiety. Smith (1985) observed that effective breathing is necessary for vitality; that insufficient breathing leaves the person in a state like "a fire with an inadequate draft" (p. 119). Healthy breathing involves the entire body (p. 120).

There are numerous ways to work with breathing. The first is to note to the client the occasions in which he or she holds a breath or breathes in a shallow or constricted manner. For some clients, it may be useful to teach them the art of deep breathing, in which the breath is started (inhaled) in the abdomen, moves up through the chest, and is released thoroughly in the exhalation, often with the aid of a vocal sound. When clients can breathe deeply and do not hold back or interrupt the breathing cycle, they are more likely to experience what they feel.

Another way to increase breathing awareness is to instruct the client to count the in-breath and the out-breath (Gilligan, 1997). For example, you might say, "As the breath comes in through the nostrils, filling up the lower diaphragm, say silently, 'breathing in, one.' As the breath goes out, say silently, 'breathing out, one' " (Gilligan, 1997, p. 76). The next breath is counted as two, then three, and so on. Other clients may use word mantras with their breath such as *let* on the in-breath and *go* on the out-breath.

Gilligan (1997) noted that the restriction of breathing is often such a chronic activity that it becomes unconscious or without awareness. He has suggested asking clients to recall an "antagonistic image, thought, or a feeling" and whether they sense it "inside" or "outside" their breath (p. 76). He observed that usually "difficult processes are experienced *outside* the breath" (p. 76). When the difficult experience is brought inside the breath, an important shift in relationship to the troubling experience usually occurs.

One of the advantages of breathing interventions is that breathing is a universal phenomenon. All people—regardless of differences in race, gender, age, class, religion, sexual orientation and so on—breathe! Many have learned, over time, to shut down their breathing, resulting in a variety of somatic and emotional symptoms.

Incomplete Sentences.   Another possibility to help clients elicit and express feelings is with the use of incomplete sentences. Usually, after some work has been done on breathing, the counselor "feeds" the client with an incomplete sentence stem and the client finishes the sentence with the first thing that comes to mind, continuing to say the same root of that sentence with different completions until there is a point at which the client seems finished. Then another sentence stem is "fed" by the counselor.

Examples of incomplete sentences developed by Branden (1971) to elicit feelings include:

> Something I'm feeling is . . .
> When I look at you, I feel . . .
> As you look at me, I feel . . .
> If I felt mad (or scared or shy or happy, etc.), I . . .
> One of the things that I do when I feel mad is . . .
> One of the things that might make me feel mad is . . .
> One of the ways that feeling mad helps me is . . .
> A good thing about feeling mad is . . .
> A bad thing about feeling mad is . . .
> The rule we had in my family about feeling mad was . . .

Understanding and Regulating Feelings

Expression of feelings is useful but such expression needs to be accompanied by making sense of these feelings and learning how to integrate them effectively into daily life and relationships with self and others. Emotional arousal or expression of emotions alone is insufficient for good therapeutic outcomes—expression needs the added component of reflection about the feelings (Warwar & Greenberg, 2000). Reflection or making meaning of emotional experience helps clients to understand their feelings and to regulate them. Emotion diaries are a way for clients to write a narrative about their emotional experiences. Emotion logs, which we described earlier, are a visual tool clients can use to help them recognize and record selected aspects of their emotional experiences.

Emotion Diaries.   Emotion diaries help clients understand feelings by writing a narrative account or story about one's emotional experience of a traumatic event. Pennebaker (1990) found that writing about the feelings associated with an upsetting event for 20 minutes at a time, with at least four different entries in the diary, had a significant effect on improving health and immune system functioning, as well as a reduction in the disturbing memories of the event. The positive effects of emotion diaries include not only writing about current incidents as a client experiences them, but also about events that occurred at an earlier time yet still elicit painful feelings for the client. Emotion diaries are a good way to help clients cope with and understand the sad and tragic events of everyday life (Greenberg, 2002, p. 31).

In addition to understanding feelings, regulating affect is a way for clients to contain feelings so that they are not overwhelmed by them. Affect regulation has an increasingly important role in the modern world filled with both natural and manmade disasters. Disturbing emotions such as sadness, shame, fear, anger, and powerlessness can overwhelm a client. Many clients believe the only way they can regulate these overwhelming feelings is to shut them down, but as Greenberg (2002) and others have found, this strategy is not useful in the long run. Other clients try to avert feeling these feelings by self-medicating, in the abuse of substances, or by self-harming, such as cutting themselves. These clients, in particular, can benefit by learning to regulate undesirable emotions with more self-soothing feelings (Greenberg, 2002, p. 212). The following strategy described by Greenberg is useful for helping clients learn affect regulation skills.

DEALING WITH DIFFICULT EMOTIONS

1. Imagine a situation or personal interaction that produces this difficult emotion. This might be a conversation with a parent or partner that leaves you feeling difficult emotions of rage, worthlessness, or undesirability.
2. As the emotion emerges, shift your attention to the process of sensing. Describe the sensations. Describe their quality, intensity, and location and any changes in these. Breathe.
3. Pay attention to accompanying thoughts. Describe the mental process in which you are engaging, whether it be thinking, remembering, or criticizing. Breathe.
4. Focus on another softer, good feeling, such as love, joy, or compassion. Imagine a situation or personal interaction in which you feel this. Feel it now. Allow the feeling to fill you.

5. Talk to the old, difficult feeling from your space in your new, healthier feeling. What can you say to the bad feeling that will help transform it to a better feeling? Say this. (p. 214)

In using interventions to work with client feelings, it is important to recall the cautions we mentioned in Chapter 7 regarding culture. Some clients from some cultural groups may feel uncomfortable with these kinds of strategies because their cultural group does not focus on feelings or on revealing feelings to a nonfamily member. Other clients may be much more concerned with survival, class, and social issues, and so focusing on affect seems trivial and irrelevant to them.

WORKING WITH CLIENT BELIEFS AND ATTITUDES

Beliefs and attitudes represent meanings, interpretations, or thoughts a client has about a situation—sometimes referred to as *cognitions*. Beliefs are potent because they affect clients' perceptions about themselves, others, and their lives.

Clients encounter all sorts of difficulty based on their beliefs and attitudes because they may be distorted and based on incomplete information. For instance, clients who are depressed or highly anxious tend to view themselves, others, and the world in a negative way (A. T. Beck, 1976; J. S. Beck, 1995). A major focus of these interventions is on changing the way the client thinks. Cognitive therapists believe that by changing the way a client thinks, his or her emotional distress and problematic behavior also can be changed (Berlin, 2001; Dobson, 2001). In this section of the chapter, we describe two related but somewhat different ways of working with client feelings: the A-B-C-D-E analysis and cognitive restructuring.

A-B-C-D-E Analysis

The A-B-C-D-E analysis is an intervention strategy based on a cognitive counseling approach known as *rational-emotive therapy (RET)*, developed by a psychotherapist named Albert Ellis. (Ellis has relabeled RET as *REBT*, or *rational-emotive behavior therapy.*) According to Ellis, emotional distress is created by faulty, illogical, or irrational thoughts. In other words, if someone feels emotionally upset, it is not a person or a situation that creates the emotional upset but rather the individual's beliefs or thoughts about the situation. Reduction in emotional distress is created when the individual's irrational thinking is changed to rational thinking, through interventions such as the A-B-C-D-E analysis.

In the first part of this strategy, the client learns to recognize the *activating event (A)*, usually a situation or person that the client finds upsetting. The activating event is often what prompts the client to seek counseling ("My relationship is on the rocks," "I lost my job," "My partner is a jerk," "I don't have any friends," "Why don't boys like me?" "I got passed over for the team," etc.). The most important aspect of this part of the strategy is to refocus clients from attributing their distress to this activating event to their thoughts about it. For example, the counselor might respond, "I realize it is upsetting to you not to make the team; however, it is not this situation in and of itself that is making you feel so bad but rather your thinking about this situation."

In the next part of the strategy, the client's specific thoughts or *beliefs (B)* about the activating event are explored and identified. The client may have both rational and irrational thoughts, but it is the irrational thoughts that contribute to the emotional distress and that need to be targeted for change. Rational thoughts are ones that are consistent with reality, are supported by data, and result in *moderate* levels of emotional upset (e.g., "I didn't play as well as other people in the tryouts and they got picked and I didn't"). Irrational thoughts are not based on facts or evidence and lead to high levels of emotional distress (e.g., "Because I didn't make the team I am a jerk"). Irrational beliefs often take the form of either catastrophization ("It will be awful when . . . ") or "musturbation" ("I must . . . ," "I should . . . ," "I have to . . . ").

The counselor then links the irrational beliefs with the resulting emotional and behavioral *consequences (C)*—that is, what clients feel and how they act as a result (e.g., "I feel so bad. I just can't seem to snap out of it. I didn't want to go back to school because I'm so ashamed of not making the team"). The counselor shows the client how his or her specific irrational beliefs led to these consequences. For instance, the therapist might respond, "You are feeling awful and staying away from school because you now view yourself as a nobody—it is not that you got passed up that is making you feel and act this way, it is the way you're now thinking about yourself."

The real work of the strategy comes next in the *disputation (D)* phase. Disputation involves disputing or challenging the client's irrational beliefs with the intent of eliminating them and helping the client acquire more rational thinking. The counselor uses questions to dispute the client's irrational beliefs. Some examples of questions suggested for cognitive disputation by Walen, DiGiuseppe, and Wessler (1992) include:

Is that true? Why not?
Can you prove it?
How do you know?
Why is that an overgeneralization?
Why is that a bad term to use?
How would you talk a friend out of such an idea?
What would happen if—?
If that's true, what's the worst that can happen?
So what if that happens?
How would that be so terrible?
Where's the evidence?
How is a disadvantage awful?
Ask yourself, can I still find happiness?
What good things can happen if X occurs?
Can you be happy even if you don't get what you want?
What might happen?
How terrible would that be?
Why would you be done in by that?
What is the probability of a bad consequence?

How will your world be destroyed if X happens?
As long as you believe that, how will you feel?
"Whatever I want, I must get." Where will that get you?
Is it worth it? (pp. 97–99)

When the disputation process has been effective, it will be apparent in new *effects (E)*, such as lessened emotional distress and changes in behavior (e.g., "I still don't like the fact I didn't make the team but I know I am not a jerk just because of that"). It is important for the counselor to help clients recognize when these emotional and behavioral shifts in effects occur.

Cognitive Restructuring

Cognitive restructuring is based in theory on the work of Aaron T. Beck, a cognitive therapist, and on the practice of Donald Meichenbaum, a cognitive-behavioral therapist. Cognitive or rational restructuring involves not only helping clients learn to recognize and stop self-defeating thoughts but also to substitute these thoughts with positive, self-enhancing, or coping thoughts. Beck (1976) suggested three approaches to restructuring self-defeating thoughts:

1. What is the evidence?
2. What is another way of looking at it?
3. So what if it happens?

In the first part of cognitive restructuring, clients learn to stop obsessive, illogical, or negative thoughts as they occur. This involves discrimination training in which they are made aware of what "they tell themselves" before, during, and after problem situations. Clients might be instructed to note and record their negative thoughts before, during, and after stressful or depressing situations for one or two weeks.

After clients are aware of the nature and types of their self-defeating thoughts, the counselor helps them work toward identifying more positive or coping thoughts that can replace the negative ones. These coping thoughts are considered to be incompatible with the self-defeating thoughts.

Coping thoughts are designed to help clients picture dealing with problem situations effectively, although not perfectly. In this way, they are considered better than mastery thoughts, which focus on perfection, because they expose the clients to possible mistakes and prepare them to recover from errors they may make in life (McMullin, 2000). It is best to personalize these coping thoughts for each client. Clients also need to learn coping thoughts to use before, during, and after problem situations. For example, a client who fails tests due to anxiety might concentrate on thoughts such as "I will be calm" or "Keep your mind on your studies" before an exam. During an exam, clients learn to concentrate on the exam and to stay calm instead of worrying about flunking or thinking about their nervousness. After using some coping thoughts, clients can be taught to reward or congratulate themselves for coping—instead of punishing themselves for worrying.

When clients have identified some possible alternative coping thoughts to use, they can practice applying these thoughts through overt (roleplay) and covert (imaginary) rehearsal. The rehearsal may take the form of a dialogue or a script and may be read aloud by the client or put on index cards or audiotape. McMullin (2000) observed that for most clients, a period of at least six weeks is necessary for the practice of coping thoughts.

A sample cognitive restructuring dialogue used for rehearsal by a high school client who feared competitive situations is provided by Cormier and Nurius (2003):

> OK. I'm sitting here waiting for my turn to try out for cheerleader. Ooh, I can feel myself getting very nervous. (*anxious feeling*) Now, wait, what am I so nervous about? I'm afraid I'm going to make a fool of myself. (*self-defeating thought*) Hey, that doesn't help. (*cue to cope*) It will take only a few minutes, and it will be over before I know it. Besides only the faculty sponsors are watching. It's not like the whole school. (*coping thoughts*) Well, the person before me is just about finished. Oh, they're calling my name. Boy, do I feel tense. (*anxious feelings*) What if I don't execute my jumps? (*self-defeating thought*) OK, don't think about what I'm not going to do. OK, start out, it's my turn. Just think about my routine—the way I want it to go. (*coping thoughts*) (p. 452)

Identifying and internalizing coping thoughts seem to be crucial in order for clients to really benefit from cognitive restructuring. Gradually, clients should be able to apply their newly found coping skills to the in vivo situations as these occur. If cognitive restructuring is successful, clients can detect increased use of coping thoughts and decreased level of stress in their actual environment. In vivo practice seems crucial for the efficacy of this strategy in order to promote the clients' confidence in their newly learned beliefs (Meichenbaum, 1993).

The use of cognitive strategies with diverse groups of clients has received increased attention in the last few years. However, as Hays (1995) has pointed out, the values inherent in cognitive interventions reflect those of the mainstream culture. Kantrowitz and Ballou (1992) elaborated: "The rational thinking orientation of cognitive therapy and cognitive restructuring reinforces worldviews and cognitive processes that are stereotypically both Euro-American and masculine," running the risk that other, different worldviews and cognitions may be ignored or even rejected (p. 81). Also, as Brown (1994) asserted, there are instances for some clients where the supposedly irrational beliefs may be reasonable or even lifesaving, given the individual's life and environmental context (p. 61). Also, the process of challenging or disputing these beliefs may not fit with some clients from particular cultural groups. Therefore, a useful caveat is to cultivate awareness in using cognitive strategies. Be flexible in the way you implement these strategies and be sensitive to the client's reaction.

WORKING WITH CLIENT BEHAVIORS

There are a variety of strategies designed to help clients modify their behavior. Behavioral interventions are based on the assumption that behavior is learned; therefore, inappropriate or maladaptive behavior can be unlearned while more adaptive behavior can be acquired (Wilson, 2000). Behavioral approaches also rely heavily on a scientific method (Wilson, 2000). This means that the therapeutic interventions and their outcomes are tested in some empirical way to establish the efficacy of the strategy or strategies being used. In this section, we describe three strategies designed to work with client behaviors: social modeling, behavior rehearsal, and self-management.

Social Modeling

Social modeling, based on observational learning, refers to a process familiar to all human beings. If people are nothing else, they are observers. From earliest childhood, humans watch and imitate. Through this vicarious experience is acquired a great amount of knowledge and skills. The limitations to observational learning include a person's ability to observe, the attractiveness of the model, and the generalizability of the event to be learned.

As a helping strategy, *modeling* is used to help a client acquire desired responses or to extinguish fears—through observing the behavior of another person, the model. This observation can be presented in a live modeling demonstration by the counselor or in symbolic form through written and media-taped models.

Live Modeling.   Live models can include the counselor, who demonstrates the desired behavior, or teachers or peers of the client. Usually, you will provide a modeled demonstration by a roleplay activity in which you take the part of the client and show a way to respond or behave. Live modeling is particularly useful in instances in which the client does not have response alternatives available. The modeled demonstration provides cues that the client can use to acquire new responses. For instance, a client who wishes to acquire self-expression skills may benefit from seeing you or a peer demonstrate such skills in roleplayed situations.

Symbolic Modeling.   Although live models have much impact on the client, they are often difficult to use because of the lack of control in ensuring their systematic demonstration of the desired behavior. To correct for this, many counselors make use of symbolic models through audiotapes, videotapes, or films in which a desired behavior is introduced and presented. For example, symbolic models could be used with clients who want to improve their study habits. Reading about effective study habits of successful people and their scholastic efforts is a first step in helping clients specify those behaviors involved. Next, clients can listen to an audiotape or watch a videotape that describes effective study behaviors.

Characteristics of Models.   In selecting models, it is best to maximize model-client similarity. Clients are more likely to learn from someone whom they perceive as similar to themselves. Such characteristics as age, gender, race, and ethnic background should be considered in selecting effective models.

A coping model may be more helpful to some clients than a mastery model. A client may be able to identify more with a model who shows some fear or some struggle in performing than someone who comes across perfectly. For example, a very shy, timid person could be overwhelmed by a very assertive model. This could be especially true if the client is from a cultural group that does not sanction individual expressiveness and assertiveness. This client may respond more quickly if he or she is exposed to a model who starts quietly and gradually increases assertive behaviors. Clients also may learn more from modeling when exposed to more than one model. Multiple models may have more impact on a client, because the client can draw on the strengths and styles of several different people. Multiple models are especially useful with bicultural and biracial clients.

When modeling fails to contribute to desired client changes, reassess the characteristics of the selected model(s) and the mode and format of the modeled presentation. In many cases, modeling can provide sufficient cues for the client to learn new responses or to extinguish fears. In other instances, modeling may have more effects when accompanied by practices of the target response. Such practices can occur through roleplay and rehearsal strategies, as described in the next section.

Behavior Rehearsal

The strategy of *behavior rehearsal* uses roleplay and practice attempts to help people acquire new skills and behave more effectively under threatening or anxiety-producing conditions. Behavior rehearsal is used primarily in three instances:

1. The client does not have and needs to learn the necessary skills to handle a situation *(response acquisition)*.
2. The client needs to learn to discriminate between positive and negative application of the skills or between inappropriate and appropriate times and places to use the skills *(response facilitation)*.
3. The client's anxiety about the situation needs to be sufficiently reduced so that the client can use skills already learned, even though they are currently inhibited by anxiety *(response disinhibition)*.

For example, if a client wants to increase self-disclosive behavior, but does not know what self-disclosure is or has not learned the skills involved in self-disclosing, the client has a deficient repertoire in self-disclosure and needs to acquire certain skills (response acquisition). On the other hand, there are times when the skills already are in the client's repertoire, but the client needs clarification or discrimination training in when and how to employ the skills (response facilitation). Many times, people have self-disclosure skills but use the skills inappropriately. A person may self-disclose too much to someone who is disinterested and withhold personal information from a significant other. In another case, the client's anxiety perhaps has inhibited the skills (response disinhibition). In other words, a client may have learned the skills of appropriate self-disclosure but avoids self-disclosing because of anxiety the client feels in certain self-disclosive situations. In selecting response targets for behavior rehearsal, remember that the behaviors need to be consistent with the values of the client's gender and cultural socialization patterns.

The practicalities of behavior rehearsal consist of a series of graduated practice attempts in which the client rehearses the desired behaviors, starting with a situation that is manageable and is not likely to backfire. The rehearsal attempts may be arranged in a hierarchy according to level of difficulty or stress of different situations. Adequate practice of one situation is required before moving on to another scene. The practice of each scene should be very similar to the situations that occur in the client's environment. To simulate these situations realistically, use any necessary props and portray the other person involved with the client as accurately as possible. This portrayal should include acting out the probable response of this person to the client's new or different behavior.

Behavior rehearsal can be overt or covert. In *covert* behavior rehearsal, clients practice the target behavior by *imagining* themselves performing the response in certain situations. For instance, clients might imagine themselves successfully presenting an important speech or initiating a discussion with a friend or a boss. In *overt* rehearsal, the client *acts out* the target responses in roleplayed scenarios. Both covert and overt rehearsal seem to be quite effective (Kazdin, 1982). A client could probably benefit from engaging in both of these forms of behavioral rehearsal. Initially, the client might practice covertly and later act out the responses in roleplayed enactments. Covert rehearsal also can be used easily by clients as homework, since imaginary practice does not require the presence of another person.

Feedback is an important part of roleplay and rehearsal strategies. It is a way for the client to recognize both the problems and successes encountered in the practice attempts, as well as a way of observing and evaluating one's performance and of initiating corrective action. However, feedback should not be used indiscriminately. Feedback may be more effective if the client is willing to change, if the feedback given is adequate but not overwhelming, and if the feedback helps the client identify other alternatives.

Following rehearsal attempts, clients can be encouraged to evaluate their performances. You will be another important source of feedback. Remember to reinforce the client for gradual improvement. Feedback also can be supplied by videotaped and audiotaped playbacks of the client's practices. These taped playbacks may be more objective assessments of the client's performance. At first, you can go over the tapes together and point out the strengths and limitations apparent in the practice. Gradually, the client should be able to analyze the taped playback alone—providing self-analysis and self-reinforcement for the practice efforts.

Modeling, Rehearsal, and Feedback: Components of Skill Training.   The strategies of modeling, rehearsal, and feedback can be combined as a skill-training package. These strategies often are used to teach clients problem-solving skills, decision-making skills, communication skills, and assertion skills. For example, in assertion training, you begin by having the client identify one situation in which he or she wants to be more assertive. Then specify what assertive behaviors are involved and what the client would like to say or do. The situation is modeled and roleplayed consistently in the interview until the client can be assertive without experiencing any anxiety. Following successful completion of the task outside the interview, assertion training can continue for other kinds of situations involving self-assertion by the client. Successes at assertiveness will soon generalize to other situations, as well; that is, it will become increasingly easier for clients to be assertive on their own without assistance and feedback. Again, remember that the skill training must be culturally relevant to the client.

As an illustration, suppose you are working with a student who reports a lack of assertive classroom behaviors. You and your client would first specify the desired assertive skills. The skills selected would be appropriate for the student's age, gender, race, and cultural background. You may need to observe the student in the classroom setting to identify these target behaviors. In counting the number of times the student engages in assertive classroom behavior (asking questions, voicing opinions, engaging in group discussion, giving reports, volunteering for chalkboard work, initiating conversations with the teacher, etc.), you can obtain an accurate idea of the kind of assertive behaviors that are most prevalent in the client's repertoire and the ones the student needs most to strengthen. You can provide either live or symbolic models of these specific assertive behaviors. After the client has seen, listened to, or read about these modeled behaviors, he or she can demonstrate and practice small steps of such assertive classroom behaviors in the interview. Following practice attempts in which the client is able to demonstrate repeated efforts of a given behavior within the interview, he or she should be encouraged to practice it on a daily basis in the classroom.

Self-Management

Many people are legitimately concerned about the long-term effects of helping. In an effort to promote enduring client changes, counselors have become more concerned with client self-directed change. This interest has led many counseling researchers and practitioners to explore the usefulness of a variety of helping strategies called *self-control* or *self-management* (Wilson, 2000).

The primary characteristic of a self-management strategy is that the client administers the strategy and directs the change efforts with minimal assistance from the counselor. Self-management strategies are very useful in dealing with a number of client issues and may promote generalization to life settings of what clients learn in the interview. Self-management strategies are among the best strategies designed to strengthen client investment in the helping process. Self-management may eliminate the counselor as a "middle" person and ensure greater chances of client success because of the investment made by the client in the strategies for change. Two of the most useful self-management strategies include self-monitoring and self-reward.

Self-Monitoring.   Recent emphases in behavioral approaches suggest the efficacy of a number of self-control procedures, of which self-monitoring is primary. Self-monitoring involves having clients count and/or regulate given habits, thoughts, or feelings. Self-monitoring seems to interfere with the learned habit by breaking the stimulus-response association and by encouraging performance of the desired response, which is then often reinforced by the individual's sense of progress following its accomplishment.

There are two issues that affect the self-monitoring strategy—reactivity and reliability. *Reactivity* means that the process of noticing one's own behavior closely can cause the behavior to change. *Reliability* refers to the accuracy with which the client counts the behavior. For counseling purposes, you and your client should attempt to structure the self-monitoring in a way that maximizes the reactivity. Therefore, in implementing the procedure, you will need to consider what, how, and when to self-monitor.

What to Monitor.   An initial step involves selecting the behavior to monitor. Usually, individuals will achieve better results with self-monitoring if they start by counting only one behavior—at least initially. Clients may, for example, count positive feelings about themselves, or thoughts of competency, or, as we saw earlier in this chapter, feelings and emotions. The counting encourages greater frequency of these kinds of thoughts and feelings. Clients may count the number of times they tell themselves to do well on a task, or they may count the number of behaviors related to goal achievement (e.g., the number of times they tell their partner "I love you," the number of times they initiate conversations or participate in class discussions, etc.). Clients also can monitor both *process* and *outcome* behaviors. For example, a client could monitor the outcomes of a study program, such as the grades on tests, reports, and papers. Equally, if not more important, is the act of self-recording the processes involved in studying, such as going to the library, finding a quiet study place, preparing for a test, researching a report, and so on. As Watson and Tharp (2002) stated, "Pay attention to the process so you can improve it, and the goal will happen" (p. 87). The important thing is that clients monitor behaviors that *they* value and care to change and that are consistent with their culture.

How to Monitor.   The particular method the client uses to count the target response will depend on the nature of the selected response. Generally, clients will count either the *frequency* or *duration* of a response. If they are interested in knowing how often the response occurs, they can use a frequency count to note—for example, the number of times they smoke, talk on the telephone, initiate social conversations, or think about themselves positively. Sometimes, it is more useful to know the amount of time the behavior occurs. A person can count the duration or length of a behavior in these cases. For example, clients might count how long they studied, how long they talked on the telephone, or the length of depressed periods of thought. Occasionally, clients may find it useful to record both the frequency and duration of a response. In choosing to count the occurrences of a behavior either by the number or by the amount of time, there is a simple rule of thumb recommended by Watson and Tharp (2002). They have suggested using frequency counts if it is easy to count the number of separate times the behavior is performed, and duration counts if separate occasions are not easy to count or if the target behavior continues for several minutes at a time. Obviously, there are some times when a client may monitor both frequency and duration—for example, the number of cigarettes smoked in a day as well as the amount of time spent in smoking cigarettes in a day.

In some cases where the target response occurs very often or almost continuously, or when the onset and termination of the target responses are hard to detect, the frequency and duration methods of recording may not be too useful. In these instances, clients could record with an interval method. In the interval method of recording, they could divide the time for recording (8:00 A.M. to 8:00 P.M.) into time intervals such as 30 minutes, one hour, or two hours. During each time interval, they simply record the presence or absence of the behavior with a "yes" if the behavior occurred or a "no" if it did not.

Clients will need to record with the assistance of some recording device. These can range from simple devices—such as notecards, logs, and diaries for written recordings—to more mechanical devices—such as a golf wrist counter, a kitchen timer, a wristwatch, a tape recorder, or a hand-held computer. The device may increase the reactivity of self-monitoring if it is obtrusive; yet it should not be so noticeable that it is embarrassing or awkward for clients to use. The device should be simple to use, convenient, portable, and economical.

When to Monitor. The timing of self-monitoring can influence the change produced by this strategy. Generally, there are two times when clients can record: before the response (prebehavior monitoring) or after the response (postbehavior monitoring). In prebehavior monitoring, the client reveals the intention or urge to engage in the behavior before doing so. For instance, the client records times when she or he has an urge to eat a dessert or a snack but does not. In postbehavior monitoring, the client records after the behavior has occurred. For example, the client records after each time she or he exercises. The effects of self-monitoring may depend on the timing and on whether there are other factors competing for the client's attention at the time the response is recorded. Although Kanfer and Gaelick-Buys (1991) have stated that there are insufficient data to judge whether pre- or postmonitoring is most effective, we suggest the following two rules of thumb:

1. *To decrease the monitored behavior:* Since you want to decrease the number of cigarettes you smoke (or the number of self-critical thoughts you have), each time you have the urge to smoke but do not (or start to criticize yourself but refrain from doing so), then count this on your log.
2. *To increase a behavior:* Since you want to increase the number of times you verbally express your opinions to someone else (or the number of positive, self-enhancing thoughts), count and record on your log immediately after you express an opinion (or as soon as you are aware of thinking something positive about yourself or your accomplishments).

Counting, or quantifying, behaviors is the initial step in self-monitoring. The second and equally important step in self-monitoring is charting or plotting the behavior counts over a period of time. This permits clients to see progress that might not otherwise be apparent. It also permits clients to set daily goals that are more attainable than the overall goal. Clients can take weekly cumulative counts of self-monitored behaviors and chart them on a simple line graph. After graphing the data, the public display of the graph may set the occasion for both self- and external reinforcement.

To summarize, self-monitoring is most likely to produce desired behavioral changes when the following conditions exist (Cormier & Nurius, 2003):

1. The client is motivated to change the behavior to be monitored.
2. The client monitors a limited number of behaviors and these behaviors are discrete.
3. The monitoring act is closely related in time prior to or after the monitored behavior.
4. The client receives some feedback from the monitoring that is compared with the client's goals.

In Figure 9.1 we showed you an example of a log for monitoring emotions. In Figure 9.2 we provide two other examples of self-monitoring logs, one for couples to use in monitoring the content and quality of marital interactions, and another for clients to use to record anxiety responses.

Self-Reward.   Research suggests that the effects produced by self-monitoring may be greater and more permanent if self-monitoring is accompanied by other therapeutic strategies, such as self-reward (Kanfer & Gaelick-Buys, 1991). Self-monitoring can always be combined with other helping strategies as a way to collect data concerning the occurrence of goal behaviors. As we noted in the previous section, self-monitoring also can be used intentionally to induce therapeutic change. However, the therapeutic gains from self-monitoring may be maximized with the explicit use of other self-management strategies to increase or decrease a response.

Self-reward involves the self-presentation of rewards following the occurrence of a desired behavior. It is intended to strengthen a behavior. Self-reward functions like external reinforcement. A *reinforcer* is something that, when administered following a target response, tends to maintain or increase the probability of that response in the future.

There are two ways clients can use self-reward. First, they can give themselves rewards after engaging in specified behaviors. For example, clients could imagine being on a sailboat after doing daily exercises or could buy themselves treats after daily studying. Second, they could remove something negative after performing the desired behaviors. For instance, an overweight client could remove a "fat picture" from the wall after losing a certain number of pounds. In most cases, we recommend the first approach (self-presentation of a positive stimulus) because it is more positive than the second.

There are three major factors involved in helping a client use a self-reward strategy: what to use as rewards, how to administer the rewards, and when to administer the rewards.

Types of Rewards.   First, you will want to help your clients select appropriate rewards. Clients should choose things that are truly reinforcing. There are different types of rewards to use. An example of a verbal-symbolic reward is self-praise, such as thinking, "I really did that well." Imaginal rewards involve visualizing or fantasizing scenes that

FIGURE 9.2   Self-Monitoring Logs

EXAMPLE 1

Content and quality of marital interactions

Record the type of interaction under "Contents." For each interaction, circle one category that best represents the quality of that interaction.

		QUALITY OF INTERACTION				
TIME	**CONTENT OF INTERACTION**	*Very pleasant*	*Pleasant*	*Neutral*	*Unpleasant*	*Very unpleasant*
6:30 A.M.		++	+	0	−	− −
7:00		++	+	0	−	− −
7:30		++	+	0	−	− −
8:00		++	+	0	−	− −

EXAMPLE 2

Self-monitoring log for recording anxiety responses

Instructions for recording:

DATE AND TIME	FREQUENCY OF ANXIETY RESPONSE	EXTERNAL EVENTS	INTERNAL DIALOGUE (SELF-STATEMENTS)	BEHAVIORAL FACTORS	DEGREE OF AROUSAL	SKILL IN HANDLING SITUATION
Record day and time of incident	Describe each situation in which anxiety occurred	Note what triggered the anxiety	Note your thoughts or things you said to yourself when this occurred	Note how you responded— what you did	Rate the intensity of the anxiety: (1) a little intense (2) somewhat intense (3) very intense (4) extremely intense	Rate the degree to which you handled the situation effectively: (1) a little (2) somewhat (3) very (4) extremely

Source: Interviewing and Change Strategies for Helpers: Fundamental Skills and Cognitive-Behavioral Interventions (with Info-Trac), 5th edition, by S. Cormier and P. Nurius. © 2003. Reprinted with permission of Wadsworth, a division of Thomson Learning: www.thomsonrights.com. Fax 800-730-2215.

produce pleasure and satisfaction. Material rewards include tangible events such as an enjoyable activity, a purchase, or tokens or points that can be exchanged for something. Tokens or points are useful when a client cannot have the reinforcer follow soon after the desired response. The tokens or points can be collected during a day (or a week) and then exchanged for a selected reinforcer at the end of the day or week based on a designated number of points or tokens. Rewards also can be current or potential. A current reward is something enjoyable that occurs on a daily basis, such as eating, reading, or getting the mail. A potential reward is something that could occur in the future that would be satisfying and enjoyable. Taking a trip and going out for a meal are examples of potential rewards.

Clients should be encouraged to select a variety of rewards, including both current and potential, material, imaginal, and verbal-symbolic. This may prevent one reward from losing its potency or impact. You can help clients select rewards by having them identify some ongoing and potentially satisfying thoughts and activities. An occasional client may have difficulty in identifying rewards. In lieu of using a very enjoyable activity as a reward, this client might choose a more mundane daily activity, such as answering the telephone or walking up or down stairs.

Using a frequently occurring activity as a reward is based on the *Premack principle*, which states that a high-probability behavior can be used to reinforce a low-probability behavior (Premack, 1965). For instance, something a student engages in frequently, such as getting up from the desk, can be made contingent on something the student does infrequently, such as completing assignments or work problems. The rewards used can be tailored to each client, since not all events or fantasies are reinforcing for all persons. The selected rewards should relate to the client's personal history, be acceptable to the client, and be something the client wants to do and is capable of doing (Kanfer & Gaelick-Buys, 1991). The rewards should also be *culturally* relevant to each client. What seems rewarding for one person may not be at all rewarding for another.

Delivery of Rewards.   After selecting rewards, clients will need to work out ways to administer the rewards. They should know what has to be done in order to present themselves with a reward. You might encourage them to reward themselves for *gradual* progress toward the desired goal. Daily rewards for small steps are more effective than delayed rewards for a great improvement.

Timing of Rewards.   Clients also need to present the rewards at certain times in order to maximize the self-reward strategy. The reward should come only *after* target behavior has been performed in order to have the most impact. Also, *immediate* rewards are more effective than delayed rewards. *Immediate* self-reinforcement is especially important "whenever the target behavior involves very strong habits such as substance use or 'feared objects' such as flying" (Watson & Tharp, 2002, p. 213).

Client Commitment to Self-Management.   A critical problem in the effective use of any self-management strategy is having the client use the strategy regularly and consistently. Clients may be more likely to carry out self-management programs given the presence of certain conditions:

1. The use of the self-management program will provide enough advantages or positive consequences to be worth the cost to the client in terms of time and effort. The self-management program must do more than simply meet the status quo.
2. The client's use of the program may be strengthened by enlisting the support and assistance of other people—as long as their roles are positive, not punishing. Former clients, peers, or friends can aid the client in achieving the goals through reinforcement of the client's regular use of the self-management strategies.
3. The counselor maintains some minimal contact with the client during the time the self-management program is being carried out. Counselor reinforcement is quite important in successful implementation of self-management efforts.

You can provide reinforcement (anything that serves to increase the frequency of a desired response) easily through verbal approval ("That's great," "I like that") or by knowledge of progress ("You did very well," "You did the task so well," "You've done a great job in improving your study habits"). Have the client drop in or telephone during the course of the self-management program. This enables you to provide immediate encouragement to the client.

Many of the behavioral strategies have been used quite effectively with diverse groups of clients, perhaps because these strategies focus on action and change rather than insight and exploration (Sue & Sue, 2003). Still, it is important to remember that some of the notions underlying behavioral interventions are decidedly Eurocentric in that they focus on an internal locus of control and responsibility. As Casas (1988) noted, "As a result of life experiences associated with racism, discrimination, and poverty," some clients have developed a cognitive set of "an external locus of control and responsibility" that is antithetical to these strategies (pp. 109–110). Again, we stress the importance of considering the client's world view and of adapting the behavioral strategies to the client's gender and culture.

WORKING WITH CLIENT INTERACTIONAL PATTERNS AND RELATIONSHIPS

With any individual client who seeks counseling, the client is part of a larger interpersonal network, sometimes referred to as an *interpersonal system*. In any interpersonal system such as a marriage, a family, a work department, or a peer group, all segments of the system are interrelated, and change in one part affects the entire system. In those interpersonal systems to which the client belongs, the client typically interacts in predictable patterns. These patterns can be seen within the context of the counseling system as well as within the various systems to which the client belongs. In other words, the counselor can see the client's typical interpersonal pattern not only in the kinds of interactions the client reports with other persons but also in the way this interpersonal pattern is reenacted within the counseling relationship. Thus, in working with interactional patterns of the client, the counselor can intervene at two different levels: use of interventions that deal directly with the counselor-client system and use of interventions that have an impact on the client's interactional style with other persons. We will describe both levels of these strategies in this portion of the chapter.

Reenactment of Interactional Patterns in Counseling

Clients begin to develop predictable interactional patterns in their family of origin. Interactional patterns are affected by many factors, including family construction and birth order (Adler, 1958), family rules and communication patterns (Watzlawick, Beavin, & Jackson, 1967), and general level of health or dysfunction of the family system (Haley, 1997; Miller, 1981). For many people who become clients, their family of origin experience was problematic in three major ways (Teyber, 2000):

1. There was a lack of a strong bond between the parents, sometimes referred to as a lack of a "primary parental coalition" (Minuchin, 1974).
2. There were disruptions or interruptions in the ways parents met children's developmental needs for nurturance, structure, separateness, and attachment.
3. There were child-rearing practices that were either too authoritarian or too permissive in nature.

To cope with this, children, as they grow older, develop a characteristic way of interacting with others. People who use an Adlerian counseling model refer to this as a "lifestyle" (Adler, 1958); those who use a transactional analysis model refer to this as a "script" (Woolams & Brown, 1979). We will talk about three characteristic interpersonal patterns from a developmental/dynamic model (see also Horney, 1970). Clients generally cope in interpersonal systems by (1) moving toward people, (2) moving away or withdrawing from people, or (3) moving against or resisting other people.

People who *move toward* others are likely to be perceived by others as understanding and accommodating. These sort of people are usually helpful and cooperative but have trouble being appropriately assertive, direct, and, above all, angry. This sort of lifestyle or interpersonal pattern is designed to elicit from others the support and nurturing that was missed as a child. With a client who behaves like this toward the counselor, the counselor must be careful not just to provide acceptance but also to focus on the general interpersonal style of the client—what the client has missed from his or her family and is trying to elicit from the counselor as well as, no doubt, from numerous other people.

Clients who characteristically *move away* or *withdraw from* people will demonstrate the same behavior in the counseling relationship. They may seek help but they will attempt to maintain as much emotional distance as possible and to remain emotionally unconnected from the counseling per se. Although at one level these clients are trying to push the counselor away, at another level they want desperately for the counselor to stay connected to them. These clients pose quite a challenge for counselors. To respond reflexively and give up on the client is nontherapeutic. At the same time, if the counselor attempts to become too emotionally connected, these clients will feel alarmed and anxious because this is so unfamiliar. The counselor will need to stay present and engaged at a pace that follows the client's lead, but above all, the counselor must not give up on these individuals.

Clients who *move against* people are likely to try to directly intimidate the counselor or to passively resist the counselor's efforts. They may behave in ways either to take control of the session or to "push the counselor's buttons" and make the counselor feel inadequate. These kinds of clients may be especially difficult for beginning counselors who may respond countertherapeutically with fear, competition, or counterhostility (Teyber, 2000). Again, as with the other instances we have described, it is important for the counselor not to respond reflexively and give these clients what they are trying to elicit. With these individuals, the counselor must avoid getting involved in a battle or power struggle and focus instead on what the clients may be trying to get and/or avoid with their interpersonal styles and the likely impact of such on their lives.

The difficulty in these three interpersonal coping styles lies in the fact that they are used "inflexibly in all types of situations," including life choices such as careers and partners (Teyber, 2000, p. 187).

Why do clients act out their typical interactional pattern with counselors? Quite simply, it is a form of a test. They feel that the counselor will respond in the same old way as most everyone else, but they hope against hope that the counselor will provide a different and more helpful response. When the counselor does, they will not have to keep reenacting their same old pattern and can move beyond the point at which they become "stuck"—not only with the counselor but with other people, as well. Teyber (2000) presented the following brief illustration of this process.

> Suppose a compliant, dependent woman says to her male therapist, "Where should we start today?" The therapist will fail the test and reenact a familiar relational scenario if he says, "Tell me about _____." . . . The therapist will pass the test and demonstrate that he is capable of engaging in a more egalitarian way than the client has been able to do with other male figures in her life when the therapist says, "I'd like to hear about what is most important to you. Let's begin with something that you would like to tell me about." (p. 216)

Teyber (2000) also noted, "The therapist can fail the client's test by responding in a way that reenacts maladaptive relational patterns, or the therapist can pass the test and provide a corrective emotional experience by behaviorally demonstrating that relationships can be different" (p. 216).

Pattern Interventions

Another level at which the counselor can respond to in the interpersonal realm involves a change or modification in the patterns of interactions around the interpersonal concerns the client reports. This is referred to as *pattern intervention* and comes from work on family therapy and Ericksonian hypnosis (Imber-Black, Roberts, & Whiting, 1988;

O'Hanlon, 1987). In the previous section, we talked about a type of pattern intervention in which the counselor attempts to change the client's characteristic pattern by having the *counselor* respond in a new and more helpful way. In the pattern intervention, the *client* changes something about the way he or she interacts in a given situation with another person or group of persons.

In pattern intervention, the counselor looks for repetitive actions on the client's part in relationships with others that are observable enough to be modified in some way—something to the client's interpersonal pattern may be added, deleted, or in some way varied. Typically, modifications are made around three aspects of an interpersonal pattern: the behaviors, the situation or context, and the sequence of behaviors (Hudson & O'Hanlon, 1991). For example, suppose you are working with a teenage girl whose presenting problem is that she has no friends. Upon exploring what patterns she uses in initiating and maintaining friendships, you describe that she has made a number of new friends in the past few years but that after several months, each friend has successively withdrawn from her, and all have told her the same thing—that she "bugs" them. When asking her what she thinks they mean by this, she rather openly states that she engages in a number of "smothering" behaviors once she makes a new friend. She follows her friends around at school, insists they eat lunch with her, and calls them frequently after school. Although she is supposedly trying to keep her friends close to her, her very actions are driving them away! In pattern interventions, you can work with helping this client modify her behaviors so that she gives her friends "space"—she requests having lunch with them only once in a while, not daily; she plans to call them perhaps once a week rather than several times a day; and so on. Of course, this is easier said than done—because with most teenagers, their primary motivation is to stay connected to their peers, no matter what!

In this example, you are helping the client modify the behaviors, the context, and the sequence of her behaviors that she engages in with her friends. Of course, it is also likely that aspects of this pattern will get reenacted with you, as well, so you will ultimately need to address the issue within your helping relationship as well as within her relationships with friends. The extent to which you do this, however, depends on the client's goals and the number of contacts or sessions that are available for working with her.

As with all the other intervention strategies we have described in this chapter, there are also caveats to consider in working with clients' interpersonal patterns and systems. A noted Jungian therapist and author, James Hillman (1996), for example, argued that too much emphasis is placed on the role of parental influence, resulting in a reductive way in which counselors look at people. In his book, *The Soul's Code*, he has cited biographies of people who have had "bad" parenting and who, in response to some internal image or dream, have gone on to live productive and fulfilled lives.

The interventions associated with the systemic model have also been criticized by those who believe that these models are based on white, middle-class U.S. families, and, as a result, contain both covert gender and ethnicity bias (Enns, 1993; Hackney & Cormier, 2001; Stevenson & Renard, 1993). As an example of such difference, Berg and Jaya (1993, p. 32) observed that many middle-class white U.S. children seem to "fight" their way out of the family in order to individualize themselves, whereas for most Asian American children, being excluded from their family system is the worst imaginable consequence; "individuation" for these children is a foreign concept. Even the definition of what a "family system" is varies across cultural groups.

As a counselor, it is incumbent on you to recognize the ways in which the values and patterns of your own interactional system may differ from those of your clients and to offer system interventions in a way that is syntonic with your clients' gender and culture. Toward this end, we recommend familiarizing yourself with the work of Boyd-Franklin (1989), Carter and McGoldrick (1999), Goldenberg and Goldenberg (2000), and Midori Hanna and Brown (1999). (See also the recommended readings at the end of this chapter.) We also recommend consideration of some questions developed by Midori Hanna and Brown (1999) for implementing these strategies in gender and culturally sensitive ways (see Figure 9.3). In the following section of the chapter, we discuss interventions to use that more directly affect a client's environmental and cultural milieu—in other words, a client's social system.

FIGURE 9.3   Questions to Assess Gender, Racial, and Cultural Factors

1. Could role inflexibility regarding tasks be related to the problem?
2. Are communication styles disempowering to the females in the family?
3. Have generational coalitions developed as a result of disempowerment in the marriage?
4. Can disempowerment stereotypes ("nag," "passsive-aggressive") be relabeled to account for the context of powerlessness?
5. Can the female therapist model more egalitarian relationships with males in the family and can male therapists affirm female strength within the family?
6. What are family rules around females' personal development and autonomy outside the family?
7. What will each family member need from the therapist in order to feel understood and accepted?
8. How does your racial/cultural/religious heritage make your family different from other families you know?
9. Compared to other families in your cultural group, how is your family different?
10. What are the values that your family identified as being important parts of your heritage?
11. At this particular time in your (family's) development, are there issues related to your cultural heritage that are being questioned by anyone? What and by whom?
12. What is the hardest part about being a minority in this culture?
13. When you think of living in America versus the country of your heritage, what are the main differences?
14. What lesson did you learn about your people? About other peoples?
15. What did you learn about disloyalty?
16. What are people in your family really down on?
17. What might an outsider not understand about your racial/cultural/religious background?

Source: From *The Practice of Family Therapy: Key Elements across Models,* 2nd edition, by S. M. Hanna and J. H. Brown (pp. 37, 38, 43). © 1999. Reprinted with permission of Wadsworth, a division of Thomson Learning: www.thomsonrights.com. Fax 800-730-2215.

WORKING WITH CLIENT CULTURAL
AND SOCIAL SYSTEMS

Almost all of the interventions we have presented in the preceding part of this chapter are drawn from counseling theories such as intrapersonal, self-in-relations, gestalt, rational-emotive, cognitive-behavioral, Ericksonian, and family systems. These theories have been developed by founding fathers and, as such, have been critiqued by multicultural theorists as reflecting an Eurocentric bias and value system and as being somewhat culturally irrelevant for clients who feel marginalized from the mainstream.

When issues of cultural salience such as race, gender, religion, sexual orientation, and social class are considered, some of the more classic therapeutic interventions we have described may even be culturally contraindicated. According to Brown (1994), it is important to ask these questions in selecting a helping strategy:

1. Will this strategy oppress my client even more?
2. What does my strategy need to offer in working with a "multiply oppressed" client?

For those clients whose worldviews (i.e., basic perceptions and understanding of the world) do not reflect the "rugged individualism" of the Eurocentric tradition, other interventions that are more culturally appropriate are needed that address group, community, and sociopolitical causes, as well as the individual causes the client presents.

The Community Genogram

Clients and their issues are connected to and impacted by the cultural and social systems to which they belong. Counselors also are affected by their own cultural and social systems as well. The impact of communities and social groups can be positive, negative, or mixed. The concept of a *genogram* was developed originally as a tool used in family therapy to view the chronology of a family's life cycle—that is, the effect of various family generations on the client over time and over various developmental stages (Carter & McGoldrick, 1999).

Ivey (1995) has developed the community genogram as a way to depict the interaction between a client and the community and cultural systems. As Ivey and colleagues (2002) noted, "One major community event can change the individual's total culture. In turn, one individual can affect the total culture as well" (p. 18). A genogram is a tool to "ensure that individual issues are seen in their full contextual background" (p. 10). Ivey and colleagues describe four goals of the community genogram:

1. to generate a narrative story of the client in community context;
2. to help the client generate an understanding of how we all develop in community;
3. to understand the cultural background of the client, and
4. to focus on personal, family, and group strengths (pp. 10, 11).

(*Note:* We agree with Ivey and colleagues that before developing this sort of story and understanding with your clients, it is first important to develop this awareness with yourself, the helper of clients!)

There are two basic processes to using the community genogram. The first process involves developing a visual picture of the client's culture and community. The second process involves developing a strengths or asset-based story or narrative of several positive images reflected in the visual picture. For specific guidelines within these two processes, refer to Figure 9.4. Gutierres, Russo, and Urbanski (1994) concluded that community-based interventions are critical, for example, in working with American Indians and their families in substance use treatment.

FIGURE 9.4   The Community Genogram: Identifying Strengths

PART ONE	PART TWO
Develop a Visual Representation of the Community	*Search for Images and Narratives of Strength*
1. Consider a large piece of paper as representing your broad culture and community. You should select the community in which you primarily were raised, but any other community, past or present, may be used.	1. Focus on one single community group or the family. You or the client may want to start with a negative story or image, but do not work with the negative until positive strengths are solidly in mind.
2. Place yourself or the client in that community, either at the center or other appropriate place on the paper. Represent yourself or the client by a circle, a star, or other significant symbol.	2. Develop an image that represents an important positive experience. Allow the image to build in your mind, and note the positive feelings that occur with the image. If you allow yourself or the client to fully experience this positive image, you may experience fears and/or strong bodily feelings. These anchored bodily experiences represent positive strengths that can be drawn on to help you and your clients deal with difficult issues in therapy and in life.
3. Place your own or the client's family or families on the paper, again represented by the symbol most relevant. The family can be nuclear or extended or both.	
4. Place the important and most influential groups on the community genogram, again representing them by circles or other visual symbols. School, family, neighborhood, and spiritual groups are most often selected. For teens, the peer group is often particularly important. For adults, work groups and other special groups tend to become more central.	3. Tell the story of the image. If it is your story, you may want to write it down in journal form. If you are drawing out the story from a client, listen sensitively.
	4. Develop at least two more positive images from different groups within the community. It is useful to have a positive family image, spiritual image, and cultural image. Again, many will want to focus on negative issues, but maintain the search for positive resources.
5. Connect the groups to the individual, perhaps drawing heavier lines to indicate the most influential groups.	

(continued)

FIGURE 9.4 **Continued**

	PART TWO
	Search for Images and Narratives of Strength
	5. Summarize the positive images in your own words and reflect on them. Encourage clients to summarize their learning, thoughts, and feelings in their own words. As you or your client thinks back, what occurs? Record the responses, for these can be drawn on in many settings in therapy or in daily life.

Source: Theories of Counseling and Psychotherapy: A Multicultural Perspective (5th ed., pp. 11–12) by A. E. Ivey, M. D'Andrea, M. B. Ivey, and L. Simek-Morgan. Published by Allyn and Bacon, Boston, MA. Copyright © 2001 by Pearson Education. Reprinted by permission of the publisher.

Ecomaps

Another intervention that is useful for working with client cultural and social systems is the ecomap. An *ecomap* is a visual tool used to map the "ecology" (hence, *eco*), or the client's relationship to social systems in his or her life, including relationships, resources, and systems that are strong, stressful, and unavailable or tenuous (Hepworth, Rooney, & Larsen, 2002). For example, Lott (2002) described how social institutions involving education and housing distance, exclude, and discriminate against economically poor and low-status persons. A sample ecomap for a couple client is shown in Figure 9.5. In this figure, note that the clients, depicted in the middle of the map, are connected to various social systems by different types of lines:

1. A solid line (————) connects the couple to systems that are strong.
2. A broken line (– – – – – –) connects the couple to systems that are negative or stressful.
3. A dotted line (··················) connects the couple to systems that are unavailable or tenuous.

Helping Roles and Indigenous Practices

In working with client cultural and social systems, a variety of roles are used to complement and extend the traditional role of counselor/helper. These additional roles are described by Atkinson, Thompson, and Grant (1993) as follows:

Adviser: One who provides information and guidance and who engages in problem solving with clients

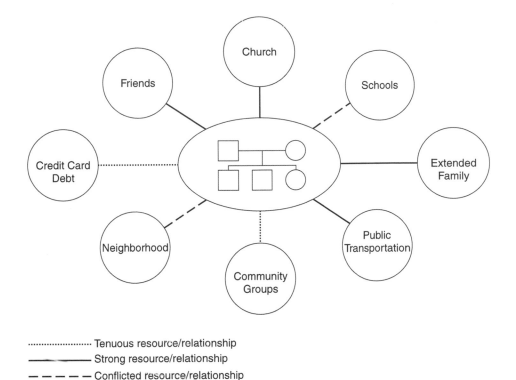

.... Tenuous resource/relationship

————————— Strong resource/relationship

— — — — — Conflicted resource/relationship

FIGURE 9.5   Sample Ecomap

Source: Adapted from *Direct Social Work Practice: Theory and Skills* (with InfoTrac), 6th edition, p. 347, by D. H. Hepworth, J. A. Larsen, and R. H. Rooney. © 2002. Reprinted with permission of Wadsworth, a division of Thomson Learning: www.thomsonrights.com. Fax 800-730-2215.

Advocate: One who represents and advocates for clients to other people and organizations

Change agent: One who actively tries to impact the client's social and cultural environment, especially aspects of it that are discriminatory and/or oppressive

Facilitator of indigenous support systems and practices: One who recognizes and actively uses the support people and systems indigenous or belonging to the client's culture. This may include the use of extended family or kinship, community elders, and religious and spiritual resources such as a shamanic healer. This also may include the use of or the referral to someone trained and skilled in using healing methods indigenous or belonging to the client's culture such as a *currandismo* (Mexican folk healer) or a tai chi instructor.

Many of the helping traditions from non-Western cultures are centered in spiritual and religious beliefs and systems. Often, the healers within these cultural systems are religious or spiritual leaders. In a sample of American Indian substance users, Gutierres, Russo, and Urbanski (1994) found that over one-half of their sample had used American Indian medicine and had participated in native spiritual ceremonies. As Lee (1996) noted, "Helping or healing . . . often involves religious or spiritual rituals that invoke higher powers or forces to assist in resolving problems" (p. 89). For example, a client who has lost a significant family member or who is faced with a life-threatening illness may participate in a healing ritual to grieve the loss or to cleanse the body of impure thoughts, deeds, or spirits. Lee continued, "In many indigenous helping systems, healers believe in many levels of human experience, which often include a spirit world where it is believed that answers to human destiny can be discerned" (p. 89). In some cultures, the healer, such as a shaman or a medicine man, makes a journey to this spirit world on behalf of a client who may be ill, for example. Often, this journey is made to the sound of a drum or other percussion instrument or to a chant or song. For example, in the autobiography of Lori Arviso Alvord (1999), she described the ritual of a Navajo blessing ceremony over the new intensive care unit in the traditional hospital in which she worked as a physician:

> The *hataalii* (medicine man) stood next to his wife. They were both dressed in traditional clothing. . . . In his hand the *hataalii* held a feather and a bowl of sacred water. He began to sing. . . . He stepped over to the row of doctors and waved an eagle feather. Over each of our bodies, he twirled the feather and sprinkled us with water. His voice rang out, rhythmic and atonal, that familiar sound of Navajo chant . . . this ceremony medicine could make it possible for Navajo patients to feel safe being treated in the new ICU. (Alvord & Van Pelt, 1999, p. 105)

This sort of healing ceremony reflects the notion that for many non-Western cultures, healing is holistic with "little distinction between physical and mental well-being. Many indigenous healers perceive human distress as an indication that people have fallen out of harmony with *both* their internal and external environment" (Lee, 1996, p. 90). This is especially important when one considers that the word *healing* means "wholeness."

Another good example of the use of an indigenous-based intervention was demonstrated for Hispanic youth by Costantino, Malgady, and Rogler (1994). They found that the use of culturally sensitive stories and pictures that depicted Hispanic cultural elements—such as foods, games, sex roles, and Hispanic families and neighborhoods (stores or *bodegas*)—were effective in reducing anxiety and conduct problems in school. They concluded that "after studying diverse age bands in several studies, we can conclude that storytelling of cultural material is an effective modality using folktales (*cuentos*) with very young children, heroic biographies with older adolescents, and composing stories about familial and ethnic pictures with older children and early adolescents." This is probably so because of the youths' active participation "in symbolic activities that enmesh culture" (p. 19).

An important concept in using counseling strategies to effect change is that of *self-efficacy*, a cognitive process that mediates behavioral change (Bandura, 1989, 1997). When self-efficacy is high, clients feel a sense of personal agency, confidence, and empowerment. High self-efficacy not only influences feelings, beliefs, behaviors, and interactions, but also a person's biochemistry. Increasingly, self-efficacy is also being identified as a significant factor both in the use of prevention and risk programs and in the academic and career performance of diverse groups of clients (Cormier & Nurius, 2003). Self-efficacy seems to be an important factor in promoting change for female clients and for clients of color, especially when it is paired with some of the strategies that focus on external social systems as well as an internal sense of confidence in oneself.

APPLICATION EXERCISE 9.1
INTERVENTION STRATEGIES

In this exercise, three hypothetical client cases are described. After reading over each case, describe what you believe the client's probable counseling goal would be and the related intervention strategies that could be used to help each client reach these goals. Consider goals and strategies for all of the five areas we discussed in this chapter: feelings, beliefs, behaviors, interactional patterns, and cultural/social systems. You may do this activity alone, with a partner, or in a small group discussion. You may wish to exchange your responses and ideas with other helpers or share your thoughts with your instructor.

A. CASE 1

Asani is an Asian American at a large university; she is overwhelmed by the size of the university, having lived in a small town all her life. She is concerned about her shyness and feels it is preventing her from making friends. Asani reports being uncertain about how to reach out to people. She is also concerned about her performance on tests. Although she believes her study habits are adequate, she reports that she "blows" the tests because she gets so uptight about them. Asani believes her grades are a reflection of herself and her family. She is worried about bringing dishonor to her family if she gets low grades.

PROBABLE COUNSELING GOALS

1. _____
   _____

2. _____
   _____

3. _____
   _____

POSSIBLE COUNSELING STRATEGIES

1. _____
   _____
   _____

(continued)

APPLICATION EXERCISE 9.1 CONTINUED

2. _____

_____

_____

3. _____

_____

_____

B. CASE 2

Mr. and Mrs. Yule have been married for seven years. Both are in their sixties, and this is their second marriage; their previous spouses died. Mr. and Mrs. Yule are concerned that they rushed into this second relationship without adequate thought. They report that they argue constantly about everything. They feel they have forgotten how to talk to each other in a civil manner. Mrs. Yule states that she realizes her constant nagging upsets Mr. Yule; Mr. Yule discloses that his spending a lot of time with his male buddies irritates Mrs. Yule.

PROBABLE COUNSELING GOALS

1. _____

_____

2. _____

_____

3. _____

_____

POSSIBLE COUNSELING STRATEGIES

1. _____

_____

_____

2. _____

_____

_____

3. _____

_____

_____

C. CASE 3

Michael is a 13-year-old boy attending a middle school in an urban area. He is constantly starting fights and getting into trouble. He says he does not know how or why but suddenly he is punching other kids. Only after the fights does he realize his temper has gotten out of hand. He reports that he considers himself to be kind of "hot headed" and he likes that about himself. He reports spending a lot of time on the streets and he feels this greatly helps him survive. He says that although he is close to his mother, he rarely sees her, as she works two to three jobs to support the family. He has had no contact with his father since he was a young boy.

PROBABLE COUNSELING GOALS

1. _____
_____

2. _____
_____

3. _____
_____

POSSIBLE COUNSELING STRATEGIES

1. _____
_____
_____

2. _____
_____
_____

3. _____
_____
_____

SUMMARY

In working with clients, all of whom present unique concerns and circumstances, you may find great use for the strategies described in this chapter. However, there are several cautions to consider in trying to use a counselor strategy effectively. The first caution in strategy implementation is to avoid oversimplification of the procedure. Although a procedure may seem relatively simple to implement, even with little experience, any therapeutic endeavor can be effective or ineffective, depending on how it is administered. Second, you must practice using strategies. You will not be an expert when you first start using them, but your skill will grow as you practice. Also remember that strategies are rarely used in isolation. Several different strategies or combinations of procedures may be necessary to deal with the complexity and range of concerns presented by a single client. As an example, suppose a counselor treats a client's alcoholism but ignores the anxiety for which alcohol is used as a tranquilizer. The strategies used to decrease the drinking behavior may not be too effective unless the counselor and client also use strategies to deal with the client's limited coping skills, self-defeating thoughts, and environmental issues that maintain the drinking.

Remember, too, that the effectiveness of counseling strategies depends, to some degree, on the strength and trust of the counseling relationship as well as the degree to which these strategies are used in a gender- and culture-friendly way. Responding to a client's social and environmental milieu is as important in strategy implementation as responding to a client's presenting feelings, beliefs, and behaviors.

Also, it is important to realize the limitations of counseling objectives and strategies and of counselors. One of the most frustrating experiences that counselors report is the experience of being thwarted in their attempts to help clients change and grow. Beginning counselors often approach the counseling process with a lot of zest, zeal, and unwavering idealism. Although a certain amount of this is useful, it can also lead to discouragement with oneself and with clients. Almost all clients will resist your attempts to help in some way. Some clients who see you at the request of someone else may be openly oppositional. Other clients may desire to change but because of biochemical imbalances may require medication for such things as depression or anxiety management. Clients with addictions may also find the process of recovery especially difficult. Clients from very dysfunctional family systems may find the weight of the system working against their own individual efforts to change. So, as you approach your growth and development and your own efforts in working with clients, it is important to remember that there are some limits to what happens in the counseling process and that almost all client resistance to change is about fear (Teyber, 2000). As clients become more able to trust themselves and you, your efforts and theirs will be rewarded.

REFLECTIVE QUESTIONS

1. In this chapter, we discuss a variety of interventions to work with the *whole person* (e.g., the client's feelings, beliefs, behaviors, interactional patterns, and cultural/social systems). As you have read and worked with these interventions, which ones feel most natural and comfortable for you? Which ones do you believe you would have the most trouble with? Why?

2. What places in your own body do you consistently hold in feelings? How do you become aware of these? What do you do to release them?

3. Can you identify situations for yourself in which your beliefs have affected the way you feel and act?

4. What persons have you used in your life for role models? What are their characteristics that appeal to you?

5. How do you apply self-management to everyday behaviors for yourself?

6. What is your characteristic interactional pattern? Can you trace it back to your family of origin? How do you think this pattern will affect the way you interact with your clients?

7. Refer to Figure 9.3 and, with a partner or in a small group, discuss these questions for yourself, your life, and your own history.

RECOMMENDED READINGS

Beck, J. S. (1995). *Cognitive therapy.* New York: Guilford.

Berlin, S. (2001). *Clinical social work: A cognitive-integrative perspective.* New York: Oxford University Press.

Carter, B., & McGoldrick, M. (1999). *The expanded family life cycle: Individual, family, and social perspectives* (3rd ed.). Boston: Allyn and Bacon.

Cormier, S., & Nurius, P. (2003). *Interviewing and change strategies for helpers: Fundamental skills and cognitive-behavioral interventions* (5th ed.). Pacific Grove, CA: Brooks/Cole.

Dobson, K. S. (Ed.). (2001). *Handbook of cognitive-behavioral therapies* (2nd ed.). New York: Guilford.

Gilligan, S. (1997). *The courage to love: Principles and practices of self relations psychotherapy.* New York: Norton.

Goldenberg, H., & Goldenberg, I. (2000). *Family therapy* (5th ed.). Pacific Grove, CA: Brooks/Cole.

Greenberg, L. S. (2002). *Emotion-focused therapy: Coaching clients to work through their feelings.* Washington DC: American Psychological Association.

Hackney, H., & Cormier, L. S. (2005). *The professional counselor* (5th ed.). Boston: Allyn and Bacon.

Hays, P. A. (1995). Multicultural applications of cognitive-behavior therapy. *Professional Psychology, 26,* 309–315.

Hepworth, D. H., Rooney, R. H., & Larsen, J. A. (2002). *Direct social work practice: Theory and skills* (6th ed.). Pacific Grove, CA: Brooks/Cole.

Hudson, P. O., & O'Hanlon, W. H. (1991). *Rewriting love stories.* New York: Norton.

Ivey, A. E., D'Andrea, M., Ivey, M. B., & Simek-Morgan, L. (2002). *Theories of counseling and psychotherapy: A multicultural perspective* (5th ed.). Boston: Allyn and Bacon.

Kanfer, F. H., & Goldstein, A. P. (Eds.). (1991). *Helping people change* (4th ed.). New York: Pergamon.

Midori Hanna, S., & Brown, J. (1999). *The practice of family therapy* (2nd ed.). Pacific Grove, CA: Brooks/Cole/Wadsworth.

Morgan, B., & MacMillan, P. (1999). Helping clients move toward constructive change: A three-phase integrated counseling model. *Journal of Counseling and Development, 77,* 153–159.

Nelson, M. L. (2002). An assessment-based model for counseling strategy selection. *Journal of Counseling and Development, 80,* 416–421.

Teyber, E. (2000). *Interpersonal processes in psychotherapy* (4th ed.). Pacific Grove, CA: Brooks/Cole.

Watson, D. L., & Tharp, R. G. (2002). *Self-directed behavior: Self-modification for personal adjustment* (8th ed.). Belmont, CA: Wadsworth.

Wolpe, J. (1990). *The practice of behavior therapy* (4th ed.). New York: Pergamon.

CHAPTER TEN

COMMON CHALLENGES FOR BEGINNING COUNSELORS

T. ANNE HAWKINS, SHERRY CORMIER, AND JANINE BERNARD

Beginning counselors often experience fears and worries about their new role (Bernard & Goodyear, 2004). As most faculty and supervisors know, these feelings are normal and are experienced more intensely as beginning helpers move closer to their initial practicum and internship experiences. It is not a stretch to conclude and be comforted by the idea that even psychotherapy giants Albert Ellis, Carl Rogers, Alfred Adler, Fritz Perls, Carl Jung, Rollo May, Karen Horney, Virginia Satir, and Sigmund Freud inevitably struggled with some of the same fears and worries that you may be currently experiencing. They, too, were faced with developing and applying new skills, testing out unfamiliar environments, meeting new clients for the first time, applying confusing and sometimes convoluted theories to practice, and responding to the feedback and evaluation of others (which wasn't always favorable or kind).

You also may be surprised to know that although these fears and worries typically decrease over time, remnants may linger as you face new challenges, are confronted with old fears, navigate unfamiliar terrain, and learn and try out new skills. Thus, a discussion of these issues benefits not only beginning helpers but also counselors who know the value of retooling. This chapter provides an overview of some of these fears and worries, as well as related issues concerning ways to prepare for ethical and supervisory challenges that you and your colleagues may experience.

COMMON CONCERNS OF BEGINNING COUNSELORS*

In the first section of this chapter we discuss common concerns of beginning counselors. These include managing stress and personal issues; managing anxiety, in all

---

*This section of the chapter was written by T. Anne Hawkins, MA, LPC, doctoral student, Department of Counseling Psychology, West Virginia University.

shapes and forms; and managing the inevitable gulf between theory and practice. We also present some of the distorted cognitions that underlie these common concerns.

Managing Stress and Personal Issues

For many students in the helping professions, learning how to manage stress is key to their ongoing personal and professional development. How you manage stress today may predict how you manage it (or let it manage you) in your future. Obvious stressors for students in the helping professions include establishing a professional identity; managing the logistics of training programs (finances, accessing resources, and navigating numerous polices, procedures, and deadlines); juggling family and relationship responsibilities; managing and responding to competitiveness; meeting expectations of faculty, advisors, and supervisors; and meeting mounting academic responsibilities.

Less obvious are stressors that relate to establishing personal competency and identity. Hazler and Kottler (1994) have suggested that training for the helping professions by its nature can be destabilizing. It requires changes in how you view yourself, others, and your world. For example, you often become "other" focused and are challenged to consider the value of process rather than content, and meaning rather than events. As you navigate your training in the helping professions, questions about the meaning of life and your role in the world may surface. Relationships with significant others, friends, and family may look and be experienced very differently as you proceed through your training program. You may find that as you examine and change your values and priorities that your expectations for intimacy in these relationships increase. These changes can initially create conflict and stress.

Stress and conflict also are inevitably evoked as core interpersonal issues that are triggered by course and clinical work. Unresolved interpersonal issues (that is, struggles with trust and emotional intimacy, competency, perfectionism, low self-esteem, and so on) can create seemingly insurmountable barriers as you navigate coursework, as you confront potential power struggles in departments and agencies, and especially as you work with clients. For example, if you experience a high need for approval, you may struggle to serially or concurrently please family and friends, faculty, advisors, peers, site supervisors, faculty supervisors, site colleagues, clients, clients' families, and clients' referral sources.

These and other unresolved interpersonal issues may negatively impact your development as a counselor and your work with clients. Hazler and Kottler (1994) provided the following list of common unresolved issues that many counselors experience:

- Being adult children of alcoholics
- Being victims of childhood sexual/physical/verbal abuse
- Undergoing a separation, divorce, or other family problem
- Living through an age-related developmental transition
- Being substance abusers or having other addictions
- Living through culture-, race-, or gender-related developmental transitions
- Lacking self-esteem
- Dealing with dependence/independence issues with a significant other (p. 84)

More enduring problematic personality traits may also affect your relationships with peers, faculty, supervisors, and clients. Counselors who are rigid, dogmatic, easily threatened by others, controlling, extremely vulnerable, self-centered, or narcissistic may experience difficulties as they attempt to make sense of peer and supervisor relationships and especially as they develop relationships with clients.

As a result of these and similar issues, many students seek counseling for themselves. Not only can the process of self-exploration be healing but it can also provide beginning counselors with valuable information about the vulnerable experience of being a client. Despite the value of this experience, many students struggle with the stigma they associate with seeking psychological help. However, a great many students and counselors do seek help for themselves, and the most common reasons reported for seeking counseling include:

- Depression/general unhappiness
- Marriage/divorce issues
- Relationship issues
- Self-esteem and confidence issues
- Anxiety

Clearly, there are a number of personal reasons why experienced and especially beginning counselors might seek counseling. McCleod (1998) suggested that engaging in personal counseling increases the effectiveness of helpers. He believes that successful counselors exhibit higher levels of general emotional adjustment and experience a greater capacity for self-disclosure.

Although it may seem convenient to seek counseling from a faculty member in your department, this option establishes dual relationships and raises privacy rights and ethical issues. We discuss dual roles and relationships in greater detail in a later section of this chapter. Alternatively, counseling may be available at no cost or for a nominal fee at many college and university counseling centers. Those who have completed their professional training may seek counseling from community agencies or counselors in private practice settings.

Anxiety: All Combinations and Flavors

Exams, research papers, audio or video counseling tapes, clients who don't show up, clients who keep showing up, clients who adore and/or despise you, progress notes, confusing treatment plans, complicated individualized educational plans, and faculty and counseling supervisors who magically know the "right" words for every situation—it's a wonder that beginning helpers ever wade through all of their hurdles!! Somehow, though, you manage the anxiety that these situations and responsibilities provoke and you graduate, pass licensing and certification exams, and become a professional helper, ultimately assisting clients in finding meaning and support.

This process is not without its challenges, particularly early in the journey. Typically, beginning helpers struggle with anxiety about competency and evaluation. Given the great responsibility of the work that you have chosen, the secrets you cradle, and the sometimes fragile helping relationships in which you find yourself, some anxiety is certainly warranted. Low degrees of anxiety may, in fact, drive beginning helpers to excel, but higher levels can create "analysis paralysis"—a state that makes it difficult for beginning helpers to retrieve and articulate words, to conceptualize and track client issues, to recall session content, and, most significantly, to attend to and be present for clients (Baird, 2002). The ambiguity that often characterizes the counseling process can compound this anxiety, particularly for students who take comfort in order, structure, and predictability. Unresolved interpersonal issues regarding personal and professional competency, pleasing others, establishing and maintaining boundaries, and inaccurate self-evaluation can inadvertently shift the focus of counseling sessions from the client to the counselor.

Beginning helpers may find themselves caught up in a new but strangely familiar quest for the perfect theory, intervention, or interpretation. They may become so immersed in a theory that they indiscriminately apply it in every counseling relationship (and social situation). They may also become so focused on achieving competence that they confuse it with perfection. With so much riding on their performance, the focus may shift from the needs of the client to "What am I going to say next and how will I say it?" and, perhaps most familiarly, "Will I be good enough?" Students may lose sight that they are expected to be beginners, not experts. They may measure their competency against that of senior faculty members and/or seasoned professionals at their field placement sites.

This need to be the "all-knowing" or "perfect" counselor can significantly impede the helping process (Baird, 2002). Ironically, it may create distance between counselors and clients, decreasing feelings of empathy, approachability, and shared worldview. Beginning helpers who struggle with this need to be perfect also may experience the impostor phenomenon. Harvey and Katz (1995) described the *impostor phenomenon* as the overshadowing sense of fraudulence and incompetence that exists despite disconfirming data. Beginning counselors who experience this phenomenon may find themselves focusing on their mistake or missteps, searching endlessly for evidence of their incompetence, exaggerating both the frequency and magnitude of their mistakes, and, ultimately, losing sight of the reality that *all* counselors make mistakes. They may be unaware of or resistant to the fact that mistakes can encourage increased self-awareness, genuineness, and flexibility on the part of counselors.

Many beginning helpers also experience varying degrees of evaluation anxiety. Making audio- and videotapes for a counseling class requirement can feel like a daunting, overwhelming assignment. Developing and presenting a case presentation can trigger old, unresolved perfectionism and competency issues. Meeting a client or a supervisor for the first time also can evoke many similar anxieties and concerns. Clients with difficult relational styles or particularly defensive coping responses can strike anxiety and fear in even the most experienced of counselors. It may help you to know that many of your colleagues also may be experiencing similar feelings and thoughts. Students in the helping professions commonly find themselves struggling with a variety of distorted cognitions, which can impact their feelings and behaviors as they work with clients. Following is a list of some of these distorted cognitions (some may even sound familiar to you!). We also list alternative cognitions for you to contemplate when finding yourself in the midst of "cognitive pollution."

DISTORTED COGNITIONS	ALTERNATIVE COGNITIONS
"If I have any problems or unresolved issues in my life, I can't be an effective counselor."	"Every counselor has problems and unresolved issues. If I work on issues, I'll be a better counselor."
"If my clients don't get better, it's my fault and/or I'm a terrible counselor."	"Clients are responsible for their own change process. I can help, but ultimately it is their responsibility."
"If my clients don't come back, I'm a lousy counselor."	"Clients don't come back for a variety of reasons. I need more information before I draw a conclusion."
"I'm the counselor now; I have to know everything."	"I don't have to know everything. I'm a beginning counselor; I'm still learning."

Managing the Theory and Practice Gulf

Bridging the gulf between theory and practice can be difficult for even the most competent and committed student. For example, you may have read about, and read about, and read about, and even practiced progressive relaxation with a colleague, but have never applied the techniques in session with a "real client" when, unexpectedly, the opportunity presents itself. This learning edge, or *zone of proximal development*, as described by Baird (2002), depicts the point just beyond a student's current level of knowledge or skill. When you are in this zone, you may experience anxiety, confusion, dissonance, discomfort, and sometimes excitement. Often, these unsettling feelings propel forward movement, urging students to take learning risks, to extend themselves, and to try out new skills in session with a client. In this moment, you are in the "zone" and are faced with the challenge of trying out a new skill or resorting to an intervention with which you are more familiar. What choice will you make? What skills or interventions will you use? Whose needs will be served by your choices? We discuss this further in the next section of this chapter, "Preparing for Ethical Challenges."

■ ■ ■ ■ ■

APPLICATION EXERCISE 10.1
EXPLORING COMMON CONCERNS
OF BEGINNING COUNSELORS

In this activity—which you can complete on your own, with a partner, or in a small group—explore the following open-ended questions about your concerns regarding counseling and being a counselor.

The best approach with clients is . . .

If I were a counselor on the *Survivor* series on television, I would . . .

The most annoying thing about being a counselor is . . .

Counselors are . . .

I want to be a counselor because . . .

The best way to get a client to change is . . .

The most important thing to remember about counseling is . . .

The hardest thing about counseling is . . .

Counselors who _____ should have their licenses revoked.

When I am counseling a client, I feel . . .

When I am counseling a client, I get nervous when . . .

When I am counseling a client, I get distracted when . . .

As a counselor, I wish I could . . .

As a counselor, I think I am at my best when . . .

Counselors get burned out because . . .

I want my clients to think that I am . . .

One thing I do that might get in the way with my clients is . . .

The most valuable thing I have learned in my counseling class is . . .

PREPARING FOR ETHICAL CHALLENGES*

Corey, Corey, and Callanan (2003) defined *ethics* as "moral principles adopted by an individual or group to provide rules for right conduct. . . . Ethics represents aspirational goals, or the maximum or ideal standards set by the profession, and they are enforced by professional associations, national certification boards, and government boards that regulate professions"** (p. 11). Recall that earlier we discussed the major professional organizations for helpers and their related code of ethics. (Refer to Appendix A for this list.)

It is important for all helpers to become familiar with the ethical code for their professional group because these codes serve several useful functions. First, they give you knowledge about ethical behavior on your part with your clients. As Corey, Corey, and Callanan (2003) noted, "The primary purpose of codes of ethics is to safeguard the welfare of clients by providing what is in their best interest" (p. 8). Another purpose of ethical codes is to provide accountability—to help ensure that all helping professionals practice within the scope of the ethical guidelines for their profession. As a result, these codes not only govern your behavior but also the behavior of those colleagues with

*This section of the chapter was written by Sherry Cormier, professor, Department of Counseling, Rehabilitation Counseling, and Counseling Psychology, West Virginia University.

**This and all other quotes from this source are from *Issues and Ethics in the Helping Professions* (Non-InfoTrac Version), 6th edition, by G. Corey, M. S. Corey, and P. Callanan. © 2003. Reprinted with permission of Wadsworth, a division of Thomson Learning: www.thomsonrights.com. Fax 800-730-2215.

whom you work. Violations of ethical codes can result in sanctions against the practitioner who has violated the code.

Often, after reviewing your ethical code, you might feel frustrated because the codes provide general, broad guidelines for ethical conduct rather than specific cookbook-like recipes for knowing exactly what to do in every ethical dilemma you face. Although we review some of the major guidelines for ethical conduct in this section of the chapter, and in other chapters of the book as well, neither our discussion nor the ethical codes are going to be enough to ensure that you behave in an ethical and responsible way with clients (Corey, Corey, & Callanan, 2003). Corey, Corey, and Callanan (2003) elaborated on this when they stated that "codes are not intended to be a blueprint that removes all need for the use of judgment and ethical reasoning . . . as each client's situation is unique and calls for a different solution. The most difficult part of being an ethical counselor is having to make decisions and then assuming personal responsibility for the consequences (Lanning, 1997). This process needs time to be done well, and it should include consultation" (p. 7). For these reasons, we will also introduce you to Corey, Corey, and Callanan's ethical decision-making model in this section of the chapter as well.

Confidentiality, Informed Consent, and Privacy

The concept of confidentiality and privacy is discussed in Chapter 5 in greater detail. Suffice it to say, however, that violations of confidentiality are a major reason why helpers are sued by clients for malpractice. Welfel (2002) reported that practitioners indicate that confidentiality is the most frequent ethical dilemma they face. All major professional organizations for helpers stipulate that clients have the right to have their communications safeguarded by their helper, with the exceptions of some situations. This safeguarding pertains not only to face-to-face communications but also to electronic sources. Since confidentiality belongs to the client, it is generally not an issue when the client provides a written authorization to allow the counselor to release information about the client. But, as Glosoff, Herlihy, and Spence (2000) observed, the ethical dilemma is posed when there is a demand or state law that suggests a counselor should release information the client does not want released. For example, all 50 states have laws requiring helpers to disclose child or elder abuse. Yet, in some circumstances, a child or an elderly person may not want the helper to notify the appropriate authorities of the abuse. It is important to note that one way to protect both the client and yourself is to inform clients at the outset of any limitations to confidentiality based on your state laws and your professional code of ethics. This is referred to as *informed consent.*

Informed consent is a way to give clients an active role in the helping process and to protect their rights by providing information to them about the helping process. Ethical codes stipulate that helping professionals are expected to discuss any and all aspects of counseling and treatment that impact clients, such as the right to confidentiality, including all the exceptions to it; the nature of the therapeutic relationship; the nature of the counseling and change process; the type of records kept; information about fees, insurance reimbursement, rationale, benefits, and risks of any treatment strategies used; and so on. Informed consent statements should also specifically address the eight exceptions to confidentiality. Welfel (2002, pp. 76–89) described these eight exceptions as follows:

1. When the client requests a release of information
2. When a court of law orders release of information
3. When a client files an ethical complaint or a lawsuit against the counselor
4. When a client initiates civil legal action against another person that includes claims of psychological harm and refers to counseling services used to alleviate such harm
5. When state statutes mandate disclosure, such as in instances of elder or child abuse
6. When the client poses an immediate threat or danger to self or others, such as suicide or homicide
7. When the client discloses he or she is planning criminal action in the future (note that this is required in some states but not all)
8. When, in some situations, a client discloses that an identifiable third party is at high risk of contracting the client's communicable and fatal disease

Informed consent begins in the initial interview and continues throughout the remainder of the helping process (Welfel, 2002). If the client is a minor or is deemed not competent to give consent, a parent or a legal guardian then provides the consent. Regulatory boards in many states now require practitioners to provide informed consent via a written disclosure statement. Keel and Brown (1999) stated, "A professional disclosure statement will reflect the distinctive qualities and characteristics of the individual helper as well as the purpose, goals, techniques, procedures, limitations, risks, and benefits of services provided" (p. 14). An important part of informed consent and a disclosure statement is the client's right to *privacy*.

Chapter 5 discussed the recent role of the Health Insurance Portability and Accountability Act (HIPAA) federal regulations as well as some state laws governing the privacy of individual clients and their health records. Corey, Corey, and Callanan (2003) stated that privacy is a constitutional right of every individual to "decide the time, place, manner, and extent of sharing oneself with others" (p. 199). Before HIPAA, privacy was protected by the client's signed informed consent statement. Following HIPAA, practitioners are now required to give each client a Notice of Privacy Practices (NPP), which spells out what your agency's privacy policies are and what protected health-related information can be released to a "covered entity" (that is, another person or persons) without client consent or authorization. This NPP must be given to clients in the initial interview. Now, under HIPAA, consent "is no longer required and is now only an acknowledgment of being notified of one's rights. The 'consent' is blanket, required for receiving treatment, not time limited, and is not in any sense informed. It allows disclosure much more freely. . . . This is a very low floor of privacy" (Zuckerman, 2003, p. 20). Disclosure is limited to diagnosis, treatment plans, appointment times, and symptoms, as well as routine treatment, payment, and health care operations. For nonroutine disclosures, or for disclosure of any other information, such as private psychotherapy notes, a specific written client authorization is required. For further detailed information on HIPAA and mental health, you might consult the manual authored by Zuckerman (2003) and the websites of various professional organizations.

Freeny (2003) observed that the effects of the HIPAA regulations on mental health therapeutic relationships are largely unknown at this point. He stated, "The privacy rules assert a client's right to not only know your privacy policies, but also to access, review, and correct" information in their official records you keep. Furthermore, as the practitioner, "you must make clear how they can request an account of disclosures and how they can limits disclosures. Yet, ironically, HIPAA mandates that you also make clear that you're not required to honor your client's requests, a curious and contradictory starting point for a new therapeutic relationship" (p. 45). One useful part of the new HIPAA regulations is that practitioners are also required to conduct privacy and security overviews of office procedures, record-keeping procedures, and the transmission of clinical information in and out of the office. For example, are telephone conversations private? Who can view computer screens? Who else has access to client information? How is your client-related information on your computer secured and backed up? Is a fax machine used to transmit client information? How is client email handled? As Corey, Corey, and Callinan (2003) noted, the use of various telecommunication devices can pose a number of potential ethical issues in terms of safeguarding the client's right to privacy. The American Psychiatric Association (2002) concluded that *"no existing security system absolutely protects electronic records in data banks from human error or malice"* (p. 2). Cooper (2003) recommends that because of the potential privacy risks to certain telecommunication devices like faxes and email, helpers either should avoid using them or should obtain client informed consent first. Heinlen, Welfel, Richmond, and Rak (2003) have recommended that any and all webcounseling be conducted according to a set of professional standards for the ethical practice of webcounseling such as the ones provided by the International Society of Mental Health Online (ISMHO) available at http://www.ismho.org. (See also Appendix A.)

Dual Relationships and Boundary Issues

Boundary issues involve some form of limit setting. In ethical conduct, this sort of limit setting occurs in several areas. One area has to do with training, education, and competence. It is important to practice within the areas that you have received training and/or certification. For example, it would be considered unethical to do a vocational assessment unless you have been trained in that area, have a degree in rehabilitation counseling, or are a certified rehabilitation counselor. Generally, the most ethical course of action involves using interventions in which you have received some training and experience. If, for example, you have never been exposed to gestalt therapy, except in a textbook, it is prudent to seek supervision and training before trying a gestalt intervention on your own with a client.

It is also important to consider what your competence is with age groups, populations, and cultural groups. As Welfel (2002) suggested, "The boundaries of competence extend not just to intervention strategies . . . but also to new populations, age groups, and cultural groups" (p. 54). For example, you may be trained to deal with depression in Euro-American adult clients, but dealing with depression in a child or adolescent, or in a refugee from another country may present differently and require different interventions. All of the major ethical codes require enough knowledge of cultural factors to be able to work effectively with varying clients. Welfel (2002) asserted that counselors have "a duty to recognize the unique parameters" of a case and "to seek additional training or consultation to help the client, or refer him to another counselor already competent with these issues" (p. 54). A challenge to this would be when you work in a rural area and do not have many referral sources or consultation sources to use. "The ethical challenge for rural counselors is to provide competent service across a wide range of issues, age groups, and populations, while acknowledging that they are not super-counselors who can do everything" (Welfel, 2002, p. 55). In these situations, Welfel suggested that if the risk of harm is high and the chance to help is less high, the counselor should not intervene. However, if the risk of harm is low and the chance to do good is high, then the intervention is more warranted (p. 55).

In a similar vein, it is risky to use interventions or treatments with clients who fall outside what would be considered the common or typical standards for practice by most helping professionals. According to Corey, Corey, and Callanan (2003), if your procedures fall outside of "the usual methods employed by most professionals," you are more vulnerable "to a malpractice action" (p. 183). Honoring the usual standards of practice has become even more important in recent years because there are now empirically developed guidelines for practice for various kinds of psychological and emotional disorders. This means that for depression, for example, interventions based on either cognitive therapy or interpersonal therapy have been found through research studies to be superior to or more efficacious than other kinds of interventions (Nathan & Gorman, 2002). One cautionary note involving these practice guidelines (often referred to as *evidence-based treatments*) is that they have not been validated on diverse groups of clients (for example to a refugee with depression), so their applicability is less clear (Quintana & Atkinson, 2002). (For information about evidence-based treatments, see Gibbs, 2003; Nathan & Gorman, 2002; Wampold, Lichtenberg, & Waehler, 2002; or www.apa.org/divisions/div12/est.) All of these challenges to competence require limit-setting or boundary management on your part as the practitioner.

Another very important kind of boundary management has to do with the relationship you develop with clients—specifically, with the kinds of roles reflected by your behavior. "Whenever counselors have other connections with a client in addition to the therapist-client relationship, a dual or multiple role relationship exists" (Welfel, 2002, p. 155). The ethical challenge is to honor a division or a boundary between "the professional and personal lives of counselor and client" (p. 155). In instances when this boundary is not honored, there is a blurring of roles and what can be referred to as *boundary crossing* or *boundary violations.* Codes of ethics indicate that practitioners should avoid dual- or multiple-role relationships when possible for several reasons. First, a dual relationship "implies that the counselor is vulnerable to other interests that compete with promoting the welfare of the client" (Welfel, 2002, p. 160). Second, "when a counselor has another role in the client's life, the client's emotional reaction is confused" (Welfel, 2002, p. 161). Finally, there is a power differential in all helping relationships, meaning that the practitioner holds more power than the client, resulting in the fact that the client who feels powerless may feel coerced to participate in a dual- or multiple-role relationship.

Boundary violations between helper and client can be nonsexual or sexual. Nonsexual dual or multiple relationships include the following:

1. Accepting a friend or relative as a client
2. Providing counseling to an employee
3. Employing a client
4. Going into business with a current and/or former client
5. Providing counseling to a student and/or a supervisee
6. Allowing a client to enroll in a course taught by the counselor
7. Inviting a client to a party or going to a social event with a client
8. Selling something to a client (Welfel, 2002, p. 165)

Although some of these nonsexual dual relationships are clearly prohibited by ethical codes, a few fall into a "gray area" but are still strongly discouraged for the three reasons we mentioned above. This is especially true when practicing in an urban area where it is "almost always possible to make other arrangements" (Welfel, 2002, p. 169). However, being able to completely avoid any dual role for rural practitioners is more challenging; in some ways, they face a "more demanding standard" and need greater ethical sensitivity about these boundary issues (p. 172). One way that rural practitioners can manage complex boundary decisions is with detailed informed consent statements at the beginning of the helping process (Jennings, 1992).

All ethical codes in the helping field prohibit sexual intimacy of any kind in the counselor-client relationship. Most of the codes also state that if a counselor has had a previous sexual relationship with a person, that person should never become the counselor's client. According to Corey, Corey, and Callanan (2003), "It is clear from the statements of the major mental health organizations that these principles go beyond merely condemning sexual relationships with clients. The existing codes are explicit with respect to sexual harassment and sexual relationships with clients, students, and supervisees" (p. 272). A sexual relationship with a client is perhaps the most serious ethical violation that exists and is also the most common reason for a malpractice suit. Counselors can face both civil and criminal charges for sexual boundary violations with clients as well as other serious consequences such as loss of licensure. A sexual dual relationship is the most damaging kind of boundary violation that exists, and is often preceded in the helping relationship by much more subtle behaviors such as excessive self-disclosure by the counselor (Smith & Fitzpatrick, 1995).

It is important to note the distinction between sexual *feelings* about a client and sexual *behavior* with a client. A general guideline is that a sexual feeling toward a client is not an unusual occurrence, but acting on these feelings is always harmful and in violation of the ethical codes. This is a good example of a situation in which it is simply imperative to seek consultation with an instructor, colleague, or supervisor! The ethical codes also stipulate that sexual relationships with former clients should be avoided.

There now appears to be a trend in ethical code revisions toward prohibiting any post-termination sexual relationships as well, due to possible exploitation factors, continued imbalance of power, and the lack of clarity about when and whether the professional relationship actually terminated (Corey, Corey, & Callinan, 2003, p. 281). In addition to the gravity of sexual boundary violations, it is also important to remember that other boundary violations can still feel just as damaging to clients (p. 275).

Ethical Decision Making

Given the complexity of the various ethical codes and the complexity of client issues, it is useful to develop a way to make decisions about ethical dilemmas. Recall that the ethical codes are not cookbook-like recipes. They do contain guidelines, which in some cases, like sexual dual relationships, are very explicit. In other situations, the guidelines are less clear and require challenging decisions to be made by the helper. In this section, we present the Corey, Corey, and Callanan ethical decision-making model to help you sift through and think critically about the application of the ethical codes to various ethical dilemmas that will arise for you during practice. According to the authors (2003, p. 18), the ethical decision-making process is not often a cognitive, linear, or stepwise model—it is complex, involves emotions, and can be a somewhat circular process that requires critical and reflective thinking and recognition of emotions.

Corey, Corey, and Callanan have described their ethical decision-making model with the following eight steps:

1. *Identify the problem or the dilemma.* Most ethical dilemmas have some degree of ambiguity about them, which is what makes them a dilemma! Corey, Corey, and Callanan (2003, p. 20) suggested deciding whether the dilemma is an ethical, legal, moral, professional, or clinical problem, or more likely, some combination of these. There are two important guidelines to follow in making decisions about ethical dilemmas: consultation and documentation. *Consultation and documentation start with this step and continue throughout the process.* In a nutshell, we advise that whenever you are faced with an ethical dilemma, consult immediately with your supervisor(s), a colleague, or, at times, even an attorney. And document, document, document the consultations in which you participate.

2. *Identify the potential issues involved in the dilemma.* According to Corey, Corey, and Callanan (2003, p. 20), this means assessing the "rights, responsibilities, and welfare" of all those involved and impacted by your decision(s). For example, if you are faced with a decision to report about a client who is suicidal and a danger to oneself, what are the issues involved in protecting the client from harm and in safeguarding the client's well-being?

3. *Review the relevant ethical codes.* What do the ethical codes say about this dilemma? How do you feel about the position of the ethical codes? If the codes are ambiguous, consider consulting with the ethical board or committee of your professional organization or the state in which you are working.

4. *Review the relevant laws and regulations.* In many ethical dilemmas, there are both state and federal statutes and regulations that impact ethical and legal practices. Consider whether there are any of these that affect your particular dilemma. What does your state say, if anything, about breaking confidentiality if the client is considered to be a danger to oneself? Does the place where you work have any regulatory guidelines or policies that also affect your decision?

5. *Obtain consultation.* Consultation should start at the beginning of the ethical decision-making process. Corey, Corey, and Callanan (2003) have recommended consulting with more than one professional and consulting with persons who have a variety of perspectives. Further, they stated that consultation is important not only because it helps you think through the best decision but it also shows that you have tried to adhere to the best practice standards by consulting with others and finding out what they would do under the same or similar circumstances.

6. *Consider possible and probable courses of action.* At this stage of ethical decision making, you are basically engaging in a brainstorming process. In brainstorming, your initial task is to identify all and any solutions, rather than judging or evaluating the effectiveness of each solution at this point in the process (evaluation of each option is the next step). Often, it is useful to include the client in this brainstorming process, too.

7. *Evaluate the possible consequences of various decisions.* After identifying potential solutions through brainstorming, start to scrutinize each solution very carefully. Weigh the benefits and risks of each solution for all those impacted by your decision. Again, it is often very useful to assess the potential consequences with your client, as well.

8. *Decide on what seems to be the best possible course of action.* After gathering all your information and seeking consultation, at this point you can decide on the best course of action—the one with the most benefits and the least costs, and the one that puts the client's well-being at the top of the list without violation of ethical and/or legal codes and statutes. It is still wise to decide on the course of action with a consultation that you document in writing, and often, again, with involving the client, too.

■ ■ ■ ■ ■ ▬▬▬▬▬▬▬▬▬▬▬▬▬▬▬▬▬▬▬▬▬▬▬▬▬▬▬▬▬▬▬▬

APPLICATION EXERCISE 10.2
PREPARING FOR ETHICAL CHALLENGES

In this activity we describe two case vignettes. Read each case carefully. Then apply the ethical decision-making model to identify the potential dilemmas, to review relevant ethical codes and laws, and to brainstorm and evaluate the best course of action for the dilemmas. You may wish to complete the activity on your own at first and then discuss your findings and ethical decision-making process with a group.

A. CASE 1

You are practicing or working in a rural setting. You keep meeting some of your clients at social and community events. What are the ethical challenges to confidentiality, privacy, and boundaries in this situation? What do you think is the best course of ethical action to take in this general situation and why?

B. CASE 2

You are working in a local high school. One evening one of your clients obtains your home telephone number and calls you in a very distraught state. She indicates that she was pregnant and had an abortion several months ago (before she started seeing you for counseling). Now she is having severe misgivings about her decision and is feeling very guilty. She has not told anyone about this, including her boyfriend or her parents—only now is she telling a soul and that is you! She begs you not to tell anyone. What do you believe is the best ethical action to take in this situation and why?

PREPARING FOR SUPERVISION CHALLENGES*

In a nutshell, *supervision* can be defined as "overseeing," although we provide a more sophisticated definition in the next section, "The Parameters of Supervision." From the time you begin a professional preparation program, such as we described in Chapter 1, throughout your field placements, and even after you obtain your degree(s) and begin employment, you will be supervised or "overseen" by someone. This is usually a novel experience for most people. Because supervision seems to make individuals feel scrutinized, especially initially, we end this chapter with a section on what supervision is and how you can best prepare for it and utilize it for your own professional growth and development.

The Parameters of Supervision

In order to understand supervision, one must consider what happens in supervision, who provides the supervision, and in what context supervision occurs. It makes sense to start with a definition. *Clinical supervision* is

> an intervention that is provided by a senior member of a profession to a junior member or members of that same profession. This relationship is evaluative, extends over time, and has the simultaneous purposes of enhancing the professional functioning of the junior member(s), monitoring the quality of professional services offered to the clients she, he, or they see(s), and serving as a gatekeeper for those who are to enter the particular profession. (Bernard & Goodyear, 2004)

*This section of the chapter was written by Janine Bernard, professor and chair, Department of Counselor Education, Syracuse University.

We will now examine this definition more closely by looking at its parts:

1. *Supervision is an intervention.* Clinical supervision is different from counseling and teaching, though it is related to both. There are competencies and skills involved in supervision that allow the supervisor to help the supervisee* gain competence and insight into the dynamics of counseling. Supervision does not just happen—it is planned.

2. *Supervision is provided by a more advanced practitioner and involves evaluation.* A clinical supervisor is more advanced than the supervisee, at least on some important variables. Supervision also has an evaluative aspect. It is conducted, in part, to evaluate the counselor. This *summative evaluation* will occur after there has been enough supervision to expect a certain degree of competence. However, throughout the supervision experience, there is an evaluative component. When the supervisor suggests that a counselor go in a different direction with a client, that supervisor is making a judgment regarding what has transpired during counseling up to this point.

3. *Supervision extends over time.* An important aspect of supervision is establishing some clarity regarding the supervision contract. In other words, the relationship between counselor and supervisor will be different depending on how long the two will be working together and under what conditions. An assumption of supervision, however, is that the supervision relationship will last long enough to allow for some developmental progress for the supervisee.

4. *The supervisor monitors and serves as a gatekeeper.* While conducting supervision, the supervisor is always aware that the supervisee represents only one level of the supervisor's responsibility. Ethically and legally, the supervisor also must monitor the quality of the counseling that is being delivered to the supervisee's clients.

Responsibilities of Supervisors and Supervisees

You and your supervisor have certain responsibilities to each other. These responsibilities include having formally scheduled contacts with one another on a regular basis, as well as access to supervision on an as-needed basis for crises or emergencies. Another responsibility involves providing each other with information about your cases, especially the management of difficult and problematic cases. You and your supervisor are ethically obligated to safeguard the communication of your clients in a confidential manner. Additionally, your supervisor is required to track your work with clients, monitor the quality of it, and provide you with regular and periodic feedback, including suggestions for improvement. Your supervisor also is ethically bound to restrict his or her relationship with you to just supervision. In other words, during the time you are being supervised, you do not have another kind of relationship with your supervisor that could compromise supervision. If a supervisor is also your close friend or coun-

---

*Also referred to as *trainee* and *counselor.*

selor, this is considered a *dual relationship*, which is considered unethical by the American Counseling Association Code of Ethics (1995a), as discussed earlier.

Another important distinction is that between *clinical supervision* and *administrative supervision*. Your employer in a mental health center, for example, is your administrative supervisor, since this person has the power to hire and/or fire you, to increase your salary, to determine your job description, and so forth. However, this person is not automatically a clinical supervisor. A clinical supervisor must be working with you in some manner to improve your counseling ability.

Finally, *context* refers to more than the work or training setting in which supervision occurs; it refers also to larger social and political contexts. Your supervisor must share some values with you in order to be an effective supervisor. He or she must also help you appreciate that both counseling and supervision relationships are determined, in part, by the parameters reflected in a diverse society. Addressing these issues is an essential part of appreciating context within supervision (Leong, 1994).

Haynes, Corey, and Moulton (2003, p. 138) suggested a number of contextual competencies that need to be present in effective multicultural supervision. Among these are the following:

1. Explore racial dynamics in the supervisory relationship.
2. Assist supervisees in developing cultural self-awareness.
3. Provide knowledge regarding cultural diversity.
4. Assess cases using a multicultural conceptualization.
5. Practice and promote culturally appropriate interventions.
6. Provide and model social justice.

The Focus of Supervision

What is your supervisor looking for? For beginning counselors or counselors who are working with a new supervisor, this is a common and legitimate question. In fact, *role ambiguity* (i.e., not knowing what is expected of you) has been documented as a common issue for novice counselors (Olk & Friedlander, 1992). Here are some of the areas that most supervisors use to assess and evaluate supervisees:

- Intervention knowledge and skills
- Assessment knowledge and skills
- Relationships with staff and clients
- Responsiveness to supervision
- Awareness of limitations, knowing when to seek help
- Communication skills
- Ethical and legal practice
- Multicultural competence
- Judgment and maturity
- Openness to personal development
- Compliance with field placement policies and procedures (Haynes, Corey, & Moulton, 2003, p. 257)

■ ■ ■ ■ ■ ▬▬▬▬▬▬▬▬▬▬▬▬▬▬▬▬▬▬▬▬▬▬▬▬

APPLICATION EXERCISE 10.3
THE FOCUS OF SUPERVISION

For your own part, you can begin to determine the focus of your counseling sessions by asking five simple questions:

1. Did I know what to do in the session?
2. Did I know what I wanted to do?
3. Was I comfortable at that point?
4. Was my performance that of a professional counselor?
5. What issues came up for me in the session(s) regarding any of the following:
   Interventions
   Assessment
   Relationships
   Ethics
   Multiculturalism
   My own limitations

You can do this with roleplays or tapes of sessions.

Styles and Roles of Supervisors

Now that you have a better idea of what supervisors look for in training and supervising counselors, we will discuss the choices supervisors make about their own behavior. As you will soon discover, if you have not already, different supervisors have different styles. Sometimes their style makes you feel confident and supported, and sometimes their style has a less positive effect on you (Berger & Buchholz, 1993). At least some of this has to do with the role they choose as they work with you (Bernard, 1979, 1997).

The Role of Teacher.   The most common role for supervisors during the initial training of counselors is the *teacher role*. (For purposes of clarification, we shall use the word *instructor* to mean the person responsible for teaching a particular course, leaving the word *teacher* to mean a particular role or style the instructor may or may not wish to assume.) When in the teacher role, the supervisor takes responsibility for knowing what the counselor needs to do or learn. Therefore, the supervisor might instruct the counselor about a new technique, model a new intervention, or make other direct suggestions regarding the counselor's work. When the supervisor acknowledges the rightness or wrongness of a particular counselor strategy, the teacher role is being used. When a supervisor is in the teacher role, there is no question who is in charge.

The Role of Counselor.   When supervisors focus on the interpersonal or intrapersonal dynamics of their counselors or trainees, they are most likely in the *counselor role*.

The goal of the supervisor in this role is most often the personal growth of the counselor. Historically, this role has been widely used by supervisors, based on the assumption that the most legitimate way for counselors to grow professionally is to grow personally. Although the last two decades have offered differing opinions of this premise, there are times when the counselor role is the necessary and most desirable option for the supervisor to use. Furthermore, later in your career, supervisors are more likely to rely on the counselor role to stimulate your growth (Skovholt & Ronnestad, 1992). (It is important, however, for the supervisor to be careful to avoid a dual relationship and to suggest a referral to someone else if extensive counseling for personal issues is needed.)

The Role of Consultant.   When the goal of the supervisor is to encourage trainees to think on their own and to trust their own insights, the *consultant role* is most appropriate. When in this role, supervisors limit themselves to being a resource for their trainees. The authority for what will transpire in the supervisee's counseling is more equally shared. As a result, the consultant role conveys a degree of mutual trust and professional respect not necessarily found in the other two roles. On the other hand, respect is based on the expectation that the counselor can and will put forth the effort to use this role suitably.

The Need for Different Roles.   One well-documented model of supervision is the *developmental model,* which describes counselor growth as advancing through sequential skill levels (Borders, 1986; McNeil, Stoltenberg, & Pierce, 1985; Stoltenberg & Delworth, 1987; Worthington, 1987). Depending on the developmental level of the counselor, different supervisor roles may be warranted.

Research indicates that trainees prefer their supervisors to be in the teacher role initially (e.g., Bear & Kivlighan, 1994; Rabinowitz, Heppner, & Roehlke, 1986; Stoltenberg, Pierce, & McNeil, 1987). This is because novice counselors tend to be unsure of themselves, and the teacher role gives the structure and sense of security that they need at first. After they have received considerable training, they are more likely to prefer a consultant approach. When the supervisor is in this role, it allows the counselors to stretch their wings and use their supervisor primarily as a resource. Throughout training and beyond, the counselor role may be needed (if not welcome) because trainees occasionally hit personal snags that block their therapeutic efforts.

You might be asking, What if I don't like my supervisor's style? What can I do about it? First of all, you might determine if you encourage a certain role behavior. For example, if you approach supervision by asking a lot of questions, you are inviting your supervisor to assume the teacher role. If you try to convince your supervisor that you felt very anxious in your last session, you are (perhaps inadvertently) requesting the counselor role. When you make definitive statements about your work, you are encouraging a consultant role from your supervisor.

Second, if you believe that the problem is not in your approach but due to your supervisor's preference, you can ask if another role might be tried for a while. Again, knowing about the supervision process allows you to influence it. You might want to have your supervisor in the consultant role rather than in the teacher or counselor role.

One trainee approached her supervisor with this request. Her supervisor's reaction was, "I think that's a good idea. I agree that I've been too active in supervision. On the other hand, if it's going to work, I think you need to come to supervision more prepared. Perhaps you could review your tapes [audiotapes of counseling sessions] ahead of time and be prepared to identify segments that gave you difficulty and give your opinion of what went wrong." The trainee found this a reasonable plan. You might have noticed that the supervisor was *teaching* the counselor how to use him as a *consultant*. This kind of transition is often needed when a change of supervision role is to occur.

As a final note, we would like to mention that many, if not most, supervisors use all three styles in their work. It is not necessary that you be able to track your supervisor's style at all times. Rather, the issue of supervision role becomes relevant when you are trying to pinpoint why you are feeling stressed under supervision or why you do not think you are progressing as quickly as you would like. The supervisor's role may or may not be the problem, but it is one more important piece of the puzzle for you to consider.

Avoiding Supervision

As we stated elsewhere, supervision is evaluative in nature. Counseling is a very personal activity, and feedback about your counseling can be taken very personally, leaving you feeling highly anxious and threatened by the prospect of receiving supervision. It can be difficult to separate your value as a person from your success as a helper when your motivation to help is strong. Therefore, we will address the issue of avoiding supervision. Most counselors who avoid supervision do so psychologically, not physically, although there are counselors who avoid supervision by missing or coming late to their supervision sessions.

Bauman (1972), in what now is considered a classic article, pointed out that counselors can play games to avoid dealing with their skill issues. He outlined some of the postures presented by supervisees that, in effect, help them avoid supervision. Bauman's list of five "games" is as relevant today as it was when it was published, and includes such strategies as submission, turning the tables, "I'm no good," helplessness, and projection.

Submission.   In the *submission* game, trainees yield immediately to the superior knowledge of the supervisor. Discussion is not warranted because the trainee begs out as a result of obvious inferior judgment. He or she accepts all feedback unquestioningly—almost, it seems, before hearing it. Under such conditions, the trainee communicates complete malleability and unaccountability.

Turning the Tables.   We alluded to the game of *turning the tables* earlier when we discussed the counselor who solicits the teacher role from the supervisor through extensive questioning. The trainee approaches supervision with an infinite list of questions to solicit advice from the supervisor. The trainee, therefore, is in control of the supervision session and keeps the supervisor at arm's length.

"I'm No Good."   The game of *"I'm no good"* is more active than the submission strategy. Here, the trainee must convince the supervisor that he or she is on the verge of becoming a counselor casualty. The trainee magnifies counseling mistakes, placing the supervisor in the role of diminishing those self-deprecating remarks and assuring the trainee that there is hope. One possible consequence of this game is to invite the supervisor into a counselor role.

Helplessness.   Yet another variation on the same theme, *helplessness* is a stance protesting lack of experience as a reason for the supervisor to take full responsibility for the direction of the trainee's counseling. The trainee's energy seems to be directed at convincing the supervisor that the case is too unique, too advanced, too vulnerable to legal ramifications, and so on, for the trainee to take primary responsibility.

Projection.   Finally, a frequently used avoidance posture is to project the mistakes one has made in counseling onto the supervision process itself. The most salient example of *projection* is when the trainee protests that sessions that are observed by the supervisor are far more stilted and self-conscious than sessions that occur in the absence of the supervisor (or when the tape recorder is turned off). The message is that, for whatever reason, the supervisor never really sees the trainee's highly developed (or even adequate) counseling skills.

Liddle (1986) has asserted that trainee resistance stems from an attempt to avoid a perceived threat. She has listed five possible sources of threat in supervision: (1) evaluation anxiety; (2) performance anxiety (living up to one's own standards of performance); (3) personal issues within the supervisee (such as having unresolved feelings about death when counseling a client who is mourning the loss of a loved one); (4) deficits in the supervisory relationship; and (5) anticipated consequences (resisting the learning of how to confront out of fear of client anger).

Does knowing about resistance help to avoid it? How do you overcome those things that threaten you in supervision? First of all, it is essential that you realize and accept that some anxiety in supervision is unavoidable (Yager, Witham, Williams, & Scheufler, 1981). It could even be said that feeling no anxiety is in itself a form of avoidance. Second, you must try to identify the sources of your anxiety if you are to resolve them. If you feel yourself avoiding supervision, you might discuss this with your supervisor. If that seems too threatening, you could find a peer you trust to help you uncover the motives or fears underlying your resistance. Finally, trainees need to find productive ways to handle their resistance rather than succumbing to a psychological avoidance of supervision. For example, pairing some of the ideas presented earlier, say that you are playing helpless with your supervisor out of a fear that learning to confront will cause client anger. Continuing to be helpless is inappropriate. However, it is highly appropriate to acknowledge your fear to your supervisor. Once you and your supervisor are dealing with the real issue, there are innumerable ways to conquer your fears. The point is to acknowledge that those fears are a normal and legitimate part of supervision (Liddle, 1986) and that avoiding them is counterproductive.

Putting Your Development as a Counselor in Perspective

Although most counselors manage to resist the urge to sabotage their supervisors, why is it that this is a chronic temptation, especially early in training? Why are the fears so poignant at this juncture? At least one answer lies in an understanding of the development of the professional counselor.

A common frustration among novice trainees is that they feel they are getting worse, not better, during the initial phases of training. What once came naturally to them (i.e., being helpful to others) now seems a monumental challenge that causes humiliation and even shame. It can be very helpful to understand the development of counseling expertise to assuage some of this frustration. In their well-regarded book, Skovholt and Ronnestad (1992) described the eight stages of professional development for counselors from pretraining to retirement. The transition from stage one to stage two is most relevant to our discussion here.

In stage one, the future counselor is in the *conventional stage*—the stage of being a natural helper in his or her world. It is in this stage that you determine that counseling might be a good profession for you, from a combination of self-evaluation and feedback from friends and family. The next stage, called the *transition to professional training*, upsets the balance that you had as a natural helper. Where you once had confidence that you had some innate ability to be of help to others, you now feel enthused but insecure. Where you once relied on what you already knew and your common sense, now you are overwhelmed with new concepts that seem to be coming from several different sources. Feeling overwhelmed is included by Skovholt and Ronnestad as one of the major reactions to this stage. There are five more stages to follow, none as fraught with insecurity as this one. That's the good news. The bad news is that there is no way to get to these more advanced stages without working through this stage and its challenges. It also should be noted, however, that the transition stage includes the acquisition of knowledge and personal introspection that delights most students and serves to balance their discomfort. The point is that your first supervisory experiences may feel the most uncomfortable for developmental reasons alone. Once you have some experience (and some success!) under your belt, supervision should become safer and more rewarding.

Preparing for and Using Supervision

All things being equal, translating supervision to direction for the counselor is a shared responsibility between the supervisor and the trainee. That is, the supervisor should conduct the session so that it is clear how you are to implement his or her suggestions. If, however, this is not clear, you should ask for clarification before you are expected to perform again. This will avoid a common complaint made by supervisors that certain trainees are enjoyable to work with, but they do not seem to follow through on supervisory suggestions.

Even if it is clear how you are to use a supervisory suggestion, it is wise to give yourself some time to review what was gleaned from supervision before your next counseling session. What seems perfectly clear in a discussion with your supervisor may become muddled or somehow out of reach during the counseling session if you have not integrated the concepts into your own frame of reference prior to the session. This failure to integrate is a common mistake made by trainees—one that causes them unnecessary feelings of discouragement and embarrassment. The key to maximizing supervision is to invest additional energy between supervision and subsequent counseling sessions. This will help you avoid having to expend energy after the session to recover from disappointment of lack of success.

If you invest time and energy during the supervision process, you will gradually be able to engage in *self-supervision*, defined as a process whereby counselors can reflect on "intrapersonal, interpersonal, and clinical issues that influence their work" (Morrissette, 2002, p. xvii). When you supplement your regular supervision with self-supervision, what you have to offer to your clients will be of even higher quality.

■ ■ ■ ■ ■

APPLICATION EXERCISE 10.4
JOURNALING

Keeping a journal enhances your ability to be reflective and to explore your actions, thoughts, and feelings about aspects of your professional practice. "Reflective journals allow students to raise important questions, reflect on activities and progress, and consider new approaches and resources" (Morrissette, 2001, p. 75). Morrissette (p. 75) suggested the following steps in keeping a reflective journal about your professional helping activities:

1. Your first journal entry should be a short narrative reflecting on the persons, circumstances, situations, and values that drew you to counseling as a profession.
2. Subsequent entries can focus on your educational experiences and/or your field placement experiences, noting the following:
   ■ What was the most significant experience I had this week?
   ■ What questions did the experience raise for me personally? Professionally?
   ■ How can I use what I learned from this experience in my development as a professional helper?

SUMMARY

In this chapter we considered the transition that occurs from student to professional. Specifically, we addressed some common concerns that face helpers as they begin seeing actual clients. These include managing stresses induced by the training program and evaluation of one's work, challenges to one's competency and identity, and potential conflict in interpersonal relationships. Many students seek personal counseling for themselves to deal with these and other such challenges, such as anxiety and the impostor phenomenon. Students also have to bridge the gap between theory and practice. We described a number of ethical challenges that face counselors, such as confidentiality and its limits, informed consent, and privacy. We pointed out the risks to confidentiality in using telecommunication. We also discussed boundary issues and dual roles and dual relationships, noting that although these are generally to be avoided, sometimes exceptions are made when working in rural areas. Dual relationships can be problematic when either nonsexual or sexual, although clearly a sexual relationship with a client is always unethical and must always be avoided. We commented on the need to adhere to professional standards of practice, such as those listed on professional organizations' websites in Appendix A. Given the complexity of the various helping ethical codes and the complexity of client issues, we described a model for making ethical decisions. We also explored some components of clinical supervision, such as the parameters and focus of supervision and the style and role of supervisors.

Clinical supervision exists only when all these segments operate in union. Regardless of focus, role, or style, supervision is most often described as the most rewarding part of a counselor's training. Likewise, supervisors report a high degree of satisfaction in their work with supervisees. Both parties are reflecting the distinct pleasure of passing on and safeguarding the profession of counseling.

REFLECTIVE QUESTIONS

1. Reflect on and discuss the primary stresses that face you at this stage of your life. What strategies do you have for managing stress?

2. What do you see as some benefits for getting personal counseling for yourself? What obstacles might stand in the way of this?

3. Describe what your concerns are at this stage of your training and education.

4. Has our discussion about confidentiality changed your views in any way? What do you see as the advantages and the pitfalls of providing disclosure to clients about the limits of confidentiality in an initial session?

5. Discuss some ways to maintain a client's privacy. How might a practitioner unintentionally violate a client's privacy?

6. Identify potential situations in which it might be easier for you to relax boundaries with a client and establish another relationship in addition to the counseling one.

7. What do you think are the ethical risks in using electronic communication with clients?

8. Everyone approaches a new experience with certain expectations. List three things you hope to receive from supervision. List three things you know that you do not want from supervision. Discuss.

9. Knowing yourself as you do, what issues should be a focus during one of your initial sessions with your supervisor?

RECOMMENDED READINGS

Baird, B. (2002). *The internship practicum and field placement handbook* (3rd ed.). Upper Saddle River, NJ: Prentice-Hall.

Bernard, J. M., & Goodyear, R. K. (2004). *Fundamentals of clinical supervision* (3rd ed.). Boston: Allyn and Bacon.

Corey, G., Corey, M. S., & Callanan, P. (2003). *Issues and ethics in the helping professions* (6th ed.). Pacific Grove, CA: Wadsworth.

Corey, M. S., & Corey, G. (2003). *Becoming a helper* (4th ed.). Pacific Grove, CA: Wadsworth.

Freeny, M. (2003, March–April). No hiding place: Will patient privacy become a thing of the past? *Psychotherapy Networker,* 42–45.

Haas, L. J., & Malouf, J. L. (2002). *Keeping up the good work: A practitioner's guide to mental health ethics* (3rd ed.). Sarasota, FL: Professional Resource Press.

Harvey, C., & Katz, C. (1995). *If I'm so successful why do I feel like a fake? The impostor phenomenon.* New York: St. Martin's Press.

Haynes, R., Corey, G., & Moulton, P. (2003). *Clinical supervision in the helping professions: A practical guide.* Pacific Grove, CA: Wadsworth.

Hazler, R. J., & Kottler, J. A. (1994). *The emerging counseling profession.* Alexandria, VA: American Counseling Association.

Heinlen, K. T., Welfel, E. R., Richmond, E. N., & Rak, C. F. (2003). The scope of Webcounseling: A survey of services and compliance with NBCC *Standards for the Ethical Practice of Web-Counseling. Journal of Counseling and Development, 81,* 61–69.

McCleod, J. (1998). *An introduction to the counseling profession* (2nd ed.). Buckingham, England: Open University Press.

Morrissette, P. J. (2002). *Self-supervision: A primer for counselors and helping professionals.* Lillington, NC: Edwards Brothers.

Smith, D. (2003, January). 10 ways practitioners can avoid frequent ethical pitfalls. *Monitor on Psychology,* 50–55.

Welfel, E. R. (2002). *Ethics in counseling and psychotherapy* (2nd ed.). Pacific Grove, CA: Wadsworth.

Zuckerman, E. (2003). *HIPAA help: A compliance manual for psychotherapists.* Armbrust, PA: Three Wishes Press.

WEBSITES FOR ETHICAL CODES AND RELATED STANDARDS OF PROFESSIONAL ORGANIZATIONS

American Association of Marriage and Family Therapy
(http://www.aamft.org)

American Association of Pastoral Counselors
(http://www.aapc.org)

American Counseling Association
(http://www.counseling.org)

American Mental Health Counselors Association
(http://www.amhca.org)

American Psychological Association
(http://www.apa.org)

American School Counselor Association
(http://www.schoolcounselor.org)

Association for Multicultural Counseling and Development
(http://www.bgsu.edu/colleges/cdhd/programs/AMCD)

Canadian Psychological Association
(www.cpa.ca)

Code of Professional Ethics for Rehabilitation Counselors
(http://crcertification.com)

International Association of Marriage and Family Counselors
(http://www.iamfc.org)

International Society for Mental Health Online
(http://www.ismho.org)

National Association of Social Workers
(http://www.naswdc.org)

National Board for Certified Counselors
(http://www.nbcc.org)

National Organization for Human Services Education
(http://www.nohse.com)

COUNSELING STRATEGIES CHECKLIST

Most counselor trainees view the opportunity for supervision as a mixed blessing. They know that their performance has weaknesses that are more easily identified by an observer. On the other hand, they feel vulnerable at the prospect of having someone view and assess their interview behavior, particularly when they cannot see that person. There are no easy solutions to this problem. Learning to feel comfortable is uniquely a function of your own goals and the observer's awareness of your discomfort. Therefore, you must identify the implications of your counseling goals in terms of your own risk taking, and you must be prepared to communicate your fears.

The Counseling Strategies Checklist (CSC) is suggested as one means of assessing your performance. It is divided into categories that conform to the skills chapters in this text. The instructor or supervisor may want to use parts of the checklist for each interview, rather than attempt to complete the total checklist each time you are observed. The checklist provides a point of departure for you and your supervisor to discuss the progress of the interview, as well as your input and its effect on your client.

HOW TO USE THE COUNSELING STRATEGIES CHECKLIST (CSC)

Each item in the CSC is scored by circling the most appropriate response. The items are worded so that desirable responses are "Yes." "No" is an undesirable response. Following each section of the CSC there is space for observer comments. You can use this to record general impressions and specific observations. One way we like to use the CSC is to note to what degree the counselor's responses are culturally appropriate for each client. Specific assessment of multicultural competencies can be found in Part VII of the checklist.

After the instructor or supervisor has observed and rated the interview, the two of you should sit down and review the ratings. Where noticeable deficiencies exist, you and the supervisor should identify a goal or goals that will remedy the problem. Beyond this, you should list two or three action steps that permit you to achieve the goal. After three or four more interviews, have the observer evaluate you again, and compare the two sets of ratings to determine whether progress was evident.

Part I: Counselor Attending Behavior (Nonverbal)

1. The counselor maintained eye contact with the client.   Yes   No

2. The counselor displayed several different facial expressions during the interview.   Yes   No

3. The counselor's facial expressions reflected the mood of the client.   Yes   No

4. The counselor often responded to the client with facial animation and alertness.   Yes   No

5. The counselor displayed intermittent head movements (up-down, side-to-side).   Yes   No

6. The counselor refrained from head nodding when the client did not pursue goal-directed topics.   Yes   No

7. The counselor demonstrated a relaxed body position.   Yes   No

8. The counselor leaned forward as a means of encouraging the client to engage in some goal-directed behavior.   Yes   No

9. The counselor demonstrated some variation in voice pitch when talking.   Yes   No

10. The counselor's voice was easily heard by the client.   Yes   No

11. The counselor used intermittent one-word vocalizations ("mm-hmm") to reinforce the client's demonstration of goal-directed topics or behaviors.   Yes   No

Counselor Attending Behavior (Verbal)

12. The counselor usually spoke slowly enough so that each word was easily understood.   Yes   No

13. A majority (60 percent or more) of the counselor's responses
    could be categorized as complete sentences rather than
    monosyllabic phrases.   Yes   No

14. The counselor's verbal statements were concise and to   Yes   No
    the point.

15. The counselor refrained from repetition in verbal statements.   Yes   No

16. The counselor made verbal comments that pursued the topic   Yes   No
    introduced by the client.

17. The subject of the counselor's verbal statements usually   Yes   No
    referred to the client, either by name or the second-person
    pronoun, *you.*

18. A clear and sensible progression of topics was evident in the   Yes   No
    counselor's verbal behavior; the counselor avoided rambling.

Comments: _____

_____

Part II: Opening the Interview

1. In the first part of the interview, the counselor used several   Yes   No
   different nonverbal gestures (smiling, head nodding, hand
   movement, etc.) to help put the client at ease.

2. In starting the interview, the counselor remained silent or   Yes   No
   invited the client to talk about whatever he or she wanted,
   thus leaving the selection of initial topic up to the client.

3. After the first five minutes of the interview, the counselor   Yes   No
   refrained from encouraging social conversation.

4. After the first topic of discussion was exhausted, the counselor Yes   No
   remained silent until the client identified a new topic.

5. The counselor provided structure (information about nature,   Yes   No
   purposes of counseling, time limits, etc.) when the client
   indicated uncertainty about the interview.

6. In beginning the *initial* interview, the counselor used at least one
   of the following structuring procedures:

   a. Provided information about taping and/or observation   Yes   No

   b. Commented on confidentiality and privacy; stated limits   Yes   No
      of confidentiality

   c. Made remarks about the counselor's role and purpose of   Yes   No
      the interview

   d. Discussed with the client his or her expectations about   Yes   No
      counseling

Comments: _____

_____

Part III: Termination of the Interview

1. The counselor informed the client before terminating that the   Yes   No
   interview was almost over.

2. The counselor refrained from introducing new material   Yes   No
   (a different topic) at the termination phase of the interview.

3. The counselor discouraged the client from pursuing new topics   Yes   No
   within the last five minutes of the interview by avoiding asking
   for further information about it.

4. Only one attempt to terminate the interview was required before   Yes   No
   the termination was actually completed.

5. The counselor initiated the termination of the interview through   Yes   No
   use of some closing strategy such as acknowledgment of time
   limits and/or summarization (by self or client).

6. At the end of the interview, the counselor offered the client Yes No
an opportunity to return for another interview.

Comments: _____

_____

Part IV: Goal Setting

1. The counselor asked the client to identify some of the Yes No
conditions surrounding the occurrence of the client's problem
("When do you feel _____ ?").

2. The counselor asked the client to identify some of the Yes No
consequences resulting from the client's behavior ("What
happens when you _____ ?").

3. The counselor asked the client to state how he or she would Yes No
like to change his or her behavior ("How would you like for
things to be different?").

4. The counselor and client decided *together* on counseling goals. Yes No

5. The goals set in the interview were specific and observable. Yes No

6. The counselor asked the client to orally state a commitment Yes No
to work for goal achievement.

7. If the client appeared resistant or unconcerned about Yes No
achieving change, the counselor discussed this with the client.

8. The counselor asked the client to specify at least one action Yes No
step he or she might take toward his or her goal.

9. The counselor suggested alternatives available to the client. Yes No

10. The counselor helped the client to develop action steps for goal attainment.   Yes   No

11. Action steps designated by counselor and client were specific and realistic in scope.   Yes   No

12. The counselor provided an opportunity within the interview for the client to practice or rehearse the action step.   Yes   No

13. The counselor provided feedback to the client concerning the execution of the action step.   Yes   No

14. The counselor encouraged the client to observe and evaluate the progress and outcomes of action steps taken outside the interview.   Yes   No

Comments: _____

_____

Part V: Counselor Differentiation

1. The counselor's responses were usually directed toward the most important component of *each* of the client's communications.   Yes   No

2. The counselor followed client topic changes by responding to the primary idea communicated by the client.   Yes   No

3. The counselor usually identified and responded to the feelings of the client.   Yes   No

4. The counselor usually identified and responded to the behaviors of the client.   Yes   No

5. The counselor verbally acknowledged several (at least two) nonverbal affect cues.   Yes   No

6. The counselor encouraged the client to talk about his or her feelings.	Yes	No
7. The counselor encouraged the client to identify and evaluate his or her actions.	Yes	No
8. The counselor asked questions that the client could not answer in a yes or no fashion (typically beginning with words such as *how, what, when, where, who*, etc.).	Yes	No
9. Several times (at least two) the counselor used responses that supported or reinforced something the client said or did.	Yes	No
10. Sometimes the counselor restated or clarified the client's previous communication.	Yes	No
11. The counselor used several (at least two) responses that summarized ambivalent and conflicting feelings of the client.	Yes	No
12. The counselor encouraged discussion of negative feelings (anger, fear) expressed by the client.	Yes	No

Comments: _____

_____

Part VI: The Process of Relating

1. The counselor made statements that reflected the client's feelings.	Yes	No
2. The counselor responded to the core of a long and ambivalent client statement.	Yes	No
3. The counselor verbally stated his or her desire and/or intent to understand.	Yes	No

4. The counselor made verbal statements that the client reaffirmed without qualifying or changing the counselor's previous response. Yes   No

5. The counselor made attempts to verbally communicate his or her understanding of the client that elicited an affirmative client response ("Yes, that's exactly right," and so forth). Yes   No

6. The counselor reflected the client's feelings at the same or a greater level of intensity than originally expressed by the client. Yes   No

7. In communicating understanding of the client's feelings, the counselor verbalized the anticipation present in the client's communication (i.e., what the client would like to do or how the client would like to be). Yes   No

8. When the counselor's nonverbal behavior suggested that he or she was uncertain or disagreeing, the counselor verbally acknowledged this to the client. Yes   No

9. The counselor answered directly when the client asked about his or her opinion or reaction. Yes   No

10. The counselor encouraged discussion of statements made by the client that challenged the *counselor's* knowledge and beliefs. Yes   No

11. Several times (at least two) the counselor shared his or her own feelings with the client. Yes   No

12. The counselor encouraged the client to identify and discuss his or her feelings concerning the counselor and the interview. Yes   No

13. The counselor voluntarily shared his or her feelings about the client and the counseling relationship. Yes   No

14. The counselor expressed reactions about the client's strengths and/or potential. Yes   No

15. The counselor made responses that reflected his or her liking and appreciation of the client.　　　　　　　Yes　No

Comments: _____

_____

Part VII: Multicultural Competencies*

1. The counselor displayed an awareness of his or her own racial and cultural identity development and its impact on the counseling process.　　　　　　　Yes　No

2. The counselor was aware of his or her own values, biases, and assumptions about other racial and cultural groups and did not let these biases and assumptions impede the counseling process.　　　　　　　Yes　No

3. The counselor exhibited a respect for cultural differences among clients.　　　　　　　Yes　No

4. The counselor was aware of the cultural values of each client as well as of the uniqueness of each client within the client's racial and cultural group identification.　　　　　　　Yes　No

5. The counselor was sensitive to nonverbal and paralanguage cross-cultural communication clues.　　　　　　　Yes　No

6. The counselor demonstrated the ability to assess the client's level of acculturation and to use this information in working with the client to implement culturally sensitive counseling.　　　　　　　Yes　No

7. The counselor displayed an understanding of how race, ethnicity, and culture influence the treatment, status, and life chances of clients.　　　　　　　Yes　No

*From *Pathways to Multicultural Counseling Competence: A Developmental Journey*, 1st edition, by B. Wehrly. © 1996. Reprinted with permission of Wadsworth, a division of Thomson Learning: www.thomsonrights. com. Fax 800-730-2215.

8. The counselor was able to help the client sort out the degree to which the client's issues or problems are exacerbated by limits and regulations of the larger society.   Yes   No

9. The counselor was able to assess and identify the locus of the client's problem etiology.   Yes   No

10. The counselor was able to help the client deal with environmental frustration and oppression.   Yes   No

11. The counselor was able to recognize and work with the client dealing with multiple oppressions.   Yes   No

12. The counselor *worked with* the client to bring about change rather than *doing for* the client.   Yes   No

13. The counselor and client *worked together* to determine mutually acceptable and culturally sensitive goals.   Yes   No

Comments: _____

_____

REFERENCES

Adler, A. (1958). *What life should mean to you.* New York: Capricorn.

Alvord, L. A., & Van Pelt, E. C. (1999). *The scalpel and the silver bear.* New York: Bantam.

American Association for Marriage and Family Therapy. (1998). *Code of ethical principles for marriage and family therapists.* Washington, DC: Author.

American Counseling Association. (1995a). *Code of ethics.* Alexandria, VA: Author.

American Counseling Association. (1995b). Summit results in formation of spiritual competencies. *Counseling Today, 30.*

American Counseling Association. (1997). Governing council minutes of the September 1997 governing council meeting. Alexandria, VA.

American Psychiatric Association. (2002). *Documentation of psychotherapy by psychiatrists, 2002* (Data file). Available from the American Psychiatric Association website: http:www.apa@psych.org.

American Psychological Association. (2003). *Ethical principles of psychologists* (rev. ed.). Washington, DC: Author.

American School Counselor Association. (1998). *Ethical standards for school counselors.* Alexandria, VA: American Counseling Association.

Association for Specialists in Group Work. (2000). Professional standards for the training of group workers. *The Group Worker, 29*, 1–10.

Atkinson, D. R., Thompson, C. E., & Grant, S. K. (1993). A three dimensional model for counseling racial/ethnic minorities. *The Counseling Psychologist, 21*, 257–277.

Axelson, J. (1999). *Counseling and development in a multicultural society* (3rd ed.). Pacific Grove, CA: Brooks/Cole.

Baird, B. (2002). *The internship, practicum and field placement handbook* (3rd ed.). Upper Saddle River, NJ: Prentice-Hall.

Baker, S. B. (1999). *School counseling for the twenty-first century.* Upper Saddle River, NJ: Prentice-Hall.

Bandura, A. (1989). Human agency in social cognitive theory. *American Psychologist, 44*, 1175–1185.

Bandura, A. (1997). *Self-efficacy: The exercise of self-control.* New York: Freeman.

Banikiotes, P. G., Kubinski, J. A., & Pursell, S. A. (1981). Sex role orientation, self-disclosure, and gender-related perceptions. *Journal of Counseling Psychology, 28*, 140–146.

Bauman, W. F. (1972). Games counselor trainees play: Dealing with trainee resistance. *Counselor Education and Supervision, 11*, 251–256.

Bear, T. M., & Kivlighan, D. M., Jr. (1994). Single-subject examination of the process of supervision of beginning and advanced supervisees. *Professional Psychology: Research and Practice, 25*, 450–457.

Beck, A. T. (1976). *Cognitive therapy and the emotional disorders.* New York: International Universities Press.

Beck, J. S. (1995). *Cognitive therapy.* New York: Guilford.

Benjamin, A. (1990). *The helping interview.* Boston: Houghton Mifflin.

Berg, I., & Jaya, A. (1993). Different and same: Family therapy with Asian-American families. *Journal of Marital and Family Therapy, 19*, 31–38.

Berger, S. S., & Buchholz, E. S. (1993). On becoming a supervisee: Preparation for learning in a supervisory relationship. *Psychotherapy, 30*, 86–92.

Berlin, S. (2001). *Clinical social work: A cognitive-integrative perspective.* New York: Oxford University Press.

Bernard, J. M. (1979). Supervisor training: A discrimination model. *Counselor Education and Supervision, 19*, 60–68.

Bernard, J. M. (1997). The discrimination model. In C. E. Watkins, Jr. (Ed.), *Handbook of psychotherapy supervision* (pp. 310–327). New York: Wiley.

Bernard, J. M., & Goodyear, R. K. (2004). *Fundamentals of clinical supervision* (3rd ed.). Boston: Allyn and Bacon.

Bohart, A. C., Elliott, R., Greenberg, L., & Watson, J. C. (2002). Empathy. In J. C. Norcross (Ed.), *Psychotherapy relationships that work* (pp. 89–108). New York: Oxford University Press.

Bohart, A., & Greenberg, L. (1997a). Empathy and psychotherapy: An introductory overview. In A. Bohart & L. Greenberg (Eds.), *Empathy reconsidered* (pp. 3–32). Washington, DC: American Psychological Association.

Bohart, A., & Greenberg, L. (Ed.). (1997b). *Empathy reconsidered.* Washington, DC: American Psychological Association.

Borders, L. D. (1986). Facilitating supervisee growth: Implications of developmental models of counseling supervision. *Michigan Journal of Counseling and Development, 17,* 7–12.

Borders, L. D., Bernard, J. J., Dye, H. A., Fong, M. L., Henderson, P., & Nance, D. W. (1991). Curriculum guide for training counseling supervisors: Rationale, development, and implementation. *Counselor Education and Supervision, 31,* 58–80.

Boyd-Franklin, N. (1989). *Black families in therapy: A multisystems approach.* New York: Guilford.

Bozarth, J. (1997). Empathy from the framework of client-centered theory and the Rogerian hypothesis. In A. Bohart & L. Greenberg (Eds.), *Empathy reconsidered* (pp. 81–102). Washington, DC: American Psychological Association.

Brammer, L. M., Abrego, P. J., & Shostrom, E. L. (1993). *Therapeutic counseling and psychotherapy: Fundamentals of counseling and psychotherapy* (6th ed.). Englewood Cliffs, NJ: Prentice-Hall.

Branden, N. (1971). *The disowned self.* Los Angeles: Nash.

Brown, L. (1994). *Subversive dialogues: Theory in feminist therapy.* New York: Basic Books.

Brown, L. S., & Ballou, M. (1992). *Personality and psychopathology: Feminist reappraisals.* New York: Guilford.

Buie, D. (1981). Empathy: Its nature and limitations. *Journal of the American Psychoanalytic Association, 29,* 281–307.

Carter, B., & McGoldrick, M. (1999). *The expanded family life cycles: Individual, family, and social perspectives* (3rd ed.). Boston: Allyn and Bacon.

Casas, J. M. (1988). Cognitive behavior approaches: A minority perspective. *The Counseling Psychologist, 16,* 106–110.

Castillo, R. J. (1997). *Culture and mental illness.* Pacific Grove, CA: Brooks/Cole.

Chung, R. C.-Y., & Bemak, F. C. (2002). The relationship of culture and empathy in cross-cultural counseling. *Journal of Counseling and Development, 80,* 154–159.

Claiborn, C. D., Goodyear, R. K., & Horner, P. A. (2002). Feedback. In J. C. Norcross (Ed.), *Psychotherapy relationships that work* (pp. 217–234). New York: Oxford University Press.

Cooper, G. (2003, March–April). Clinician's digest. *Psychotherapy Networker,* 15–18.

Corey, G. (2001). *Theory and practice of counseling and psychotherapy* (6th ed.). Pacific Grove, CA: Brooks/Cole.

Corey, G., Corey, M. S., & Callanan, P. (2003). *Issues and ethics in the helping professions* (6th ed.). Pacific Grove, CA: Wadsworth.

Cormier, S., & Nurius, P. (2003). *Interviewing and change strategies for helpers: Fundamental skills and cognitive behavioral interventions* (5th ed.). Pacific Grove, CA: Brooks/Cole.

Corsini, R., & Wedding, D. (Eds.). (2000). *Current psychotherapies* (6th ed.). Itasca, IL: Peacock.

Costantino, G., Malgady, R. G., & Rogler, L. H. (1994). Storytelling through pictures: Culturally sensitive psychotherapy for Hispanic children and adolescents. *Journal of Clinical Child Psychology, 23,* 13–20.

Cournoyer, B. (2000). *The social work skills workbook* (3rd ed.). Belmont, CA: Wadsworth/Brooks/Cole.

Daw, J. (1997). Cultural competency: What does it mean? *Family Therapy News, 28,* 8–9, 27.

Dean, L., & Meadows, M. (1995). College counseling: Union and intersection. *Journal of Counseling and Development, 74,* 139–142.

Dobson, K. S. (Ed.). (2001). *Handbook of cognitive-behavioral therapies* (2nd ed.). New York: Guilford.

Edwards, C., & Murdock, N. (1994). Characteristics of therapist self-disclosure in the counseling process. *Journal of Counseling and Development, 72,* 384–389.

Efthim, P. W., Kenny, M. E., & Mahalik, J. R. (2001). Gender role stress in relation to shame, guilt, and externalization. *Journal of Counseling and Development, 79,* 430–437.

Egan, G. (1976). *Interpersonal living: A skills/contract approach to human relations training in groups.* Monterey, CA: Brooks/Cole.

Egan, G. (2002). *The skilled helper: A problem-management and opportunity-development approach to helping* (7th ed.). Pacific Grove, CA: Brooks/Cole-Wadsworth.

Ekman, P., & Friesen, W. V. (1967). Head and body cues in the judgment of emotion: A reformulation. *Perceptual and Motor Skills, 24,* 711–724.

Ekman, P., & Friesen, W. V. (1969). Non-verbal leakage and clues to deception. *Psychiatry, 32,* 88–105.

Enns, C. B. (1993). Twenty years of feminist counseling and therapy: From naming biases to implementing multifaceted practice. *The Counseling Psychologist, 21,* 33–87.

Enns, C. (2000). Gender issues in counseling. In S. D. Brown & R. W. Lent (Eds.), *Handbook of counseling psychology* (pp. 601–638). New York: Wiley.

Farber, B. A., & Lane, J. S. (2002). Positive regard. In J. C. Norcross (Ed.), *Psychotherapy relationships that work* (pp. 175–194). New York: Oxford University Press.

Farberman, R. K. (1997). What's leading America astray? *American Psychological Association Monitor, 28,* 1, 15.

Forrest, D. V. (1983). Employee assistance programs in the 1980's: Expanding career options for counselors. *Personnel and Guidance Journal, 62,* 105–107.

Fosha, D. (2000). *The transforming power of affect.* New York: Basic Books.

Freeny, M. (2003, March–April). No hiding place: Will patient privacy become a thing of the past? *Psychotherapy Networker,* 42–45.

Gale, A. U., & Austin, B. D. (2003). Professionalism's challenges to professional counselors' collective identity. *Journal of Counseling and Development, 81,* 3–10.

Gibbs, L. (2003). *Evidence-based practice for social workers.* Pacific Grove, CA: Brooks/Cole.

Gilbert, L. A., & Scher, M. (1999). *Gender and sex in counseling and psychotherapy.* Boston: Allyn and Bacon.

Gilligan, S. (1997). *The courage to love: Principles and practices of self-relations psychotherapy.* New York: Norton.

Gladding, S. T. (2002). Reflections on counseling after the crisis. In G. R. Walz & C. J. Kirkman (Eds.), *Helping people cope with tragedy and grief* (pp. 9–11). Greensboro, NC: CAPS Publication.

Glauser, A. S., & Bozarth, J. D. (2001). Person centered counseling: The culture within. *Journal of Counseling and Development, 79,* 142–147.

Glosoff, H. L., Herlihy, B., & Spence, E. B. (2000). Privileged communication in the counselor-client relationship. *Journal of Counseling and Development, 78,* 454–462.

Goldenberg, J., & Goldenberg, I. (2000). *Family therapy* (5th ed.). Pacific Grove, CA: Brooks/Cole.

Greenberg, L. (2002). *Emotion-focused therapy: Coaching clients to work through their feelings.* Washington DC: American Psychological Association.

Gutierres, S. E., Russo, N. F., & Urbanski, L. (1994). Sociocultural and psychological factors in American Indian drug use: Implications for treatment. *The International Journal of the Addictions, 29,* 1761–1786.

Hackney, H., & Cormier, L. S. (1996). *The professional counselor* (3rd ed.). Boston: Allyn and Bacon.

Hackney, H., & Cormier, L. S. (2001). *The professional counselor* (4th ed.). Boston: Allyn and Bacon.

Haley, J. (1997). *Leaving home* (2nd ed.). New York: Brunner-Mazel.

Hardy, K. V., & Laszloffy, T. (1995). The cultural genogram: Key to training culturally competent family therapists. *Journal of Marital and Family Therapy, 21,* 227–237.

Harper, R., Wiens, A., & Matarazzo, J. (1978). *Nonverbal communication: The state of the art.* New York: Wiley.

Harvey, J. C., & Katz, C. (1995). *If I'm so successful why do I feel like a fake? The impostor phenomenon.* New York: St. Martin's Press.

Haynes, R., Corey, G., & Moulton, P. (2003). *Clinical supervision in the helping professions: A practical guide.* Pacific Grove, CA: Wadsworth.

Hays, P. A. (1995). Multicultural applications of cognitive-behavior therapy. *Professional Psychology: Research and Practice, 26,* 309–315.

Hazler, R. J., & Kottler, J. A. (1994). *The emerging counseling profession.* Alexandria, VA: American Counseling Association.

Heinlin, K. T., Welfel, E. R., Richmond, E. N., & Rak, C. F. (2003). The scope of Webcounseling: A survey of service and compliance with NBCC Standards for the Ethical Practice of WebCounseling. *Journal of Counseling and Development, 81,* 61–69.

Helms, J., & Cook, D. (1999). *Using race and culture in counseling and psychotherapy.* Boston: Allyn and Bacon.

Hepworth, D. H., Rooney, R. H., & Larsen, J. A. (2002). *Direct social work practice: Theory and skills* (6th ed.). Pacific Grove, CA: Brooks/Cole.

Hewlett, K. (2001). Can low self-esteem and self-blame on the job make you sick? *Monitor on Psychology, 32*(7), 58.

Hill, C., & Knox, S. (2002). Self-disclosure. In J. C. Norcross (Ed.), *Psychotherapy relationships that work* (pp. 255–266). New York: Oxford University Press.

Hillman, J. (1996). *The soul's code: In search of character and calling.* New York: Random House.

Hoffman, R. M. (2001). The measurement of masculinity and femininity: Historical perspective and implications for counseling. *Journal of Counseling and Development, 79,* 472–485.

Horney, K. (1970). *Neurosis and human growth.* New York: Norton.

Hudson, P. O., & O'Hanlon, W. H. (1991). *Rewriting love stories: Brief marital therapy.* New York: Norton.

Hutchins, D., & Cole-Vaught, C. (1997). *Helping relationships and strategies* (3rd ed.). Pacific Grove, CA: Brooks/Cole.

Imber-Black, E., Roberts, J., & Whiting, R. (Eds.). (1988). *Rituals in families and family therapy.* New York: Norton.

Ivey, A. E. (1995, April). *The community genogram: A strategy to assess culture and community resources.* The annual meeting of the American Counseling Association, Denver, CO.

Ivey, A. (1999). *Intentional interviewing and counseling* (5th ed.). Pacific Grove, CA: Brooks/Cole.

Ivey, A. E., D'Andrea, M., Ivey, M. B., & Simek-Morgan, L. (2002). *Theories of counseling and psychotherapy: A multicultural perspective* (5th ed.). Boston: Allyn and Bacon.

Ivey, A., Gluckstern, N., & Ivey, M. B. (1993). *Basic attending skills*. North Amherst, MA: Microtraining Associates.

James, R. K., & Gilliland, B. (2003). *Theories and strategies in counseling and psychotherapy* (5th ed.). Boston: Allyn and Bacon.

Jenkins, A. H. (1997). The empathic context in psychotherapy with people of color. In A. Bohart & L. Greenberg (Eds.), *Empathy reconsidered* (pp. 321–342). Washington, DC: American Psychological Association.

Jennings, F. L. (1992). Ethics of rural practice. *Psychotherapy in Private Practice, 10*, 85–104.

Johnson, D. W. (2003). *Reaching out: Interpersonal effectiveness and self actualization* (5th ed.). Boston: Allyn and Bacon.

Jordan, J. (1997). Relational development through mutual empathy. In A. Bohart & L. Greenberg (Eds.), *Empathy reconsidered* (pp. 343–352). Washington, DC: American Psychological Association.

Jourard, S. M. (1963). *Personal adjustment*. New York: Macmillan.

Kanfer, F. H., & Gaelick-Buys, L. (1991). Self-management methods. In F. H. Kanfer & A. P. Goldstein (Eds.), *Helping people change* (4th ed., pp. 305–360). New York: Pergamon.

Kanfer, F. H., & Goldstein, A. P. (1991). (Eds.). *Helping people change* (4th ed.). New York: Pergamon.

Kantrowitz, R., & Ballou, M. (1992). A feminist critique of cognitive-behavioral therapy. In L. S. Brown & M. Ballou (Eds.), *Personality and psychopathology: Feminist reappraisals* (pp. 70–87). New York: Guilford.

Karasu, T. B. (1992). *Wisdom in the practice of psychotherapy*. New York: Basic Books.

Karen, R. (1992). Shame. *Atlantic Monthly, 269*, 40–70.

Kazdin, A. E. (1982). The separate and combined effects of covert and overt rehearsal in developing assertive behavior. *Behavior Therapy and Research, 20*, 17–25.

Keel, L., & Brown, S. (1999, July). Professional disclosure statements. *Counseling Today*, 14–15.

Kelley, C. (1974). *Education in feeling and purpose*. Vancouver, WA: The Radix Institute, c/o C. Kelley, 13715 Southeast 36th St., Vancouver, WA 98684.

Kelley, C. R. (1979). Freeing blocked anger. *The Radix Journal, 1*, 19–33.

Klein, M. H., Kolden, G. G., Michels, J. L., & Chisholm-Stockard, S. (2002). Congruence. In J. C. Norcross (Ed.), *Psychotherapy relationships that work* (pp. 195–215). New York: Oxford University Press.

Knapp, M. L., & Hall, J. (1997). *Nonverbal communication in human interaction* (5th ed.). Orlando: Holt, Rinehart and Winston.

Kottler, J. (1991). *The compleat therapist*. San Francisco: Jossey-Bass.

Kramer, P. D. (1993). *Listening to Prozac*. New York: Viking.

Lanning, W. (1997). Ethical codes and responsive decision-making. In J. A. Kottler (Ed.), *Finding your way as a counselor* (pp. 111–113). Alexandria, VA: American Counseling Association.

Lazarus, A. (1976). *Multimodal behavior therapy*. New York: Springer.

Lee, C. C. (1996). MCT theory and implications for indigenous healing. In D. W. Sue, A. E. Ivey, & P. B. Pedersen (Eds.), *A theory of multicultural counseling and therapy* (pp. 86–98). Pacific Grove, CA: Brooks/Cole.

Leong, F. T. L. (1994). Emergence of the cultural dimension: The roles and impact of culture on counseling supervision. *Counselor Education and Supervision, 34*, 114–116.

Lewis, J. B. (1971). *Shame and guilt in neurosis*. Lido Beach, NY: International Universities Press.

Liddle, B. J. (1986). Resistance in supervision: A response to perceived threat. *Counselor Education and Supervision, 26*, 117–127.

Lott, B. (2002). Cognitive and behavioral distancing from the poor. *American Psychologist, 57*, 100–110.

Lowen, A. (1965). *Breathing, movement, and feeling*. New York: Institute for Bioenergetic Analysis.

Mayer, J. D., & Salovey, P. (1997). What is emotional intelligence? In P. Salovey & D. Sluyter (Eds.), *Emotional development and emotional intelligence* (pp. 3–31). New York: Basic Books.

McCleod, J. (1998). *An introduction to the counseling profession* (2nd ed.). Buckingham, England: Open University Press.

McMullin, R. E. (2000). *The new handbook of cognitive therapy techniques*. New York: Norton.

McNeil, B. W., Stoltenberg, C. D., & Pierce, R. A. (1985). Supervisees' perceptions of their development: A test of the counselor complexity model. *Journal of Counseling Psychology, 32*, 630–633.

Meichenbaum, D. (1993). Stress inoculation training: A 20-year update. In P. M. Lehrer & R. L. Woolfork (Eds.), *Principles and practice of stress management* (2nd ed., pp. 373–406). New York: Guilford.

Mellody, P. (1989). *Facing codependence*. New York: Harper and Row.

Mesquita, B., & Frijda, N. (1992). Cultural variations in emotions: A review. *Psychological Bulletin, 112*, 179–204.

Midori Hanna, S., & Brown, J. (1999). *The practice of family therapy* (2nd ed.). Pacific Grove, CA: Brooks/Cole.

Miller, A. (1981). *The drama of the gifted child.* New York: Basic Books.

Miller, D. (1999). *Principles of social justice.* Cambridge, MA: Harvard University Press.

Miller, G., & Wooten, J. R., Jr. (1995). Sports counseling: A new counseling specialty area. *Journal of Counseling and Development, 74,* 172–173.

Miller, S. (1985). *The shame experience.* Haberford, PA: Analytic Press.

Miller, S., Wackman, D., Nunnally, E., & Miller, P. (1988). *Connecting with self and others.* Littleton, CO: Interpersonal Communication Programs.

Minuchin, S. (1974). *Families and family therapy.* Cambridge, MA: Harvard University Press.

Morgan, B., & MacMillan, P. (1999). Helping clients move toward constructive change: A three-phase integrated counseling model. *Journal of Counseling and Development, 77,* 153–159.

Morrison, J. (1995). *The first interview: A guide for clinicians.* New York: Guilford.

Morrissette, P. J. (2002). *Self-supervision: A primer for counselors and helping professionals.* Lillington, NC: Edwards Brothers.

Moursund, J. P., & Erskine, R. G. (2004). *Integrative psychotherapy: The art and science of relationship.* Pacific Grove, CA: Brooks/Cole.

Murdin, L. (2000). *How much is enough: Endings in psychotherapy and counselling.* London: Routledge.

Murphy, B., & Dillon, C. (2003). *Interviewing in action* (2nd ed.). Pacific Grove, CA: Wadsworth.

Myers, J. E., Sweeney, T. J., & White, V. E. (2002). Advocacy for counseling and counselors: A professional imperative. *Journal of Counseling and Development, 80,* 394–402.

Nathan, P., & Gorman, J. (Eds.). (2002). *A guide to treatments that work.* New York: Oxford University Press.

National Association of Social Workers. (1996). *Code of ethics.* Washington, DC: Author.

Nelson, M. L. (2002). An assessment-based model for counseling strategy selection. *Journal of Counseling and Development, 80,* 416–421.

Norcross, J. C. (2001). Empirically supported therapy relationships: Summary report of the Division 29 Task Force. *Psychotherapy, 38* (4).

Norcross, J. C. (Ed.). (2002). *Psychotherapy relationships that work.* New York: Oxford University Press.

O'Hanlon, W. H. (1987). *Taproots: Underlying principles of Milton H. Erickson's therapy and hypnosis.* New York: Norton.

O'Hara, M. (1997). Relational empathy: Beyond modernist egocentrism to postmodern holistic contextualism. In A. Bohart & L. Greenberg (Eds.), *Empathy reconsidered* (pp. 295–320). Washington, DC: American Psychological Association.

Ohlsen, J. J. (Ed.). (1983). *Introduction to counseling.* Itasca, IL: Peacock.

Olk, M., & Friedlander, M. L. (1992). Role conflict and ambiguity in the supervisory experience of counselor trainees. *Journal of Counseling Psychology, 39,* 389–397.

O'Neill, T. D. (1993). "Feeling worthless": An ethnographic investigation of depression and problem drinking at the Flathead Reservation. *Culture, Medicine, and Psychiatry, 16,* 447–469.

Ozer, E. M., & Bandura, A. (1990). Mechanisms governing empowerment effects: A self-efficacy analysis. *Journal of Personality and Social Psychology, 59,* 472–486.

Paisley, P., & Borders, L. D. (1995). School counseling: An evolving specialty. *Journal of Counseling and Development, 74,* 150–153.

Patterson, L., & Welfel, E. (1999). *The counseling process* (5th ed.). Pacific Grove, CA: Brooks/Cole.

Pedersen, P., & Ivey, A. (1993). *Culture-centered counseling and interviewing skills.* Westport, CT: Praeger.

Pennebaker, J. W. (1990). *Opening up: The healing power of confiding in others.* New York: Morrow.

Perls, F. (1969). *Ego, hunger, and aggression.* New York: Vintage.

Perls, F. (1973). *The gestalt approach and eyewitness to therapy.* Palo Alto, CA: Science and Behavior Books.

Power, S. J., & Rothausen, T. J. (2003). The work-oriented midcareer development model: An extension of Super's maintenance stage. *The Counseling Psychologist, 31,* 157–197.

Premack, D. (1965). Reinforcement theory. In D. Levin (Ed.), *Nebraska symposium on motivation* (pp. 123–180). Lincoln: University of Nebraska Press.

Prochaska, J., DiClemente, C., & Norcross, J. C. (1992). In search of how people change. *American Psychologist, 47,* 1102–1114.

Prochaska, J., & Norcross, J. C. (2002). Stages of change. In J. C. Norcross (Ed.), *Psychotherapy relationships that work* (pp. 303–314). Oxford: Oxford University Press.

Prochaska, J. O., & Norcross, J. C. (2003). *Systems of psychotherapy: A transtheoretical analysis* (5th ed.). Pacific Grove, CA: Brooks/Cole.

Quintana, S., & Atkinson, D. R. (2002). A multicultural perspective on principles of empirically supported interventions. *The Counseling Psychologist, 30,* 281–290.

Rabinowitz, F. E., Heppner, P. O., & Roehlke, H. J. (1986). Descriptive study of process and outcome variables of supervision over time. *Journal of Counseling Psychology, 33,* 292–300.

Robinson, T. (1997). Insurmountable opportunities. *Journal of Counseling and Development, 76,* 6–7.

Rogers, C. (1957). The necessary and sufficient conditions of therapeutic personality change. *Journal of Counseling Psychology, 21,* 95–103.

Rosado, J. W., Jr., & Elias, M. J. (1993). Ecological and psychocultural mediators in the delivery of services for urban, culturally diverse Hispanic clients. *Professional Psychology: Research and Practice, 24,* 450–459.

Rosenthal, T., & Steffek, B. (1991). Modeling methods. In F. H. Kanfer & A. P. Goldstein (Eds.), *Helping people change* (4th ed., pp. 70–121). New York: Pergamon.

Roysircar, G., Arredondo, P., Fuertes, J., Ponterotto, J., Coleman, H., Israel, T., & Toporek, R. (2002). *Updated operationalization of the multicultural competencies.* Washington, DC: American Counseling Association.

Roysircar, G., Sandju, D. S., & Bibbins, V. (2003). *Multicultural competencies: A guidebook of practices.* Washington, DC: American Counseling Association.

Scott, D. A., & Robinson, T. L. (2001). White male identity development: The Key model. *Journal of Counseling and Development, 79,* 415–421.

Seligman, M. (1990). *Learned optimism.* New York: Pocket Books.

Sharf, R. S. (2000). *Theories of psychotherapy and counseling: Concepts and cases* (2nd ed.). Belmont, CA: Wadsworth.

Simpkinson, A., & Simpkinson, C. (1992, January–February). Man talk/woman talk. *Common Boundary,* 30–33.

Skovholt, T. J., & Ronnestad, M. H. (1992). *The evolving professional self: Stages and themes in therapist and counselor development.* New York: Wiley.

Smith, D., & Fitzpatrick, M. (1995). Patient-therapist boundary issues. *Professional Psychology, 26,* 499–506.

Smith, E. (1985). *The body in psychotherapy.* Jefferson, NC: McFarland.

Smith, H., & Robinson, G. (1995). Mental health counseling: Past, present, and future. *Journal of Counseling and Development, 74,* 158–162.

Solomon, B. B. (1976). *Black empowerment: Social work in oppressed communities.* New York: Columbia University Press.

Sommers-Flanagan, J., & Sommers-Flanagan, R. (2003). *Clinical interviewing* (3rd ed.). New York: Wiley.

Sperry, L., Carlson, J., & Kjos, D. (2003). *Becoming an effective therapist.* Boston: Allyn and Bacon.

Steinem, G. (1992). *Revolution from within: A book of self-esteem.* Boston: Little, Brown.

Stevenson, H., & Renard, G. (1993). Trusting ol' wise owls: Therapeutic rise of cultural strengths in African-American families. *Professional Psychology: Research and Practice, 24,* 433–442.

Stoltenberg, C. D., & Delworth, U. (1987). *Supervising counselors and therapists: A developmental approach.* San Francisco: Jossey-Bass.

Stoltenberg, C. D., Pierce, R. A., & McNeil, B. W. (1987). Effects of experience on counselors needs. *The Clinical Supervisor, 5,* 23–32.

Sue, D. W. (1992). The challenge of multiculturalism: The road less traveled. *American Counselor, 1,* 6–15.

Sue, D. W. (2001). Multidimensional facets of cultural comptence. *The Counseling Psychologist, 29,* 790–821.

Sue, D. W., Ivey, A. E., & Pedersen, P. B. (1996). *A theory of multicultural counseling and therapy.* Pacific Grove, CA: Brooks/Cole.

Sue, D. W., & Sue, D. (2003). *Counseling the culturally diverse.* New York: Wiley.

Sue, S. (1998). In search of cultural competence in psychotherapy and counseling. *American Psychologist, 53,* 440–448.

Sue, S., & Lam, A. (2002). Cultural and demographic diversity. In J. C. Norcross (Ed.), *Psychotherapy relationships that work* (pp. 401–422). Oxford: Oxford University Press.

Sweeney, T. J. (1995). Accreditation, credentialing, and professionalization: The role of specialties. *Journal of Counseling and Development, 74,* 117–125.

Tannen, D. (1990). *You just don't understand.* New York: Random House.

Tannen, D. (1993). *Gender and conversational interaction.* New York: Oxford University Press.

Teyber, E. (2000). *Interpersonal processes in psychotherapy* (4th ed.). Belmont, CA: Wadsworth.

Vacc, N. A., & Loesch, L. C. (2000). *Professional orientation to counseling* (3rd ed.). Philadelphia: Brunner-Routledge.

Vera, E. M., & Speight, S. L. (2003). Multicultural competence, social justice, and counseling psychology: Expanding our roles. *The Counseling Psychologist, 31,* 253–272.

Walen, S. R., DiGiuseppe, R., & Wessler, R. L. (1992). *A practitioner's guide to rational-emotive therapy* (2nd ed.). New York: Oxford University Press.

Wampold, B., Lichtenberg, J., & Waehler, C. (2002). Principles of empirically supported interventions in counseling psychology. *The Counseling Psychologist, 30,* 197–217.

Warwar, N., & Greenberg, L. S. (2000, June). *Emotional processing and therapeutic change.* Paper presented at the annual meeting of the International Society for Psychotherapy Research, Indian Hills, IL.

Watson, D., & Tharp, R. (2002). *Self-directed behavior* (8th ed.). Pacific Grove, CA: Brooks/Cole.

Watson, J. C. (2002). Revisioning empathy. In D. Cain & J. Seeman (Eds.), *Humanistic psychotherapies handbook of research and practice* (pp. 445–472). Washington DC: American Psychological Association.

Watson, O. M. (1970). *Proxemic behavior: A cross-cultural study.* The Hague: Mouton.

Watzlawick, P., Beavin, J. H., & Jackson, D. D. (1967). *Pragmatics of human communication.* New York: Norton.

Wehrly, B. (1995). *Pathways to multicultural counseling competence.* Pacific Grove, CA: Brooks/Cole.

Welfel, E. (2002). *Ethics in counseling and psychotherapy.* Pacific Grove, CA: Brooks/Cole.

West, J. D., Osborn, C. J., & Bubenzer, D. L. (2003). *Leaders and legacies: Contributions to the profession of counseling.* New York: Brunner-Routledge.

Wilson, G. T. (2000). Behavior therapy. In R. J. Corsini & D. Wedding (Eds.), *Current psychotherapies* (6th ed., pp. 205–240). Itasca, IL: Peacock.

Wolpe, J. (1990). *The practice of behavior therapy* (4th ed.). New York: Pergamon.

Woolams, S., & Brown, M. (1979). *TA: The total handbook of transactional analysis.* Englewood Cliffs, NJ: Prentice-Hall.

Worden, M., & Worden, B. (1998). *The gender dance in couples therapy.* Pacific Grove, CA: Brooks/Cole.

Worthington, E. L., Jr. (1987). Changes in supervision as counselors and supervisors gain experience: A review. *Professional Psychology: Research and Practice, 18,* 198–208.

Worthington, E. L., Jr., & Roehlke, H. J. (1979). Effective supervision as perceived by beginning counselors-in-training. *Journal of Counseling Psychology, 26,* 64–73.

Yager, G. G., Witham, M. V., Williams, G. T., & Scheufler, C. E. (1981). *Tips for the inexperienced counselor: How to maximize your time in supervision.* Paper presented at the North Central Association for Counselor Education and Supervision Annual Meeting, Milwaukee, WI.

Zuckerman, E. (2003). *HIPAA help, A compliance manual for psychotherapists.* Armbrust, PA: Three Wishes Press.

INDEX